BLACKOUT
TO
BLESSING

How the Perfect Love of Jesus
Saved Me From the Highway to Hell

MELISSA HURAY

BEAUFORT
BOOKS

BLACKOUT TO BLESSING

Paperback: 9780825309922
Ebook: 9780825308710

For inquiries about volume orders, please contact:
Beaufort Books, sales@beaufortbooks.com

Published in the United States by Beaufort Books
www.beaufortbooks.com

Distributed by Midpoint Trade Books
a division of Independent Publisher Group
https://www.ipgbook.com/

Cover designed by Gwyn Flowers at GKS Creative

Printed in the United States of America

"He has sent me to bind up the brokenhearted, to proclaim freedom for the captives and release from darkness for the prisoners, to proclaim the year of the LORD's favor and the day of vengeance of our God, to comfort all who mourn, and provide for those who grieve in Zion—to bestow on them a crown of beauty instead of ashes, the oil of joy instead of mourning, and a garment of praise instead of a spirit of despair."

—ISAIAH 61:1-3

"Forget the former things; do not dwell on the past. See, I am doing a new thing! Now it springs up; do you not perceive it? I am making a way in the wilderness and streams in the wasteland."

—ISAIAH 43:18-19

"Something supernatural happens when you share the gospel."

—PASTOR MARK OLSON

FOREWORD

BY MIKE LINDELL

The world promotes a big lie that money and fancy programs are the only ways to buy freedom from drug and alcohol problems. But for myself and millions of other followers of Jesus Christ, all it took was a simple but sincere prayer of surrender. I've never believed addiction was a disease.

This widespread lie is woven into the fabric of America, because there is big money in pushing the deception that a high-end rehab is the answer to chronic drug and alcohol problems. If people were truly transformed, what would happen to all these treatment centers? In spite of luxury facilities, lots of amenities, and therapy methods of all kinds, recovery program outcomes have remained flat and stagnant for decades.

You know what *did* work back then? The stripped-down version of early Alcoholics Anonymous. It was beautiful in its simplicity—a good, old-fashioned "get down on your knees and surrender" type of outfit. It was the *only* option available for suffering alcoholics—and it was very effective for those who were willing and desperate enough to do just a few simple things. Why? Because the most important part was total trust in Jesus Christ.

The fear of offending others with the truth is like a cancer in our society these days, and AA's founding fathers eventually watered down the elements of the program that made it revolutionary. Instead of directing people to the *only* power that could truly save them—total surrender to Jesus Christ and repentance—addicts were allowed to choose anything from a doorknob to their dead grandmother as their savior. This was a huge mistake.

Since then, recovery has been "therapized" and standardized—and the medical community has lulled the general public into believing addiction is a disease that the "things of man" can fix. We're asleep at the wheel, doing what we're told—doing more of what *doesn't work*. Addiction is a *spiritual problem* that results when people seek fulfillment from things other than God. Period. Many need special intercessory prayer to break the strongholds that have held them captive, but they're not getting it in most treatment centers. The one true remedy for the plague of addiction has not changed because of the shifting winds of culture. The answer is still Jesus Christ.

The Minnesota Model that birthed the multi-billion dollar treatment industry blended education and psychiatry with 12-step groups and became the accepted standard of care by the 1960s. But here's the thing—you don't need to pay thirty grand to find freedom! Clinging to the disease mindset means big dollars however—and abandoning it would be devastating to research facilities, big pharma, and people who are profiting from the pain of others. The underlying message that is pushed to keep the lie going is that of "addict-as-defective"—along with incurable illness, endless meetings, and a depressing path of white-knuckling it through every day. If people get cured, the need for ongoing therapy goes away!

Belief in the "addiction is a disease" model makes people victims instead of victors—and keeps the money machine cranking.

Honestly, I haven't met many addiction counselors who reject the disease model like I do, but Melissa Huray is one of them.

Our meeting was a total divine appointment, and I don't say that lightly. Before she came along, I had been too busy to meet with any interview candidates for several weeks. I get tons of correspondence from people seeking jobs with my company, and it's impossible to meet them all. But when Melissa's name surfaced three times in one week, I knew God was trying to get my attention.

I figured she was a usual secular therapist, but was surprised to learn Melissa was a former addict herself. Not only had she been delivered through a simple but life-changing prayer like I was, she was a strong Christian whose absolute goal was to help others find TRUE deliverance from the chains of addiction. Surrendering to Jesus in a moment of sincere desperation and repentance had been the *only* permanent solution—and she deeply wished to share this truth with others.

I knew Melissa was the one to lead the Lindell Recovery Network. Over the past four years, I've often wondered what are the odds our paths would cross? I had no idea she had discovered my backstory as a former crack cocaine addict—or that she had been telling her former treatment clients about my reputation as a second-chance employer. I was also unaware she had been petitioning God in her prayer closet for a new assignment.

As time went on, her role with my company grew and I eventually became aware of the many skills she had never talked about—broadcasting and T.V. news, public speaking—and most importantly, her writing.

In January of 2021, I was under attack because of my relentless pursuit to expose election crime and preserve voting integrity. One day, Melissa sent me a story she had written called "The Real Mike Lindell." It brought tears to my eyes! Melissa shared her personal experience as one of my employees—describing me as a genuine advocate for addicts and broken people. I shared her great article on social media and her message spread everywhere.

Melissa has a real way with words and a knack for seeing beauty, truth, and sincerity in others. She has great discernment, desires to please the Lord, and is genuine, loyal, and trustworthy.

In 2021, my good friend and founder of the Operation Restored Warrior program, Paul Lavelle, approached me about starting an internet television show for the Lindell Recovery Network and suggested that Melissa Huray and his friend, former Navy Seal Jason Perry, would be the dream team to host it.

For years, I have wanted to have a show featuring only good news and call it "The Hope Report," and this was confirmation that the time was right.

Melissa has grown greatly in the past four years. I have seen her conquer fear of man, develop great boldness, and become a strong warrior for the Kingdom of Jesus. When I think back on her life journey, I can see how the Lord is now using her history of brokenness to bring hope to others. Melissa's message is important and empowering: addiction is not a disease, and true freedom is found only in breaking the chains of addiction through spiritual deliverance and a new identity in Jesus Christ.

The money-making machine of the world may not like Melissa's message that defies the tired, old narrative that addiction is a lifelong illness with no cure—but the millions of addicts who will finally find total restoration are going to be forever grateful! The answer to addiction is beautiful and it is simple: JESUS SAVES, JESUS HEALS, and JESUS RESTORES. The Holy Spirit is powerful and transformational. The end.

You probably know by now I don't care much what people think, and neither does she. God has given both of us messages to proclaim to the world and they are hills we believe in so strongly we are willing to die on them. Going against the grain is not always popular, but it is transformational to the lost. To God be the glory!

—MIKE LINDELL

PROLOGUE

SUMMERTIME 1998

Weak gray light filtering through the twisted mini blinds roused me from a drunken stupor. My roommate's crafty ways had created a Martha Stewart-esque atmosphere for our dumpy ground-floor apartment, but the tweaker blinds somehow escaped her renovation. Eye level with the yellow shag carpeting, staggering dread blasted in like a runaway train as I struggled from the floor, cradling my splitting head.

The morning felt perilous.

With my sweaty hair and tumbling mind, I was a wreck. Shaky and dehydrated, mass quantities of liquid were needed, stat.

Stumbling to the fridge for a pitcher of Kool-Aid, I gulped it with reckless need as the door gaped open. The red juice falling in rivulets from the corners of my mouth and spattering the floor was a very low priority. Another morning after had broken, and I was just trying to survive.

Though I ached to recreate the blank slate the previous night had left behind, my memories had halted at late afternoon. Hard drinking at a shady tavern in Oliver, Wisconsin, set the stage for a giant cavern between a simple tequila shooter and my present reality.

How *did* the night end? The outing at the railroad bar began midafternoon, but home would elude me for many hours. Countless mornings broke this way—frantic, panicked fumbling for snapshot clips of recollection through a head throbbing from last night's booze.

Cobbling together available facts, red satin shorts came to mind, and I saw myself in the Budweiser mirror above the bar, tanned legs crossed, peek of cleavage from my V-necked T-shirt, my face a disinterested smirk. The appreciative glances gained from nearby patrons suggested I was an exquisite jewel rarely unearthed in Oliver, Wisconsin. Self-delusion ruled me while I racked up an impressive collection of empty bottles to mark my spot at the bar, amber glass sad when empty, but alcohol shooters soon brought new life to the party. Content to just peel silver labels while I waited for what was coming, I folded the thin, curly papers into sloppy origami to pass time. The jukebox looped Bob Seger, Steve Miller, and Lynyrd Skynyrd, drowning out the thud of the longneck making sickening contact with my front teeth while bar trivia and Name that Tune provided just enough mental distraction. Older adults were always surprised by my vast musical knowledge.

"Bet ya can't guess this one."

2

An old guy in a leather biker jacket called as he swaggered back from plugging coins into the jukebox.

C'mon. Give me a challenge.

"Mungo Jerry. 'In the Summertime.' Say around 1970? Before I came along, anyway."

I lifted my beer bottle with a wink, wondering if I had evolved into *one of them*. Smug approval but no words from the Harley guy. Temporary chums, but I wasn't out of the woods yet.

Someone a little more my type had snagged a nearby stool, so far generating only bits of banal conversation. Without warning, he plunged into a spirited discussion about 12-step groups.

"It helped me not get so trashed all the time," he concluded, gesturing for the bartender.

I pondered recovery groups and my limited knowledge of them. The sober scene was as distant as the dark side of the moon, but I tried to connect.

"My dad went through AA. Like back when I was in high school. I don't remember much about it, other than him always wanting near-beer afterward."

I stared at my foot, bouncing along the baseboard of the bar, grimy toes poking out from my black flip-flops to illustrate the determination of a long walk. It was unlikely the guy was focused on my feet.

"Near-beer was like a gateway drug for him," I continued, coaxing the conversation along. "Next step was always the real thing. And I don't mean sodie-pop."

He offered a small chuckle, but forging a serious connection was a challenge. We continued sipping beer in tandem as I bided my time, coming into myself.

Frequenting bars alone was tantalizing. The possibilities of the night ahead swelled in the quiet space between us. The fabric of the anonymous culture was enticing, and I was a wayward traveler stepping into a screenplay with an unknown ending. My sweaty trek to the tavern had earned an afternoon of adult beverages without fear of police or the need to conduct a vehicle rescue mission the following day. Time to rationalize my way right into a blackout.

The bar stool would be mine for the next several hours—my objective (whether I admitted it or not): to earn the attention of an attractive stranger. This desperate quest would dominate unless something very compelling intervened—like a natural disaster, loss of power, or some other antic that resulted in my eviction from the bar. Occasionally, a passing train broke the atmosphere of apathy with a cloud of dust blasting through the doorway like free entertainment. My bemusement was lost on the regulars who simply continued their placid swilling like a row of comfortable but unchallenged cattle. Railroad dregs were nothing new to them.

My latest admirer was a bar regular living in the nearby town of Oliver—a crusty little village reduced to a population of 412 souls off Highway 105—offering only a dilapidated old schoolhouse, a general store, a vacant church, and most notably to me, the dying tavern. The watering hole near the tracks serviced local laborers along with an occasional passerby.

My local boy drinking buddy was nicely offering a sort of preauthorization into the Oliver scene. Chatting idly with increased flirtation as the night wore on, soon I'd stop remembering. Did we leave together? That very question would be agonizing later, but history indicated the mysterious stranger had been the only reason I gave up my bar stool.

The evening evaporated as unlimited drinks propelled time forward, the clock hours disappearing with the beers. Moments eroded comfortably, and no judgements existed inside the bubble of the bar. Each trip to the jukebox felt like an important assignment. Other patrons were counting on me.

WE WILL REFUSE SERVICE TO ANYONE WHO APPEARS TO BE UNDER THE AGE OF 40 screamed pointlessly from above the doorway—ineffectual considering a group of kids gathered at the back playing pinball beneath a sign blaring HANG LOOSE. The peculiar wall hanging looked like it had come from a garage sale and displayed a half-naked neon lady flickering blandly to the beat of the jukebox, her outline a coconut bra and grass skirt. The kids weren't drinking. Their presence had to do with some Wisconsin tavern exemption.

The blinding day just outside the doorway made afternoon drunkenness awfully hypocritical. Like a scratched piece of vinyl jammed in the jukebox, I begged the same question of my male friend: *"What's your name?"* Getting a true read on him was tough. Like shattered glass, his pale blue eyes darted from my face to my shorts to the clock—then back to his beer. He'd probably answered my question sixteen times already.

Close to the point of final recall—I evaluated my reflection once again—this time in the bathroom mirror. Red V-neck T-shirt, red satin shorts, tanned legs. The looking glass offered validation one last time.

A shot of tequila now marked my place, glinting pale orange in the half-light from the open door. My new friend had supplied it, and was coyly searching me for a reaction. I just smiled, made a hat-tipping gesture, and flipped the drink neatly down my throat.

It was just five o'clock now, but I had gone dark.

Oh no, I wasn't sleeping or passed out. I was walking, talking, and functioning. The difference between me and typical partiers was that my autopilot actions hid my absent memory. So much time unfolded after that last tequila shot, hours filled with God only knows what. When did I leave? How did I make it home? What had we *done*?

The most reasonable conclusion became clear later: my acquaintance and I migrated from Oliver to downtown Superior and closed down the strip, although I may as well have started a colony on Venus. With just shreds to work with, I pressed my roommate for information the following day. Recreating the night was a delicate balancing act of soliciting information while concealing my functional blackout. History suggested I'd held a complex and detailed conversation with her when I finally stumbled home, but I could easily cover my tracks. I was an expert faker.

Alcohol would be my ruin, that much was clear from the very first taste. Booze caused a horrific chemical reaction in both brain and body, but that didn't stop my quest for constant numbing. Shocking impulsivity, loss of control, and disabling blackouts punctuated every binge, but I couldn't escape the compulsion to capture one more night outside of myself.

Anna wasn't one to judge; my roommate enjoyed tipping back a few cocktails herself and had no real experience with blackouts. In her eyes, I was nothing more than a garden-variety partier. Being the only available witness, she was the key to reconciling my erased evening.

"How ya feeling today?" Anna asked with a small but non-judgmental smirk.

"Not too bad," I responded shortly, watching with careful eyes and hoping my sheepish shrug was convincing. I was most certainly not *fine*, perilously close to vomiting, and dragging around a head that felt like a thousand-pound rotten melon left in the path of an eighteen-wheeler.

Rummaging through the refrigerator, Anna sidestepped the puddle of Kool-Aid without comment—a good sign.

"Any Taco Bell left from last night? Oh, and that guy who brought you home . . . Where does he live again?"

Chatting over tacos?

"Oliver," I managed.

As Anna skillfully peeled a burrito from its soggy paper, I gently pressed for facts. "So, I just fell asleep then? After he left?"

"Not exactly," she chuckled, chewing. "He took off, and you watched *Billy Madison* for like the fiftieth time! You were laughing your butt off, remember? How come you never get sick of that movie? I don't even think it's that funny."

Faint with relief, I discovered the tape still loaded in the VCR. Anna spoke the truth. Though I remembered nothing, an unconvincing nod helped.

"Ah, that's right."

The shred of closure was comforting, but I continued to obsess about the Oliver bar guy with the pale blue eyes. Where had we gone? What had we done? The fact that I had been awake but not forming memories was disturbing, but that secret was locked up in my very own brain. *I am okay.*

Shifting to my roommate's on-again/off-again relationship was a handy way to change the subject.

"What's going on with you and Mike these days?"

Anna and Mike Huray had been high school steadies, an

innocent partnership she'd tried unsuccessfully to drag into their twenties. I knew of Mike, but mostly through Anna's stories. We had met only once—when he showed up to install a shower in the decrepit old bathroom of our duplex. It was the spring of 1998, and I'd just been introduced to Anna through a mutual acquaintance. She joined me at the Alamo, the name locals dubbed our hell-hole tenement due to its weird, Spanish-style stucco exterior. Nice, stable, orderly, cute—Mike added a functional shower to our old claw foot tub, and spent a few hours demonstrating a commanding mastery of plumbing tools.

"He's around," she answered distantly. "We might go see Huey Lewis and the News later on this summer. We're still friends. It's better off, I guess."

Mike was forgotten while Anna and I hosted many parties and wasted countless days baking in tanning beds and reading each other's fortunes with a deck of tarot cards I'd picked up at a local bookstore. Our nights were spent methodically closing down the mile-long strip of Tower Avenue watering holes.

Our living arrangement lasted six short months, with alcohol birthing volatility and a venomous parting. Drunken nights, parties with strange people, and plenty of scuffles took their toll, and Anna moved out in an ugly showdown. I soldiered on at the Alamo alone, fearful of taking on another roommate.

Running into my archrival was a raw fear of mine for years. We'd had a brutal parting, and it was likely that any future contact would be very ugly. We never did see each other again, although we coexisted in a smallish northern Wisconsin town for many years.

God moved her from my life, offering protection from unseen forces. The Bible says: "He moves mountains without their knowing it" (Job 9:5, NIV). The short time we shared the duplex was brief but impactful: my severe binge drinking already way out of control by twenty-five. As I ignorantly slipped deeper into my sinful vices, I didn't even notice the enemy slithering in beside me. Though I'd moved far away, God still protected me by severing my connection to Anna at just the right time.

But He still had a plan for Mike Huray and me. We'd cross paths again, but not until I'd experienced the worst alcoholic relapse of my life.

1

Jesus Christ always wanted to be my first love. A familiar and comfortable constant—the idea of God as Master of the Universe ran like an unbreakable thread through every season of my life. Public acceptance of the Savior of the world happened at nine, and John 3:16 became my mantra. But my newfound Christianity was not nurtured, and adolescence brought many false idols to fill my gaping heart wounds. Getting drunk and pleasing the world became my gods.

Though I had the most well-known scripture verse committed to memory, the Bible wasn't compatible with blackouts—and I paid no attention to that dusty old tome when I was busy pleasing the world. Alcohol and amnesia moved the Good Book to the backseat.

August 21, 2003, was another night that never registered. I seemed to be just a typical imbiber blending in at an outdoor festival, my functional blackout concealed by adept muscle memory. I was no stranger to walking around in a daze, but tonight I would partner with the enemy for his most ruthless attack. Not just a standard "relapse"—that lost night was a culmination of fifteen years spent playing Russian roulette with different flavors of destruction. Each harrowing escapade had quickened this convergence point, and when day broke and I was breathing, I knew a repeat performance would be fatal.

By the time I was three, I already had acquired a taste for ale. My father was never stingy with it—always happy to share when I crawled up into his big chair for a cuddle. This was bonding time with Dad. My little sips progressed to heftier gulps from his Blatz can, and eventually a few secret swigs from an adult's glass at family gatherings.

Few would peg a harmless little can of beer as a means to ruin. *It's just beer.* How could *that* be anyone's drug of choice? It was the 80s—party balls graced every bash, and wine coolers were king. But routinely pounding enough brews to stop breathing made blackouts common—and overdose highly possible. Countless occasions of alcohol poisoning could have taken my life many times, but the hand of God intervened.

Grandpa Bob's retirement party featured an unattended keg in the garage, and I was a happy hostess, filling bottomless red Solo cups for grown-ups and sipping from each before adding a final top-off. By age fourteen, I was already on track for an addiction problem.

The wait would soon be over. As freshman year ended, I flung full tilt into the wonderful world of binge drinking—my first experience with true incoherence easily branding my brain with a new battle cry: get drunk as frequently as possible!

The first blowout was unforgettable, though I still masqueraded as a normal teenager just out of reach. The gaping discrepancy was difficult because a worsening reputation followed each drunk. But gravel pit parties offered relief found in the temporary attention of drunk boys with Ford trucks and low standards. Accepting the new me was a hard pill to swallow, and I sometimes wished to recapture innocent afternoons daydreaming over teen heartthrobs in my bedroom. Ninth grade capped off with a huge drunk fest at a campground—my intoxicated self slinking in and out of tents populated by drunk guys. Fabricated stories of my escapades soon proliferated the school, and although reality was far less salacious than the savage rumors, my reputation was already shot.

Throughout high school, I managed two selves. Half of me was fascinated by the future and in love with Max Headroom, astronomy, science fiction, and anything "spacey," driven to succeed and dreaming of a career as an astronaut or English professor. The evil twin, however, guzzled keg beer, coveted an impressive wardrobe of heavy metal T-shirts, and skipped class to smoke borrowed Marlboro Reds behind the Proctor 7-Eleven—though I didn't really like smoking, and the taste made me gag.

Ecstatic to earn a spot on the basketball cheerleading squad my junior year, I'd worked doggedly to get myself (almost) down into the splits, but pretty soon my new position would be soiled. Sneaking sips of root beer schnapps between drills caused chronic lateness, and the coach glowered while pointing out the sloppy threads hanging from the hem of my skirt. Two years on the junior varsity swimming team, rigorous practices, and camaraderie with healthy people brought some brief normalcy, but even becoming a spelling and writing prodigy couldn't tame the alcoholic beast inside.

Weekdays had a *good girl* focus; I was a bookworm pursuing a moral and godly life. But as Friday night approached, ice-cold keg cups captured my thinking. Beer offered freedom and an unsteady gateway to carefree, relaxed, and self-assured adolescence. Four years of high school brought endless aluminum cans and a drunk Melissa who wasn't awkward, anxious, or clumsy—like a superhuman avatar manifesting dreamy events where the quarterback of the football team made me his conquest.

Alcohol's services weren't cheap, though. Short-term relief brought loads of pain and shame—Monday was never far off, and rather than deliver on promises made in the heat of the moment, love interests brushed by in the hallway with their eyes bouncing away in mild disgust.

Brief accolades sometimes followed the weekend parties. "Whoa, I heard that you and Eddie were making out on Friday night! Man! I didn't even know you guys LIKED each other?!"

Eddie? WHO IS EDDIE? Recoiling in shame, I pushed my indiscretions away while striving to prove my party antics isolated events. I vowed to behave better at the next shindig, but Friday just brought more drunken humiliation that seemed fun in the moment.

Sixteen and hell-bent on getting my license, drinking behind the wheel kicked off the very day I conquered the road test—my finest skill soon becoming expert navigation of dirt back roads in Dad's battered green Ford F-150 with a can of Pabst Blue Ribbon between my knees. Why not? Everyone at Proctor High School was doing it. Each weekend brought another gravel pit, my highest priority being first in line for the keg. Tipsy and teetering on a rusty tailgate before the ruins of a campfire, I gulped from my red Solo cup and took turns on a bottle of whatever was available.

Beer continued to deliver relief to my anxiety-riddled brain. When the parties in the woods dried up, festivities shifted to dilapidated frat houses with rowdy college sophomores, and along with a couple of girlfriends, I became very skilled at finding a few reliable bashes every week. I'd pass as *old enough* while perched on a burnt orange Goodwill couch with exposed stuffing (no one really cared as long as five dollars had been exchanged for a drink ticket), chattering incessantly with unbelievable hysteria. The precious keg cups worked well for a time: a simple plastic prop sloshing with cheap swill created an illusion far beyond an underage girl out past curfew.

I didn't come with an alcohol "off" switch. Though my friends were also experimenting with drinking, they didn't lose their wits and still watched the clock to make curfew. Not me. The morning after was never a concern.

Sometimes a worried friend wrestled my blessed beverages away while I violently protested. *You've had enough.* God saved me from alcohol poisoning countless times—passing out meant I was forced to stop searching for my next beer.

The harrowing mornings-after were excruciating: a stinky, dirty, frat house reeking of stale beer waited at daybreak. I was the last straggler clamoring to reconcile the madness of the lost night.

Once, I woke in a bean bag chair with my Girbaud jeans completely soaked to the knees with urine. This wasn't unusual or rare. In the blinding light of day, the ease of the endless kegs and the chatter of boys was gone, and I was left with soaking wet pants and panic. *I never went home last night.*

Through fifteen years of escalating blackouts and countless attempts at controlled drinking, I'd been married and divorced—and shared an eight-year-old daughter with my ex-husband. By the summer of 2003, I found myself bottomed out once again and had cobbled together forty-nine alcohol-free days. I'd made it eighteen months a few years back, but only through fear of jail. Unbearable self-hatred was my current motivation.

By late August, the forty-nine precious days I'd banked were in serious jeopardy as racing thoughts ached to recapture my old life. *I never drank daily. I always had a job and car—I was functional.*

At thirty years old, I seemed healthy and looked fine on the outside.

But control never lasted beyond a few days. The innocent act of cracking a beer on a hot summer day lit the fuse for another desperate attempt at responsible drinking, at least the happy and cheerful scene unfolding in my mind's eye thought I could do it. Merry laughter and casual beer sipping on a rooftop patio with an attentive male companion faithfully produced a head-shattering hangover and horrific regret every single time. The first heavenly sip brought nothing but disaster.

Living in the public eye made drinking binges risky escapades ripe with irrational fear—mostly about viewers recognizing me while out on a bender. Getting fired would've been crippling—my position as a small market news anchor at KDLH-TV in Duluth provided a flimsy sense of identity and reluctant permission for my existence.

My career at the station started with promise in 1999. Two DUI arrests the year I was hired had initiated my longest period of sobriety ever—and though the production department job paid peanuts, it brought redemption through ego boosting. Joining a real TV station and rubbing elbows with local celebrities, like lead reporter Lance Carter, seemed a harbinger of incredible promise.

Lance was so untouchable. Hovering far removed from the talent in my tiny teleprompter room overlooking the set, I could privately watch him in all his glory—preening before going live. After feathering his light brown hair, he smoothed his slim-cut suit and straightened his tie, then steeled his eyes for the camera. I felt so unworthy in his presence, I couldn't manage to say hello for a year.

But eventually, I did. Up close, Lance's trademark good looks told a different story—cheeks blooming with rosacea and masked by makeup, concealer streaks a dead giveaway. Perhaps he wasn't so pristine? Maybe no one was, not even TV people. After chatting about my news interests, Lance himself suggested I "put myself out there" and pursue reporting. *Huh? Me?* I had a sudden urge to turn and see if he was speaking to someone else. Those offhanded words of encouragement became a tiny flame directing me behind the very cameras I thought were reserved only for gifted and beautiful people.

An internship soon opened, and I hustled and made an impression. Booze flowed post-newscast, and I quickly locked step with other abusers in the world of broadcasting. Grinding it out over a couple of years eventually earned a reporting spot and ultimately a Weekend Anchor position, as well as notoriety as a local celebrity. When people at stores or restaurants approached with, "Hey, you're on the news," satisfaction filled me, the words of admiring strangers a healing balm for my frail identity.

Determined to prove my worth as a news professional, the straight life endured for a time, but I soon craved a trip back to the dark side. By August 21 of 2003, the hard-earned sober days hung in jeopardy—my AA sponsor an ornate shelf ornament I liked the idea of having but easily overlooked.

My commitment to sobriety splintered as I finalized plans for the Minnesota State Fair—while deciding my sponsor's dark warnings to avoid "people, places, and things" were antiquated sentiments in dreadful need of a twenty-first century update. Drinking battered the periphery of my thoughts like a lonely traveler wanting refuge from a storm, seeking the warm glow of an open tavern. The fair beckoned like a private island I might visit and then abandon without baggage, leaving all indiscretions behind. *I could drink once more, and build back the days before I had to tell anyone!*

Why not Beck? I'd taken a break from the constant tug-of-war that never left my thoughts to entertain our road trip that day. Beck Strickland was joining me—a burly laborer and close friend of my landlord Gerard. We were both single, and Gerard was forever trying to play matchmaker. Beck was a fixture at the duplex I rented, stopping by for beers sometimes. In fact, we'd been reacquainted the previous day at Gerard's birthday bash.

Beck had seemed excited about another date, but would likely become just another casualty of my trauma-based courting habits. I'd never dated anyone without a hidden agenda—either to be kindred party animals with no attachments, or to mold into husband material—no in-between. My alcohol addiction made healthy and stable relationships impossible, and it also trashed my body and health goals. In fact, drinking had a tremendous effect on my weight and the depression that came with it. The pounds had been racking up for the past two decades—starting back when my mother introduced me to the marigold Sunbeam scale under the bathroom sink. Prior to ten I'd been a normal-sized kid, but long afternoons alone after school had jump-started a pattern of raiding the cupboards to soothe anxiety. The television set and bottomless bags of Old Dutch potato chips offered predictable numbing. *The Electric Company*, *The Jeffersons*, and *People's Court* were my babysitters—the grating but reassuring laugh track and droning sounds of Judge Wapner reliable companions every afternoon.

As my weight trended upward, eighth grade brought hardcore crash dieting. Chronic binge drinking took over a year later—and any hope of scale stability crumbled. Alcohol never offered any favors with the hateful, bright yellow weighing device and brought on wild mood swings—ecstatic days where the needle dipped below 110, and intense crying jags brought on by numbers bouncing into the 180s.

As my twenties drew to a close, cravings for fried food and endless beer pitchers made sticking to a diet plan impossible. Several mornings a week, I'd be locked in the McDonald's drive-thru near my apartment—patiently inching toward the window for a bag of grease. My thighs were irrelevant when saddled with a crushing hangover.

As I left my West Duluth duplex that sticky August day fair-bound, the scale wasn't my friend—the devil's platform had greeted me earlier with a reading of 158 pounds. For someone just 5'3", chalking it all up to thickness was becoming a tough sell. A trip to the neighborhood K-Mart store scored some new stretchy stone-washed shorts, and nonstop visits to the tanning bed were useless bids to distract people from my growing size.

Blindsided by an intense desire to drink, I paused to grip the kitchen counter while a powerful craving swept through like a hot river of blood, making my head throb. *Not right now.* But what could take its place? Food, spending? Maybe an energy drink?

No booze now. I'd wrestle with the thought again later. I had nothing in my stash and no time to score before hitting the highway. Maybe I'd grab a coffee once we were on the road.

Beck was waiting on the porch as I rolled up to his tattered pink farmhouse. Offering a mock salute, he ambled down the sidewalk as I moved junk from the passenger seat. Watching him fold his thick frame into my compact car, I considered the two of us sharing a family life with children and a backyard sandbox. Maybe in this farmhouse? I could transform it into something shabby chic, peruse garage sales for antiques and refurbish them. The home would sparkle with a woman's touch, and at night when the kids were sleeping, we'd swing on the porch under the stars and knock back a few cocktails. Why not? My brother was able to, often enjoying a beer at a family party and forgetting his can while he tossed a football for one of the kids. I'd never lose track of an open beer. Once cracked, the taste and special burn were on my mind in sixteen different ways: *how can I sip this so people don't think I am a lush? Why is everyone else drinking so slowly? How many beers are left in the case? When does the liquor store close? Maybe I just won't go to bed tonight, that way I won't need to wake up tomorrow.*

My efforts to weave booze with life harmlessly had been dismal failures—because the liquor always won, smothering and choking out every competitor. It needed to be in first place.

Smiling in spite of myself as Beck managed to tuck himself

between the seat and the dashboard, I was silent as he closed the door apologetically. There was nothing wrong with this pleasant, harmless guy; he'd be a good man to some woman out there. Now I wondered: How would we keep a conversation going without alcohol? Chatting sober-style all the way to St. Paul was a paralyzing reality—and now drinking felt like a requirement. The mental wrangling raged as we merged onto the freeway heading south.

Beck wore a grizzly goatee flecked with a little gray, and although his frame carried more weight than it had in his military prime, he was still strong and somewhat fit. His faded NASCAR T-shirt and Checker Auto Parts baseball hat revealed not only his interests, but also total relaxation with himself. Gazing agreeably out the window, he made small talk. *How's work been going? I saw your story on the city council. What's the mayor like in person?*

My short responses weren't the slightest bit relaxed or subtle. I'd dusted my face with glitter and donned gaudy rhinestone sunglasses, with the perfectly manicured acrylic nail tips I really couldn't afford screaming, *Look at me! Someone, anyone!* Finding attention wasn't a problem these days—my drinking behaviors ensured I'd get noticed. Blending in with others was a thing of the distant past. Beck hadn't yet witnessed my dramatic progression, but he was about to get a whopper of a wake-up call.

Rolling down the interstate, the persistent idea of a social cocktail returned, and this time I let it stay. I-35 stretched out, void of emotion or opinion.

"Beck, I'm an alcoholic," I blurted out as we passed Moose Lake. His reaction would determine my next move.

"What? I've seen you drink . . . *alcoholic?* Come on. There's nothing wrong with you."

His reassuring smile was awfully convincing.

"What about the drunk driving?" Still unsettled. *Convince me!*

"So? That was years ago, wasn't it? I got busted twice when I was in the Navy. Lots of people do."

"But how do you *control* your drinking?" My sanity teetered on his response.

Beck stared out the window in contemplation as though I was asking him to explain something very technical, like a bear market or the particles of an atom.

"I grew out of it," he finally decided. "I stop before I get messed up. I just got tired of having too much, I guess."

His assessment of controlled drinking was brilliantly illuminating, making the elusive concept seem finally within reach. Maybe this time drinking *could* work. Alcohol and me, one last time. *A guiltless drink.*

"Have a few beers, it's cool. I'll keep an eye on ya."

Simple as taking out the trash. Beck smiled and flashed a flirty wink. With his approval, a flood of anticipation came. *It was okay.*

As Beck sang along to a Winger song, I retreated into my mind, pondering, strategizing. Should I? *No one would know.* My buddy would surely supervise. We passed the town of Sandstone, and his promise of protection sealed the deal.

I'm going to do it.

That little switch of resolution flipped, and once I'd slipped from white-knuckling to "Oh well, screw it," the obsession to begin again left me completely magnetized for liquor. Faking apathy like a pro allowed Beck to miss the gravity of the situation. I'd do it fast, dump it down my throat before anyone could intervene.

We finally made it to St. Paul, worked our way through the fairground gates, and parked. Three hours south of Lake Superior, the temperatures were appallingly hot. The entrance to the event was a confusing mess I wanted to demolish, hoping beer would break into view. My first trip to the famed Minnesota State Fair wasn't making an impression so far—I could've just as easily been on Mars. Alcohol dominated every thought.

Beck and I were still empty-handed after an hour of aimless wandering. Pausing to tie a sweatshirt around my waist, my pathetic whining would've rivaled that of a five-year-old begging for ice cream. *Where was the beer?* No one was even drinking!

Up ahead, the street sloped into a sea of bodies moving in unison, parents pushing strollers and passively guiding toddlers as they licked rainbow colored sno-cones. *No beer.* Oh Lord, what if there *wasn't any?* The thought of abandoning my mission was crippling, and panic escalated as we pressed on through the crowds.

"World-famous cheese curds," Beck pointed to a fluorescent orange stand hawking chunks of deep-fried cheese. "Are you hungry?"

"No, not really," I mumbled distractedly. I couldn't ruin the buzz already brewing in my brain.

Working our way through a steamy pole barn choked with people pondering goods and gadgets, I sidestepped them politely but inside wished for a bulldozer. Why were they milling about like cattle when *beer* was available? I was sad and sorry for them, placidly fingering oven mitts from Ely and holding up jars of blackberry jam someone had spent hours canning. While they wasted time haggling over Joe Blow's homemade granola, I was going to get drunk. *Too bad for them.*

Suddenly, it crushed me. I couldn't stop now if my life depended upon it. Scoring a drink was challenging, but I was willing to do *anything* for it. Sickening fear swept in as I was overcome by alcohol—my reigning king—and its inescapable power. Once I *started*, all control would be lost. The sudden revelation of my unstoppable pursuit of total obliteration punched me in the stomach with a terrific force. I almost changed my mind.

Emerging from the barn and into the hot sun, I drew in a huge breath of relief. There, not twenty feet ahead, was an oasis—a neon sign that screamed BEER GARDEN.

Beck pointed. "There's the bar. Should we grab a quick one?"

With my raging battle shielded from oh-so-casual Beck, I nodded hypnotically as euphoria escalated. I was going to get *drunk*. Remaining calm as we shuffled in line, Beck chattered about mundane things like the prices, weather, and crowds while I stood mesmerized by the man handling the taps. Attempting to smile and fool him into believing I was *normal*, I wanted to morph into a regular Jill who'd stopped by to wet her whistle. It was so hot. Did my face betray me?

The atmosphere in the beer garden was merry and lovely. Sneaking glances around, I soaked up the easy, animated behavior of people just kicking back with a couple of adult beverages. A group of guys hovering over a pub table caught my attention then. Beck and I weren't exclusive and he wasn't blocking future prospects, but I needed to get a few beers down first.

The boys were full of energy, signaling the server for another round. After a cautious glance, a bright blue polo shirt caught my eye, the oval patch above the breast identifying its owner as a *Pool Boy*. I instantly liked the cheeky reference enough to overlook the cherubic face and fine copper hair that normally wouldn't have been enticing. Our eyes locked then, and I wondered vaguely if he thought I was fat. My legs boasted a great tan, but the golden-brown shading did little to mask my hefty thighs.

Did he notice? He was husky himself, maybe just slightly chubby, which was fine and accepted for men—though not for me.

Our eyes met as I furtively watched him sip his beer. Easy. Drinking, talking, flirting, no guilt, no remorse, no regret. The magical cocktail of control was so close—and I hadn't abandoned my tireless pursuit of it. Beck ordered two giant beers and passed one over as my sane mind whispered: *There's still time to stop yourself.*

The devil's loud and persistent mental daggers made the voice of reason slip into the backdrop. *Go ahead and do it! No one cares. You can blend right in! Get the sweet relief you crave.*

The angel's pleas were much weaker: *You know what happened last time! Do you want to throw away more than a month of sobriety? You'll be crazy and out of control and hate yourself tomorrow. Another failure.*

The saint turned away because I had reached the point of no return.

I was too far gone for an intervention.

Turning back to the frosty beer in my hand, I revered that red cup of old, knowing just one swallow would vanquish the battle. *DO IT!*

The mental assault was silenced as I raised the precious plastic to my mouth and downed a mighty swig before anyone could interrupt. Could they see the struggle within, the battle between good and evil that always took place before I gave in?

The burning gulp flooded my throat, and I was changed, possessed, and fortified. Time stood still with no tomorrow and no consequences.

The relief was instant, the first slug of beer shutting down the fire within and the torturous war of words exchanged between the Holy voice and the enemy. Most of that first jumbo glass disappeared in ten minutes, liquid silk coating my soul with luxurious numbness.

Drinking buddy Beck was much more laid back, having shifted to complacent crowd scanning after only downing a few swigs.

"Guess what? Now that I've *started* drinking, there's no stopping me now," I revealed.

"Really?" he responded with great interest. "I could quit and just go watch the show. Doesn't really matter to me."

Such a simple guy. Kind, decent, and apparently not addicted.

The Tap Man soon beckoned with another cup of heaven. After lounging at the bar for a while, beer scarcity mode commenced, and I began pounding colossal cups like water checkpoints at a marathon. Beck was powerless to moderate me—each time I hit the bathroom I scored another beverage on the return trip.

While swilling bottomless brews in the setting sun, the morning after was an unpleasant nag from the very distant future that the excitement of the fair easily smothered. Outrageous flirting fooled Beck into believing our budding connection may continue beyond this one August night, and I appeared alert and animated. It was an illusion. Beneath the mania, my brain was methodically going to sleep.

As darkness crept in, Beck was forgotten while I flirted

with someone at the concession stand. Miles was the guy with the *Pool Boy* shirt I'd spotted earlier. I soon learned he owned a mobile disc jockey business in Eau Claire, Wisconsin, and before long he shared stories of his connections to famous musicians, along with his plan to get backstage that night.

"I'm a TV news reporter *and* an anchor, so I've met a celebrity or two," I bragged, passing him a business card as proof. "I'm a DJ, too. I've done events for the past ten years."

Miles smiled coyly, possibly doubting my claims.

"Which celebrities?"

Shrugging like it was everyday news, I rattled off a short list. "Rick Nielsen from Cheap Trick, Eddie Money, Collin Raye... Jesse Ventura. A bunch of politicians too . . . you know, with the TV job. Oh yeah, I met the guys from ELO, too." Thinking of the night our paths had crossed at Moondance Jam made me cringe. I'd been extremely drunk, repeating the same question endlessly: "Which one of you is Jeff Lynne?"

Jeff had left years earlier—and not on good terms.

Laughing like a hyena as Miles and I continued getting acquainted, I immensely enjoyed name-dropping and inflating myself for pointless reasons. I didn't realize then I'd been just another drunk small-town media type fawning over the rock stars, convinced I was the hottest thing going. They'd seen it all so many times before. But Miles chuckled, maybe with just a little admiration.

"Can I bum a cigarette?"

Though I wasn't a serious smoker, drinking always produced a powerful and overwhelming urge to light up. Miles sparked a Marlboro Light and passed it over, the gesture somehow seductive. Suddenly remembering Beck, Pool Boy shifted to the back burner as I puffed on the cig and stumbled back to my seat in the grandstand.

"Where have you been?" Beck asked, more amused than anything else.

He wasn't mad. He never got mad.

"Around."

Melissa had left the building. I was trashed, the gaping mouth of the blackout waiting to swallow me whole.

My next dim recollection transported me to the front of the crowd—facing the band Night Ranger with just a narrow security pit separating us. Apparently, I'd found Miles again, and he did have connections. Drunk on "Sister Christian," I was primal and impulsive, and beamed right back to 1985.

As though he'd never existed, Beck fell into obscurity as my blackout self took over. She walked for me, talked for me, said things I never would when in my right mind. By the time Boston, the headliners, took the stage, my brain was as desolate as a shuttered city. Pressed against the security barrier, I was close enough to make eye contact with the band members—but I'd never remember it later. The rest of the night was lost.

Twelve hours later, I came to.

Drunk and disoriented in a strange motel room, I hung from the bed, eye level with a cheap marigold bedspread. Someone was talking. Slowly things came into focus as I struggled to weave together the previous night. *Where am I?* Bits and pieces flooded in at warp speed, but it was as nonsensical as trying to discern shapes through frosted glass. Beck hovered overhead.

"Melissa. Wake up. We have to go. I think your car was towed."

His face was panicked, not the congenial, up-for-anything

Beck I'd grown accustomed to. My car? Where was it? Head pounding, I struggled into a sitting position as the bedspread fell away, revealing my naked body. Stumbling into the tiny bathroom, I slammed the door against Beck's troubled expression.

The old yellow retro tile in the motel john stuck to my bare feet as I crouched on the toilet, cradling my head. What had happened?

My last point of recall was drinking beer, flirting with guys, and waiting for the band. One brief flash of being stage right, but then my memories tumbled into nothingness. How had I left the fun and revelry of the fair only to be beamed to a horrifying place of sickness and emotional ruin? Forty-nine days sober and I'd drank the madness and insanity back in one superficial evening.

Gingerly guiding a finger along my left side, I winced while wondering if I'd cracked a rib. My right knee throbbed with pain, and the other was capped with an enormous magenta goose egg practically swelling before my eyes.

My battered body was a fitting companion for the rest of the hangover aftermath. Alcohol withdrawal surged in as my heart pounded with a familiar yet exquisitely hideous panic attack. My mind just tumbled over itself as I remained paralyzed, unable to think or talk.

After escaping the bathroom, I gathered my things while Beck summoned a cab. Anchored dumbly in the back of the taxi, I struggled to hold back tears as my partner in crime directed the driver. The beautiful, breezy morning and chatty and cheerful cabbie could not blot out my personal hell. My mind screamed its reckless course of insane thoughts as I sat in miserable silence. Terrified and helpless, I truly wished to die.

Fifteen minutes later, we returned to the fairgrounds. Destination unknown, I couldn't coax my mouth into forming words, I just shuffled behind Beck—speechless and on auto-pilot—searching for my clean, red Acura.

Walking without purpose, I was still half-drunk, my primary task keeping enough distance behind Beck so I wouldn't have to talk to him. As we roamed the endless parking lots, the drone of lawn mowers and ground workers cleaning up last night's party muffled my choking sobs.

Finally, we reached the impound lot and scraped together thirty bucks to release my car. I'd been choking on my tears for over an hour, but after navigating away from St. Paul onto the straight, emotionless expanse of I-35, an uncontrollable flood of emotion burst forth, with sobs wracking my entire body. Heaving with all the composure of a Raggedy Ann doll, I have never cried so hard in my entire life.

Beck sat speechlessly as I drove. He'd encountered the demon Melissa—the beast birthed by alcohol. Simple, harmless beer at an event that was supposed to be fun provided a gaping hole for the devil to do his work. I couldn't get people to fully understand. *They had to see it to believe it.*

"Mel, I had no idea you were that bad. I never should have encouraged you to drink." Beck looked genuinely regretful.

It didn't matter. I knew what I was going to do even before Beck joined the party—he was just another pawn in the enemy's master plan.

As we drove, Beck revealed more about the lost night and shared agonizing things I couldn't remember and didn't want to know. I'd been forced to submit a breath test while leaving the fairgrounds, and the police wanted to transport me to detox.

Beck was too distraught to remember the breathalyzer reading: .35? .40? Approaching lethal levels, apparently. Unable to walk, I'd tumbled down the cement grandstand stairs several times, resulting in badly bruised knees and possibly cracked ribs. *Did someone slip something into her drink?* An incredulous police officer had asked Beck.

My good-natured buddy spared me the deplorable admission to the detox center by assuring the officers he would keep watch—make sure I didn't die and all. Beck's presence likely prevented me from taking off with a nefarious stranger, and served as a barrier between a possibly fatal injury, like splitting my head open on the concrete—instead of just suffering cracked ribs, bruises, and paralyzing shame. But his services came at a cost. Something had happened between us, something I couldn't remember at all.

Something.

"Mel, I did something I'm not too proud of last night," Beck began.

I didn't bother looking at him. I knew.

Everything about that morning felt terribly wrong. I began to pray, slowly and methodically. Truly having reached the end of myself, I cried out to God, and thoughts of my late father swirled through my head.

I'd been chatting with the Big Guy since I was a small child playing in a large pile of dirt dumped in front of my house for some project I don't think ever happened. He was an inaccessible wizard-like Being way up in the sky then—not yet Jesus Christ, God in the flesh, the Man who'd walked the earth, who'd already borne this day on the cross.

Pain and desperation had driven me to bankruptcy. I stared

at my feet and screamed in my mind. *Please God, help me! Don't ever let me drink again! I cannot do this alone!*

That morning, I laid my addiction at the foot of the cross, and I surrendered, although I didn't quite know the enormity—the saving grace—that had met me the moment I sincerely cried out to Him.

2

From age five, I was forever hooked on a feeling—spinning around in the living room to get dizzy and whipping myself into a frenzy before the wide panoramic windows overlooking Caribou Lake. My sit-and-spin quickly wore out after endless hours of fun on the kitchen tile, finding ways to change my present reality into something a little more thrilling my life's goal. I loved performing and envisioned myself a future *Solid Gold* dancer while I practiced their routines, pretending I was before a packed house.

Sheltered in the north woods, my early years included a tight circle of friends, swimming with supervision only, building forts, and bike riding until twilight. My father kept me on a short leash and took a great deal of pride in my hair, something that would later seem overly controlling. While my girlfriends modeled cute Dorothy Hamill haircuts and pierced ears in the 1980s, Dad adamantly clung to his position: "If God had wanted you to have holes in your head, he would've put them there." Professional scissors never touched my long blonde locks until the summer before I entered seventh grade—Dad always did the trimming himself. Afterward, he'd douse my cheeks with a little Mennen Skin Bracer aftershave.

Sunday afternoons were spent listening to him play the piano by ear in a tiny space with knotty pine walls we called the music room.

"I'm your old man. That's a biological fact that *you* can't change." Dad had endless quips and was a gifted musician—having mastered everything from the piano and electric guitar to the ukulele. Music was his life—weekly he practiced with the Harbormasters Barbershop chorus in downtown Duluth, and also joined many breakout quartets. Mondays, it was my job to scavenge through the floor of my parents' closet for his patent leather chorus shoes—polishing them with lemon Pledge before he headed out for the night.

I loved Dad's identity as a masterful singer of four-part harmony—my favorite childhood T-shirt a white one with red piping that proclaimed to the world: "My Dad's a Barbershopper." Every year we watched him perform, and he won many competitions. Dad was always making music, and I was deeply proud of his talent.

Along with the sounds of Barbershop harmony, Dad's taste was deeply rooted in the 1960s and he joined various bands over the years—their practice time filling our house with the

British Invasion. I loved Dad's music. Hours disappeared as I sorted through stacks of old 45s and spun my favorites on my little suitcase record player. The battered copy of "Chug-a-Lug" got a ton of airplay, along with tunes by the Beatles and the Stones. I had no idea Roger Miller was crooning about getting drunk—the infectious tale about grape wine from a mason jar just made me deliriously happy. Between songs, I'd fetch Dad beers while he tinkered outside on a run-down painting truck.

"Melis, bring me an ice-cold Blast," Dad grinned, wiping sweat from his brow. "I've worked up a powerful thirst out here! Then we'll sing a tag."

I became a master mimicker—my ears constantly gravitating to a melody—learning now to copy it was easy, and exposure to Dad's constant vocal exercises taught pitch and harmony. His favorite part of a musical piece was the dramatic ending to a song when all four vocal parts reached a crescendo with unmistakable ringing as the chords locked together.

When Dad requested beer, he was referring to his preferred cheap swill—Blatz. Our three-season porch stocked it in mass quantities, and I was always allowed a few sips.

My parents barely squeaked by each month—often borrowing from my Grandma June to make ends meet. Their cars were old and rusty—savings nonexistent—but that didn't slow their impulsive spending. Dad's work history was dicey, and he explored many career pursuits and get-rich-quick schemes. Luckily, my mother's eventual employment as a bookkeeper provided a steady income to keep the family afloat.

Mom was a teen bride who'd been married just two weeks when my brother was born—and by the time I came along, finances were still tight, but they'd managed to move into their own place. A second income and a sitter were suddenly necessities. A fancy preschool was out of the question, so a lovely neighbor lady named Marge who lived right down the road became my caregiver. Marge and her husband Harold didn't have children together (though Marge was definitely "Mom" to Harold's daughter from a previous relationship). Instantly, we were close as flesh and blood.

Spirit-filled Christian Marge Mahaney was the only surrogate I would allow. Deviations from my dysfunctional family generally left me panicked and distressed, but Marge's quiet, cozy bungalow was the exception. Filled with the smells of homemade cooking and the sounds of three yapping dogs, the welcome haven was my second home, and I happily joined her family on weekend road trips. Marge oozed comfort and peace, emanating a Holy presence I couldn't quite identify but soaked up like bread from heaven.

Marge tempered my vigilant disposition with blissful tranquility, easing my fears with a gaze from her radiant face. Alone, I was consumed by worries unknown to most kids—easily distracted by fictional tornadoes, the terrifying thought of being trapped at school, and my greatest obsession—everyone I loved suddenly abandoning me in a spontaneous rapture. My home life was unsteady with panic always licking at the back door, and wariness prevailed even when things were stable. Marge's house was void of fear.

Days with my second mom were spent working in her garden, canning things, and learning a whole lot about Jesus. I blended in seamlessly with her family, joining Marge and Harold on camping trips each summer. Mom labeled Marge "religious" but didn't go into detail; always biting her tongue before saying something she'd regret—and I might repeat. My parents disdained the people they called "born agains" or "Jesus Freaks," comparing them to popular televangelists and prosperity gospel ministers of the 1980s they believed to be unstable lunatics. The underlying message of the supernatural realm was one of avoidance—it was okay to sing the Doxology about "Father, Son, and Holy Ghost" in conclusion to Reverend Grobe's lengthy sermons, but outside of our sporadic "only for show" church attendance, the things of the Spirit were off the table.

Though we didn't purposely sit down for Bible study, Marge truly lived her Christian faith, peppered everything she did with talk of what Jesus would do, and planted precious nuggets of gold into my troubled heart. She did her best to offer discipleship with the time we had, overseeing many milestones: potty training, flying kites, stomping in puddles in red rubber boots, and even my very first steps. She kept these cherished memories to herself until I was well into adulthood, perhaps wanting her extremely influential maternal role to stay humbly close to her heart.

Each summer, Marge dutifully delivered me to Vacation Bible School at her Baptist church where I learned stories about Jesus and memorized the names of all sixty-six books of the Bible. When I was nine, I was invited to accept Christ at the Northern City Baptist church.

Brandi, the bubbly youth leader, had regarded our group very seriously that last day of VBS. "Boys and girls, it's the end of our week together, and it's time for an important invitation. Who wants to ask Jesus into their heart? Come on down to the front."

Dutifully following the rest of the crowd, I knelt in the circle on the linoleum of the church basement as Brandi led us in the sinner's prayer, the "Hello My Name is" tag stuck to my shirt and branding me "Missi"—made me feel like an imposter.

Later that day, I relayed the experience to my mother with some unease. I needed to get the whole thing off my chest and felt vaguely guilty for not seeking permission before taking this *important step*. Mom seemed uncomfortable with my new conversion, assured me it was "no big deal," and hurried to change the subject.

A product of stoic Scandinavian parents who considered religion a very private matter, my parents encouraged rote observance of Christian holidays, but little else. Our family had no practice of reading the Bible or talking about God—though I remember being taught the Lord's Prayer at a young age and being directed to recite it before bed. To my parents, it was understood that we believed in a power greater than ourselves.

Though we occasionally attended church, dinner at the Chalet Lounge was my parents' more anticipated Sunday focus. Dad never used the Swiss French pronunciation *sha-lay,* instead, it was affectionately referred to as the "cha-lit"—sounding just like *mallet.* Another sideways defiance of a dad who did things on his own terms. The Chalet was a dingy bar/supper club joint (that still exists to this day, with reportedly amazing food and service), but in my limited experience, it was a high-class dining experience.

The smell of deep-fried food blew from the vents as we approached the front door, the portal inside a dark and dingy vestibule with a pay phone. Poking my finger into the coin slot in search of a forgotten quarter for the video games was an ingrained habit. Beyond the swinging door, a dimly lit restaurant awaited, loud maroon carpet leading into the bar. A pair of pool tables dominated the room, their wide expanse of bright green a garish but comfortable beacon under stained glass beer lanterns. Along the back wall, a row of arcade games awaited, with the jukebox tucked into an alcove just off the dining area.

We were regulars, so our waitress, Connie, was afforded the luxury of sharing the latest tale about her deadbeat boyfriend with Mom, rather than droning on about the boring specials. Connie already knew what we wanted. Poised with a mint green pad of grease-stained paper, she snapped spearmint gum as I examined her red Dr. Scholl's and tight Jordache jeans. *When I grow up, I want to be a waitress just like Connie.* I'd have *the usual*, my golden fish 'n' chips basket served with fries, a cup of coleslaw, and a floppy pickle spear. My brother Dave's standby was a cheeseburger with fried onions. Being known at the local supper club brought a sense of belonging.

As we huddled in our dimly lit private booth overlooking the jukebox, I grew hypnotized by the Victorian flocked velvet wallpaper facing me from the opposite side, and envisioned a normal family out for Sunday dinner. The movie playing in my head was a familiar rerun; the star of the show a precocious, bright-eyed, nine-year-old—the sort of kid adults were thrilled to show off.

Minutes later, my screenplay derailed.

"I'm gonna go get a snort," Dad whispered to Mom, then hustled off to the bar. *What does a snort mean? Is he snorting it up his nose?*

"Go play," Mom ordered, handing over a fistful of quarters. Her auburn hair was tucked behind her ears, and she fanned away smoke from her Winston as I reached for the coins. Dave and I headed off to the gaming area while Dad returned with a double shot of blackberry brandy and a fistful of pull tabs. We were forgotten as our parents attacked the pile of cardboard cocaine, on the hunt for a big winner. When my mother peeled a lucky ticket—one with a red line across the top—she gave it a kiss and set it off to the side to "let it grow" while she burned through the rest of the stack.

"Letting it grow" meant allowing the winner time to "steep" so to speak, much like a tea bag might to enhance the flavor. On the rare occasion my parents got lucky and won a few bucks, Dave and I enjoyed extra money for the vending machine in the adjacent laundromat. While the dryers roared, I'd happily exchange coins for Whatchamacallit bars and Reese's peanut butter cups. But most nights the cardboard pull tab heap held just a bunch of losers that brought a sense of gloom to our little party.

Candy bars, kiddie cocktails, and arcade games—Sundays often started out like a kid's dream, hours spent anchored at the Ms. Pac-Man machine sweating with the effort of controlling the joystick and chasing the color-changing ghosts before they transformed into evil apparitions. But dinner always stretched a little too late into the evening, and it was a school night. Panicked on the drive home, Dad kept weaving over the centerline making me fear he was headed for the ditch, and he and my mother were always fighting.

Most adults made me nervous. My evaluations of grown-ups included intensive appraisals to determine their trust level, and they usually failed the test. Ten years old and a little chubby, the expanse between me and the popular girls was widening along with my waistline. I didn't know I'd never close the gap.

Sleepover parties began warily; I'd arrive with my overnight bag and begin my parental inspection. If I sensed sweetness and warmth or the mother took special interest in me I might make it, but a cool or ambivalent reception sent me careening off the rails. In no time, I'd be on the phone begging Dad to go home, later slinking out to his waiting truck with a concessionary birthday treat bag I didn't deserve.

No one could figure out what was wrong. *Don't you want to stay? We're going to have cake and watch movies!*

I'd shake my head helplessly. *No! I just want to go.*

Carmen Davis invited me on a camping trip to Boulder Lake the summer I was ten. For weeks we talked on the phone excitedly about the getaway, and during the lead-up time, I hoped to avoid a repeat performance of my past failures with friends. The campground featured a little lodge with snacks like Doritos and Mountain Dew, a raft for jumping into the lake, and boys. I couldn't wait. My parents delivered me 40 minutes north of Duluth to the secluded campground.

After Mom and Dad disappeared down the long, winding driveway, I hung on a swing overlooking the lake, a ball of anxiety and dread swirling in my stomach as I considered the long hours away from home. Trying in vain to stuff the dread down, I was committed to *getting through it.* But as night fell, the reality of retreating to the camper and facing the chance that everyone could fall asleep before me became unbearable.

Along with being left alone in a car, I had intense phobias about going to bed—particularly being the last one awake. Carmen's parents, although funny and affectionate, were causing apprehension.

As panic percolated to an alarming level, I ran into the lodge and called Dad, begging him to come back. He had just arrived home and was not at all pleased about turning around and driving another thirty miles. He agreed, though, always promising he'd come in the middle of the night and would never leave me somewhere I didn't want to be. In spite of his issues, he never broke that vow. Carmen sat next to me in confused silence as we waited.

"Why do you want to leave? We were going to have fun!"

I shook my head pitifully; sure I had ruined our friendship for good.

The term *panic attack* was not part of anyone's vocabulary back then, and no one understood my horrible physical reactions or the terror they caused. Mom and Dad didn't say a whole lot about the matter, though I did overhear Mom whispering on the phone about my neuroses: "Melissa is going through another *stage*."

Since the crippling episodes were impossible for my fellow tweens to comprehend, I soon gained a reputation of a wimpy baby no one should bother including on their slumber party roster.

Grandma June was my dad's mother, a platinum-haired bundle of energy and to-do lists who worked hard and played even harder. Lazy and ungrateful children were two of her biggest pet peeves, and it wasn't unusual for her to saddle my brother and me with loathsome tasks to fill our down time. One Saturday morning our parents were gone and we were watching cartoons and happily slurping sweet milk from our cereal bowls when Gram's tanklike Chrysler suddenly turned into the driveway.

Dave tossed his bowl into the sink and switched the TV off.

"Here comes Gram! She's going to make us work," he yelled. "Let's HIDE!"

Through wary of his plan, I didn't want to spend my

Saturday scrubbing tile grout or purging the "boar's nest" (Gram's disdainful nickname for our cluttered basement), so I joined him in scurrying down the stairs to huddle in the moldy closet.

"Kids?" Gram had slipped her own key into the lock and was now clacking her ever-present pumps through the kitchen. "Dave? Missy?"

Gram was the only one who ever called me *Missy*.

I felt nervous, and possibly on the verge of peeing—but defying her was also making me just a bit giddy.

Dave put his finger to his lips, barely visible in the crack of light through the door.

"SHHH!"

Gram eventually left and we salvaged our Saturday . . . for a while, anyway.

But soon she was back and cornered me, probably knowing I was the weakest of the litter.

"Mis, I came by last weekend, I looked *all over* for you kids. I literally walked up and down the road until *my legs ached* . . . I went to Margie's, Mary Jo's—*no one* had seen you. WHERE WERE YOU?" Her voice had escalated to an ear-splitting crescendo by this time, and I sat paralyzed and unable to speak.

"WELL?" Gram sputtered. "WHERE *were* YOU?"

In a wee little voice I finally squeaked, "We were hiding."

Gram completely lost it. "YOU WERE *WHAT?*" She railed, her mouth cinched into a tight circle of reprehensible disbelief. "You were *HIDING?* After everything I've done for you? *No one* lies to me and gets away with it. I hate *LIARS* worse than poison!"

I crumpled into a heap of uncontrollable sobbing then, convinced I was the most horrible, disgusting, vile little girl around.

For the record, Dave was in NO trouble at all. Gram would not speak to me for months and refused to even acknowledge my presence, until my mother lost it and blew up in her face a couple of months later.

"You're always telling Melissa to be truthful, and she was, and now you're crucifying her!" Gram said nothing and didn't apologize, though her icy heart began to thaw just a little. Interesting choice of words from my mother, I do not think my ostracism equaled death on a cross. She did manage to get her point across, however.

Grandma June later received a big chunk of cash and generously handed over a crisp $100 bill to both my brother and me to blow at the Miller Hill Mall. She had always been very generous, and this was her thin attempt at an apology. I greedily accepted it. Forever with my nose in a book, my first stop was Walden Books. Breathing in the heady scent of paperbacks, I was in my element. While perusing the shelves of the young adult section, I stumbled upon the Nancy Drew series for the first time.

The Hidden Staircase caught my eye, and I was transfixed by the image of Nancy ascending the creepy set of cobwebby stairs. That captivating cover soon unleashed a compulsion to disappear into the book, to become a detective, and to help my father solve mysteries all over town. Nancy Drew, Judge Wapner, and endless bags of potato chips would soon become faithful friends, keeping me company during the lonely hours after school. Other mall stops to Spencer's Gifts and Kay Bee Toys yielded a few worthless trinkets, but that first Nancy Drew novel hooked me—prompting a major buying binge and return trip to Walden's to sweep up the rest of the series. Drunk with excitement, I strolled the mall with my little paper sacks stuffed with books.

Novels and sitcoms never failed. Our family's main hobby and bonding activity was watching television, so other role models became the families and teen girls starring on my favorite primetime shows. The bratty kid sister types in shows like *Alf, Growing Pains, Family Ties,* and *Mr. Belvedere* were my favorites, so I recorded the episodes on our clunky old Quasar VCR and rewatched them, trying to memorize the mannerisms of each character.

Iconic, skinny, sassy teens taught me how to act. Popular and witty, clad in the hippest shaker sweaters, stirrup pants, and chunky brightly colored strings of fake beads—they offered dissociation from reality and a paper-thin sense of identity. Each morning my ideal life movie would play, free of an alcoholic dad, junk cars in the driveway, and the ever-present disconnect notices threatening the loss of our phone service. As I rolled out of bed and into a purple shaker sweater, I morphed into Heather from *Mr. Belvedere* or Samantha from *Who's the Boss.* My all-time favorite though was Shannen Doherty's character on the weekly drama *Our House.* Smart, fierce, *and* an aspiring astronaut.

The other players in my life were forever ruining my acting attempts though—either Dad would be drunk or Mom would freak out because no vacuum tracks had been engraved into the carpet when she returned home from work. *I messed up. I'll start over again tomorrow.*

Sometimes, I'd experience a moment of clarity where I realized my existence was actually in a 980-square-foot converted cabin—*not* a Hollywood mansion. My goal to model an affluent and well-adjusted teen with high-functioning parents never stuck, but focus on fictional families helped.

My brother Dave was six years older—born when my parents were sixteen and seventeen. Our age difference seemed wider than the Grand Canyon, and I often felt like an only child because of it. An amazing athlete who excelled in school and had a knack for just about everything, Dave had apparently dodged the addict bullet. Friends with intact families helped provide stability, and he was always winning some award or another.

Then there was me. Clumsy, chubby, and not exactly a hot commodity when it came to sports. Attempting nonphysical stuff like piano lessons, spelling bees, and plays was safer—but I struggled to follow through. My gymnastics career was short-lived because my pudgy body caused extreme feelings of self-consciousness as I attempted to squeeze into my leotard with everyone else in the dressing room.

Dmitri, the intimidating Russian coach, was clearly disgusted by my weight and rapped me sharply in the stomach one day at practice.

"Suck in that pizza!" he barked right in front of everyone.

Lying about the number on the scale became necessary for survival.

"How much do you weigh?" he demanded, as the other petite Mary Lou Rettons watched, wide-eyed.

Through lips as dry as parchment I croaked, "Seventy."

A skeptical once-over indicated he wasn't buying it.

"If you want to be a gymnast you need to drop some weight," was his flat, emotionless response.

Mortified, I never returned to gymnastics again.

My next attempt at fitting in was Little League softball. Stationed in the forgotten back outfield was just fine with me, I hoped to conceal my painful lack of athletic ability. Not that anyone else was rock star material—our team was currently in eighth place out of ten. My parents had yet to see me in action, and I was cool with that. Dad was extremely vocal and obnoxious at sporting events, and my football and track star brother offered plenty of opportunities for family name bonus points and parental pride.

As I clambered off the bus one game day, I was surprised to find Dad's beat-up old painting truck parked in the driveway. Instantly swallowed in panic, something foreboding choked the atmosphere. *Why was he home?* As the bus disappeared in a cloud of dust, I talked myself down from the ledge. *Maybe he wasn't feeling well? Maybe he finished his job early?* Dad referred to himself grandly as a *tradesman,* but really my uncle had simply overlooked his drinking antics by providing work through the family business. He knew Dad was unreliable and slower than molasses, but dealt with it for Mom's sake.

Dad's heavy drinking kicked in around fourth grade when I was nine and my brother fifteen. I have no memory of any physical abuse, but his intimidating presence did enough talking of its own. The sharp warning crack of a belt whipping from its loops, a vice grip on the upper arm when someone needed correction, a firm kick in the rear when we'd done something dumb (like the time I accidentally stabbed him in the back with a flaming stick—I deserved what I got for that one). I'd heard ominous tales of Dad's spankings when I was a small child ("Dad would cry after paddling you" my mother insisted, and years later admitted I had wet my pants once while anticipating his wrath). One thing was certain, when Dad was angry I felt the intense urge to relieve myself, and I was extremely afraid of authority figures. For years, my brother had infused good-natured harmony when Dad and Gram were flipping their lids, but I was on my own once he left for college.

Back to that softball day near the end of the school year, the mild afternoon seemed suspended—a point in time stamped into my limbic brain that seemed necessary for survival. Closing in on the front door, the pleasant day faded once I had slipped my key into the lock. Barbershop music strained through the porch door—growing louder and intensifying my apprehension as I moved through the must-choked sun porch. Gram had lovingly filled the three-season space with aqua floral patio furniture and hanging conch shell chandeliers and dubbed it the Florida Room, wanting a little piece of the south right in the Land of 10,000 Lakes. But Dad had allowed her treasured haven to fall into disrepair.

Plenty cocky about providing a lake-home lifestyle, Dad glossed over the details and led everyone to believe he'd scrimped and pinched for a down payment on resort property. Actually, Gram had facilitated it all, offering her house to us when I was five for next to nothing. She eventually relocated to Proctor.

A relic left over from the 50s, the Caribou Lake cabin house struggled to keep up with the times and the new construction pressing in on Sunny Lane. The lake was smallish and very weedy, but on dark summer nights, the Milky Way looked stunning mirrored in its black waters. Even if Gram facilitated it all, I was grateful. Growing up on a lake was idyllic and blissful in many ways. Swimming until I was waterlogged, catching my first sizeable northern, and hanging out on the redwood dock nearly every day from May to September. Dad would often sit there too, beer in hand, scanning the expanse before him with wholehearted satisfaction. Living in the house on Caribou Lake gave him the sideways sense of being a provider, and an aura of having worked hard to provide a little slice of heaven to the ones he loved. The luster of the lake shrouded his growing alcoholism.

"Dad?" I yelled as I walked further into the house.

The ear-splitting volume level of the music was customary for "appreciating" Barbershop harmony. That's what Dad called it. Although it was a bright day, the entire house was as dark as a funeral home with the heavy drapes in the living room drawn against the exquisite afternoon. Shadows followed my father everywhere.

Stepping into the room, hypervigilance quickened my senses, along with the faintly rancid smell of a barroom at closing time. Dad struggled into a sitting position while I observed warily from my vantage point in the doorway. I didn't need to move any closer. The cues screamed he was drunk.

"Melis."

My father beckoned, his face morphing into a creaky smile that intensified my alarm.

"You remember this one?"

Moving closer to the radio, he cranked "Top of the World," an old a cappella staple I'd heard millions of times.

"Vocal Majority," he rambled on. "They're the *best*. Saw them back in Salt Lake City in '78. You have no idea, Melis. Artists these days couldn't squeeze a pimple on any one of those guys' rear ends. Karen Carpenter, though," he mumbled distractedly. "She could pull it off."

Clearly, Dad was already armpit deep into his drunken Barbershop glory days, and it was best to agree.

"Sure. It's great, Dad."

As I flicked a lamp on, the black plastic sports mug came

into view—something a young boy would covet—featuring a helmet representing each NFL team. The mug wasn't innocent, though, it held straight vodka.

"I have a game this afternoon," I said quickly, distracted by the sight of the tumbler. "Over at the ball field on Martin Road. Can I have a ride?"

Driving with Dad was petrifying, but I was stuck. The Little League park was over five miles away, and it was much too late to ride my bike. Staying after school and riding the late bus could've prevented the whole excruciating scenario, and I agonized over my poor planning. Eyes red and half shut, Dad picked up his drink and took a pull as I evaluated his disheveled flannel shirt and greasy black hair.

"Of course." His words were unmistakably slurred. "That's why I took off work early, so I could be in attendance."

My face flushed with horror knowing my drunk dad would be jeering the batters from the stands. His dry wit and odd sense of humor escaped most, but alcohol made him unbearable.

"You don't have to do that," I choked. "Just drop me off. The game will be boring anyway."

Our competitors had already secured the first place slot—cute Barbie doll types who lived in split level homes I only dreamed of—and spent their free time horseback riding or having elaborate birthday parties in their finished basements. Their sponsor was a railroad—representing the whole Proctor-train-town-thing. In its own right, it was cliquey.

Dad looked me dead-on. "What's the matter, Melis? Are you embarrassed of your old man?"

Yeah, I was mortified—but I shook my head vigorously instead.

"No! But you haven't showered. And you're acting goofy."

Dad's drunken behavior was often labeled *goofy*, although it reflected nothing remotely comical. We danced around the ugly reality. Dad was a raging alcoholic, with no one bold enough to come out and tell the emperor he wasn't wearing clothes. Drinking made him Unpredictable Dear Old Dad. Treading lightly was crucial.

"What are you drinking?" I ventured, gesturing to the beverage in question—knowing he wouldn't answer honestly.

Dad demoted his cocktail to a decorative chunk of cork on the end table. Forever obsessive about coasters, he deplored the white rings of a wet beverage cast carelessly onto a wooden surface. Then rising from the couch, he stumbled a bit as he went about stuffing things into his pockets. Whipping open his Zippo lighter in one quick motion, he fired up a Winston. Then remembering the drink, he finished it off.

"7-Up. See fer yerself."

Waving it two inches from my nose posed a challenge—a dare—but fear blunted my primal urge to call him out. No doubt he'd been hitting the bottle all day and had just drained the cup of cheap vodka—deep down I knew that with every fiber of my being—but I dismissed him with mild annoyance.

"I believe you!"

While Dad continued stumbling about the living room, I headed downstairs to change into my uniform. Our entire living space in that cabin house was less than one thousand square feet, the unfinished basement was needed for bedrooms. I occupied its dank, cool, and musty chambers for much of my childhood—with Dave and I sharing the space for years. When I started seventh grade I moved up to the music room—but until then the basement was my dwelling place. The carpet grew wet in the summer and left squishy footprints each year as water crept in from cracks in the foundation, but no one seemed to notice. Crickets found a home there too, along with spiders and even frogs. Lying in bed at night, I'd hear small field mice scurrying along the base of my bed and the wall. I took comfort in knowing they probably couldn't crawl under the covers.

Dad's lackadaisical attitude caused the cabin house to deteriorate a little more each year. He had other priorities—weekends jam-packed with drinking and entertaining the neighbors. My mother rode him constantly to address household projects needing repair, but his response was always the same.

"Get off my back!"

I yearned for a sweetly decorated bedroom with a canopy bed, roll-top desk, and mirrored dresser. My reality was not even close: a chilly, musty, unfinished basement corner with particle board walls and a moldy closet.

My uniform was snug, and I desperately wanted to ditch the annoying fat roll I attempted to hide with the band of my sweatpants. I'd been an average-sized child up until then, but around fourth grade my consumption of after-school junk food became impossible to hide. I stuck out like a sore thumb on the perfect country Little League team.

Although I had a couple of friends who also played softball, I was still an oddball; a chubby dork with the alcoholic dad who drove a rust-bucket Ford pickup.

Although we coexisted on the team, at school I was a stranger to most. During lunchtime, I scrambled to hide my leftover meatloaf sandwich and flat 7-Up poured into a mismatched plastic bottle. My mother always packed my lunch

in an enormous paper sack, the kind used to bag groceries at
our local SuperValu store, and it was hard to blend in with the
other girls toting colorful plastic Smurfette and Garfield lunchboxes. Both my chubbiness and my lack of athletic ability were
regarded with a distant sort of pity.

Dad and I made our grand entrance to the ball field in
his rust bucket at least fifteen minutes late, making me even
more conspicuous. Never on time for a thing, events were on
his clock. Slinking to my place way out in left field, I sent up
fervent prayers to God and begged the ball to stay far away.
Watching Dad from the outfield was excruciating. He was
yelling, swearing, and spewing profanities. *Could I please just
die right now?*

As we changed field positions, the coaches stage-whispered
to each other. Dad was a few feet off with his hands raised over
his head, fingers hooked into the chicken wire of the dugout
in an effort to keep his balance. His baggy painting pants were
spattered with layers of old wood stain, a gray hooded sweatshirt loosely knotted and sagging from his waist. I loathed his
presence, parked like a redneck albatross right in front of the
dugout on the infield, which was a major no-no for spectators.

"C'mon, team, let's DO IT!" he bellowed, the last two words
resounding in his usual pathetic battle cry for attention.

I studied the coaches in horror—they were gossiping about
Dad, just as I had dreaded.

"I think he's drunk," one whispered.

I wanted to dig a hole in left field and crawl into it until
the game was over.

This shameful day marked the first and last sporting event
of mine that either of my parents attended.

3

Not only was I addicted to sugar, but mirrors were my best friends. From a very young age, I would stop dead in my tracks anywhere I spotted my reflection. My deep fear was that I didn't really exist, and nonstop gazing at myself offered just a little relief. My parents teased me and vowed I'd someday grow up to be a movie star.

Living in the moment was a way of life in my household with keeping the peace at all costs necessary for survival. Dad never really grew up or learned responsibility or how to lead a family—spending most of his early years as a spoiled and pacified golden boy. Gram adored her two perfect sons, and though she dimly acknowledged alcohol caused problems, she considered it perfectly fine for just about anyone over the age of ten to drink beer.

Gram's enabling hobbled Dad's development, and her abundant handouts helped him dodge serious financial problems, though he was often out of work. During his short-lived college years, Gram provided a new car and supplied spending cash, clueless to Dad's chronic school ditching. He'd later describe almost proudly how he'd arrive home in his Ford 406 just in time to intercept his failing grade notices from the mailbox.

At just sixteen, my mother discovered she was expecting my brother. Dad was a tall, lanky, bleached-blond surfer boy when he won her attention; he and his family were blessed to spend the brutal Minnesota winters in West Palm Beach, Florida, a type of lifestyle unheard of by my mother and her sheltered friends. Dad loved to tell stories of Key West sunsets, the glorious Seven Mile bridge, and days of surfing from sunrise to sunset. They weren't rich—they occupied a very modest trailer during those snowbird winters—but Gram didn't care. Florida was her dream destination, and just being in the Sunshine State did something magical to her psyche. I've since been told I have Florida in my blood. The Ellefson clan made the most of every day—over the years I'd seen many black-and-white photos of gourmet dinners in their old Airstream, long walks on the beach, and sand dollar art—with every single sunset a special event deserving of Brandy Manhattans.

To a bundled-up Minnesotan who'd never dipped a toe out of the Upper Midwest, the surf appeal made Dad quite a catch, and he radiated integrity, gaining acclaim on the Proctor swimming team and never touching a drop of alcohol while courting my mother. She had no reason to believe booze would become a future landmine. With his fast car and all-American good looks, Dad was just about as cool as James Dean, and Mom was quickly head over heels in love. Back then, few options existed when a pregnancy occurred. Mom had dreamed of college, but that wasn't happening now.

"You *will* get married," Grandma June had insisted.

After they tied the knot in a brief, undercover ceremony two weeks before my brother's birth, Mom and Dad moved into Grandma June's basement. Grandpa Boyd had upgraded it to a year-round home—and Gram had delegated every aspect to align with her preferences. That meant lots and lots of bright aqua blue paint.

Gram *adored* all things aqua. Mom despised that shade of blue and as the years went by, developed a lot more to hate. Young Susie Q did not want to live with Dan's domineering mother, but had no other options. Barely seventeen with an infant son and no job—she was terrified of Gram's brandy binges. To earn her keep, my mother was quickly turned into a live-in maid.

Mom was naïve and timid but eventually reached her breaking point. She once shared a story of Gram demanding Mom serve her and a group of friends one night after work. Mom dutifully delivered cocktails to the banking gang as they lounged in Adirondack chairs in front of the lake and was further instructed to tend to the roast Gram had left cooking in the oven. But as the night wore on, Gram's frequent demands for brandy wore on my mother's nerves, and when she rattled the cubes in her glass for about the tenth time and yelled, "Susie! Set us up!" Mom lost it. She ran to the edge of the lake and fired the overdone roast down the hill, screaming, *"You WENCHHHHHHHH!"*

She was a bit of a spitfire back then.

Fearing Gram's wrath, Mom tore back into the house and locked herself in the bathroom. The next morning, Gram was her same old self, requesting black coffee and burnt toast "buttered to the edges," making a chore list, and firing orders. Apparently, she had no memory of my mother's reckless handling of the roast.

Gram had lost her husband of thirty years to a brain aneurysm just weeks after my parents married and grappled to fill his void with my brother—newborn baby David. Mom and Dad had moved into the basement that would one day become my musty bedroom, but Gram insisted on keeping Dave's bassinet next to her bed. When he fussed in the night, Gram quickly swept him up before Mom could respond. Her resentment grew like a wild thorn bush, but she never said much, and instead of advocating for his young wife, Dad preferred the conflict avoidance route.

Headstrong and haughty, Gram held a high position at a local bank, a big deal for a woman back then. One Halloween, my mother tagged along to a party for the bank's employees. Baby David went too, dressed up as a darling little field mouse. My mother was proud and made sure he was warm and snug, turning frequently to the backseat to check on him. Gram drove like a bat out of hell from Caribou Lake into Proctor.

"*Why are we always pushing the clock?*" she roared, blasting into the driveway of the house party. Mom stepped out of the car and opened the back door for Dave as Gram hovered nearby in her high heels, smug look, and wool trench coat. She reached out and clapped her hands.

"Give him to me. *I* want to carry him in!"

My mother wasn't having it. "He's *my* baby!"

"Oh, he is, is he?" Gram sneered, reapplying lipstick as she marched on her stilettos, eyes blazing. "Tell me, Missy, just *who* is putting a roof over your heads? Me. Don't forget it."

She snatched Dave from Mom's arms, and Mom relented, her mousy brown hair covering her freckled face in a sheet.

Rumor has it that my dad started drinking heavily after *his* dad passed away. Grandpa Boyd never drank much, and only when pressured would mix a small glass of wine with 7-Up and nurse it all night long. Dad's own father was one of few relatives on that side of the family who was not a problem drinker. My dad seemed to take after his mother. At just eighteen, he'd acquired his own family, the brandy helping to morph him from a coddled little boy into a man-child.

It started with the good old family physician's orders. Dad, struggling to cope with his own father's unexpected death, finally agreed to see a doctor about his stress and weight loss. The physician advised him to drink some blackberry brandy to settle his stomach, a recommendation Dad had no problem following. Several times a day, he sipped the thick berry-red liquor.

"Doctor's orders," he assured Mom. "To help my stomach."

Dad quit school then and picked up a gambling habit for spending cash, but continued to wear his husband and father titles like badges of honor. Oblivious to the future consequences of his constant brandy swilling, Dad rationalized it all away and, for a long time, the booze seemed to treat every ailment. He was young and strong with many years ahead.

Six years later, things had settled down somewhat, and I joined the family.

When Gram found out my parents had birthed a baby girl, she insisted in a highly irrational manner that they comply with her wishes to name me Carrie June, after her own mother and herself. Mom wasn't having it and compromised with Melissa June.

Dad, now in his early 20s and pursuing a career as an insurance agent, described himself on job applications as "Determined, detail-oriented, and efficient. Wife and two children. Excellent health." His presence on paper was outstanding, but the drinking was growing heavier: beer each night and weekend blow-outs with the Caribou Lake gang. Going to work hung over soon became a regular cost of playing too hard.

My parents loved entertaining—most weekends included gatherings with the neighbors or Dad's Barbershop buddies and their wives. The basement was my haven while the adults imbibed, and I was happy and secure with my brother near. Dave and I set up stair-hopping Slinkys and played Monopoly for hours, and when he grew bored with letting me win, he'd migrate to his Atari game console.

Dad called the low-ceilinged space the "down DAIRS" in a deep, booming voice, attempting to indicate something foreboding was lurking there and freak us out as kids. We loved having the private area during those party nights, the attractive black lacquer bar my grandfather had constructed back in the '50s was our favorite attraction. Intended to spearhead an entire basement renovation that my father never carried out, that bar was the showpiece of the room, still cool in spite of the cheap particle board foundation.

Sometimes Amy's parents joined the parties upstairs and we'd play cocktail lounge, taking turns as bartender. Perched over the glossy black top, we filled our tumblers with tropical punch Kool-Aid, pretended it was wine, then acted drunk and tumbled from our stools to the yellow shag carpeting.

Amy and I were inseparable—having shared Caribou Lake and Sunny Lane while moving through each school year together. Our mothers were best friends and met up every weekend for Scrabble and screwdrivers, our dads often worked in the garage together and even volunteered to take us trick-or-treating each year at a nearby trailer park. We pounded the pavement for hours in frigid late October until our pillowcases sagged under the weight of the abundant candy, with Dad joking about needing the pint of peppermint schnapps tucked in the pocket of his vest to keep warm.

My big brother was my idol, and I yearned to be his sidekick. Though he put up with a lot, our six-year age difference widened as the years passed and Dave eventually immersed himself in academics and sports. As he built stability for himself outside of the family, Dad's directionless approach to life caused increasing turmoil for me.

My terrible episodes of panic and fear were increasing: the racing heart and awful out-of-control feelings convinced me that I was dying.

"Friends are going to stop inviting you if you keep acting like a baby!" my mother warned, when, once again, I begged to be picked up in the middle of the night from a slumber party.

Something about my parents made me wary and unsettled. One night, Dad stopped off at a bar on our way home from a trip to the grocery store and left me in the backseat, where I experienced a crippling panic attack. I climbed over the seats to hide in the back, convinced I was going to get kidnapped. Adults and their broken promises were never-ending, and I didn't trust anyone.

My parents offered comforting but empty words as they departed for their pub crawls, *"We'll only stop for one, we'll bring you home a treat. Just watch TV, and we'll be back before you know it."*

I learned valuable lessons from an early age—most importantly the art of being alone without losing my marbles. Many 80's children were latchkey kids like me, with parents working fulltime without cash for babysitters. Being alone in the house was awful, especially during the fall and winter when darkness crept in early, but TV and junk food were my saviors. As long as the reliable old Zenith was blaring a sitcom or after-school special, I wasn't really alone. Afternoon hours were somewhat manageable, but weekend nights nearly finished me.

Conflict avoidance was another life skill I used to sidestep embarrassing or painful issues, and distraction, humor, or just zoning out in front of *M*A*S*H* with a Swanson frozen dinner also helped to keep the peace.

Learning to detach from people, opinions, disappointment, and pain was essential—turning within to my rich inner life provided escape from rejection and shame. The dazzling world of my mind's eye beckoned during the times Dad embarrassed me with his drunken antics, I wasn't invited to a party, or all the other girls in my class were invited out on dates while I sat home eating and recording sitcoms.

Family rituals were safety nets—most notably reliable prime-time shows my parents wouldn't miss. *Hart to Hart* was a favorite weekly program about a husband and wife amateur detective team that locked the family in together, but Thursdays soon became a bar ritual for my parents. *But Cheers is coming on . . . they need to make it home for Cheers!*

The new hangout that kick-started their weekend on Thursdays now was located on a dumpy block with other hole-in-the-wall drinking establishments and our dinner became take-out cheese soup from the saloon. Stretched out in front of the TV with my food, I became absorbed in my favorite sitcoms while envisioning our family strikingly similar to the actors on *Growing Pains*. The dad was witty and wise, the mom beautiful and loving—and the kids colorful, creative, and well-adjusted.

I could tolerate Thursdays. But Friday—my parents' *big* evening out—was dreadful. Dave was usually with friends, so I held down the fort while Mom and Dad went out on the town—the nights unfolding into long, lonely hours of pacing the floor convinced they'd died in a horrible car wreck. Anchored in front of the kitchen window, I'd hitch myself onto the old porcelain sink for a better view. *What if they were dead?*

Rifling through the Yellow Pages with panic, I'd dial up every tavern for miles, but the bartender seemed to be deaf.

"ELLEFSON," I yelled into the phone. "Could you please page Dan Ellefson?"

"Don Olson?" The bartender screamed over the background ruckus.

"No! DAN. D-A-N. Dan Ellefson. Is he there?"

Sometimes I fell into a restless doze on the couch only to be jolted awake by a lucid dream of a maniac breaking into the house. A door we never used loomed overhead, and although it was sealed shut with heavy winterizing plastic, I was convinced it just *had* to be the perfect portal for a killer. My mother had hung a beige doily over the glass, but across the black lake fuzzy lights strained from the place where bad men served their time. The *work farm*.

Dad's ominous tales of the minimum-security prison were frightening, but he came alive telling them while gazing into his gun cabinet. Soon I was completely convinced those horrible criminals were eager to start their killing sprees with someone like me.

My horrific fears were silenced around midnight when headlights swept the driveway and my parents stumbled in with a fast-food burger squashed into a Styrofoam box from one of their pit stops. I'd happily devour my food with relief, my terror an evaporating mist disappearing with my dinner. A full belly and the physical presence of humans were enough to lull me into a restful sleep.

4

Seventh-grade physical education was one of the worst realities of my junior high life, and my after-school junk food binges and late-night burgers weren't doing anything to bring acceptance from the popular crowd. Mr. James Masterson was my gym teacher—a husky, compact man usually clad in a black polo shirt and nondescript jogging pants, his square jaw set in a no-nonsense line. Twenty years my senior, he also happened to be my second cousin. Unfortunately, this coincidence regarding the family tree didn't come with bonus points. I still received an F one semester as punishment for my habitual failure to remember gym shoes. My mother had exploded, "HOW DO YOU FAIL GYM?!"

No one knew Jimmy and I were related, and back then I

refused to share this embarrassing reality. My gym teacher never issued any free passes to sit on the sidelines, even as I concocted every tall tale imaginable to avoid squeezing into a swimsuit in the locker room. Claiming to have my period three times was a fireproof fib, but even it had limits. Inside the gym, I was completely out of my element. Everything was a nightmare—the sweating, the squeak of sneakers halting on the heavily waxed floor, the way my thighs rubbed together as I attempted to jog, the disparaging comments from the pencil-thin boys running like the wind. *Why do you wear elastic band pants? Because you're so fat, nothing else fits!*

The fifty drawn-out minutes of P.E. were spent with my eyes glued to the clock, fixated on its painful progression leading up to the ringing of the bell that couldn't come soon enough.

A spontaneous disappearing act was impossible when it was time to line up with everyone else for team selection. Never a popular favorite during the excruciating process, my only pitiful wish was to somehow avoid last place as, one by one, my classmates were claimed. Sometimes I would get lucky and score second-to-last when just a 300-pound girl and me remained before the firing squad. Once chosen, I'd slither to my location, mentally pledging to fade into the walls.

The absolute worst part of gym class was a barbaric scheme known as the Presidential Fitness Test. This cruel activity was designed to track yearly progress but felt like nothing more than an opportunity for public humiliation. The hellish scenario began with push-ups, sit-ups, trunk lifts, and chair stepping (excruciating enough), but came to an unbearable climax as students formed a line and progressed to the dreaded pull-up bar.

Boys were instructed to perform military-style pull-ups to

failure. Girls got a slight break and directions to hang above the bar for as long as possible. Stepping into place in front of the obese girl, I hoped her dismal performance would be the most memorable event of the day.

Mr. Masterson stood solidly with his clipboard as each student filed past. Levi Garrett, a wiry cross-country runner, hoisted up to the bar and nailed eight perfect pull-ups. Following a smattering of applause, he swung down neatly and cast a smug glance backward.

Continuing in a death march, my heart thudded and adrenaline coursed through my system as a primal urge to flee swept in. Intense fear of making a scene kept my place in line.

Denise Petoletti was next on the roster. Not wildly popular—not a nerd, either—just a nondescript, bookish type clad in baggy shorts and a faded blue Michael Jackson *Thriller* T-shirt. Clambering onto the plastic chair beneath the bar, Denise easily pulled herself up as Mr. Masterson hovered below to move the chair away. The rest of us stood silently fixed on her narrow back and sneakers dancing like a marionette as she hung. Ten seconds passed, and Denise's slight body began to tremble. She faced the wall, but I still imagined her face crimson from exertion. As the seconds ticked by, Mr. Masterson stood poised with his stopwatch. Another ten. The boys gasped in surprise as Denise soldiered on. Finally, her arms gave out and she dropped to a heap on the floor.

Punching his watch, Mr. Masterson thundered, "Forty-three seconds!" Denise scurried away, embarrassed by the attention.

Now it was my turn—and my chest felt highly combustible as I anticipated the torture to come. It would be ugly; the only remaining hope was ripping the Band-Aid off fast and getting it over with. Acutely aware of all the watchful eyes, I clambered gracelessly onto the chair, pulled myself up, and promptly collapsed to the floor. Done and done. I couldn't hold my weight for ONE SECOND. Face blooming with red-hot mortification, I internally screamed for a hiding place as the kids giggled.

Avoiding their disgusted looks, I slunk away as Mr. Masterson did his best to appear unaffected.

"Nice try, Melissa. Next?"

The humiliating event was much like the scene in gymnastics class when the coach demanded I reveal my true weight. Forever burned into my mind was the core belief that I was nothing but a big, fat, weakling and that my body would forever fail me.

Though I had high hopes of dropping a ton in the three months leading up to the start of eighth grade, by Labor Day weekend I was even fatter. Instead of being excited for the big shopping spree Mom and I had planned, I was kicking myself for failing at the plan to exercise daily and consume nothing but celery stalks. The night before our mall excursion, I'd stayed up until 4 a.m. watching the Jerry Lewis Telethon and stuffing my face with glazed doughnuts.

Dragging through the stores the next day, I scanned the racks for cute getups resembling the hip fashions modeled by the stars of my TV sitcoms, but scoring the right clothes wasn't coming easily. I'd been avoiding the scale, though I knew the needle was hovering in the mid-160s.

Mom and I continued pursuing the style I craved: acid-wash jeans, V-neck sweaters, Nikes with a blue swoosh, and sweatshirts emblazoned with logos from Ivy League colleges I'd never actually attend. JCPenney was a bust—my growing size had nearly evicted me from the junior department. Mom had held up a pair of pale pink pleated pants with a questioning look, but I nixed them after learning they were size 15. Whether they fit didn't matter because something that large was not welcome in my closet.

The search for an elusive pair of size 13s continued. Mom was maxed out, wearily snagging rest stops on nearby benches surrounded by a litter of shopping bags while I searched the racks. Before long she was willing to pay any price for a coveted pair of pants and a ticket out of the mall.

"I want a pair of Guess jeans so bad," I whined, as we wandered by the County Seat. Doubtful I'd squeeze into those babies; the maximum size was a 32—straight-leg-skinny and not forgiving.

Finally, at Glass Block, a pair of $65 Calvin Klein's caught my eye. Mom gasped in horror at the price tag, but I wouldn't be swayed after slipping into them. Their cut and flat front pleats, along with the creative dressing room lighting, surely shaved twenty pounds from my frame.

Magical denim paired with purple or magenta shaker sweaters, button-down polos with popped collars, and chunky strings of fake beads moved me through the first two months of the school year without incident.

Feeling ten feet tall and bulletproof—and very encouraged that no one had fat-shamed me so far that year—I strutted into American History one November day. Walking to my desk, I overheard Carl Davidson—a tall, lanky class clown—murmuring "boom, boom, boom," and mocking me with thunderous sound effects as I moved down the aisle. The jeans instantly lost their worth and I switched to sweats.

A new sweater became another confidence-boosting piece of

armor—it featured a cat graphic with satiny pink bows, combining a precocious mix of teen sweetheart and animal lover. Though my birthday wish had been for a real live kitty, Mom (not a fan of animals in any form) substituted the cat sweater. The bus ride to school unearthed a very unpleasant smell—the tight wool of the garment caused uncontrollable sweating, forcing me to press my arms against my sides all day. I felt like the Peanuts character Pig-Pen, extremely dirty and radiating a cloud of dust, but wanted to believe I also resembled Tracey Gold from *Growing Pains*.

Carl wasn't the only one making a spectacle of my size and appearance. Terry Capra had eyed me up in English that morning, twisting in his desk chair until he was about two inches from my face. Mortified, heat rose in my cheeks as I stared at my notebook, willing him to look away.

"Why do you even try covering up your zits?" he demanded. "It doesn't work. You can still see every single one."

With a small chuckle, he returned his attention to the blackboard as I sat frozen and unable to defend myself. I turned inside and channeled Tracey Gold.

Slumped on a bus smelling vaguely of vomit, the ride home was spent thinking of Carl, Terry, and also the crowded lunch period earlier that day—I'd faced my usual challenge of finding an unoccupied chair. After snatching one I thought was free, a twiglike boy with glasses belted out, "Give it back, fatty!"

As everyone turned and scrambled to get a load of the lard ass, my ears rung with cafeteria noise and I pushed the chair back feverishly, wanting the green, cracked linoleum of the A.I. Jedlicka Junior High cafeteria to open up and swallow me whole. *Hide me! I'm ugly!*

The pain of the school day would disappear with a massive dose of sugar. Bolting to the kitchen, I ransacked Dad's secret cupboard and found glazed doughnuts among a half-eaten and slightly stale Mickey fruit pie. The pastries were crack-like, gratification and release flooding in with the doughy goodness. Mining through the freezer next—I was on a hunt for waffles and ice cream served with chunks of Hershey's chocolate. My second helping of Butter Brickle ice cream was scooped creatively from the gallon pail to hide the huge volume I'd already consumed. Shouts of neighborhood kids strained through the screen door—I'd been invited to join the gang down the road more than once, but preferred eating to socializing—and did just that until my stomach begged for mercy.

Sugar was my first addiction. Collapsing to the floor, I cradled my swollen belly and munched dry peanut butter Cap'n Crunch straight out of the box, captivated by *Family Feud*. I imagined whom I'd invite to join me in Hollywood if I was selected for a casting call. My fake game show family looked nothing like the real one.

5

By the time I hit eighth grade I was packing 165 pounds on my modest 5'3" frame. Telling myself, *You carry your weight well. No one would guess you weigh that much* kept me sane. My signature look was a baggy shirt stretched to the knees and stirrup pants with a generous waistband. Finding cute jeans was almost impossible, and I was too fat for the wildly popular designer styles—but the Guess bib overalls that debuted during junior high were generously cut and came in four sizes—S, M, L, and XL, eliminating the need for a waist measuring 32 inches or less. Soon I was begging Gram to open up her wallet once again, though she made her thoughts on my type of fashion crystal clear.

"When I was a girl, the only people who wore *JEANS* were

the men on the railroad. I wouldn't pay five cents for them!" Gram declared.

She thought denim was of the devil.

One morning near the end of eighth grade, I met Amy at her house to catch the bus. We curled up on opposite ends of the couch, watching Poison and Beastie Boys videos until it was time to leave. When I bent over to put on my shoes, my sweatshirt slipped up and bright red stretch marks were exposed.

Amy gasped. "What happened to your back? How did you get those scratches?"

I claimed I'd been clawed by a maniacal cat, but as we settled into our seats, I obsessed about the crimson gashes my mother dismissed as the harmless result of "growing" too fast.

Later that week, I had to visit our ancient family pediatrician for a tetanus shot; apparently my last one had been either at birth, or never. Dr. Reimer had a serious talk with me after reviewing my vitals.

"Melissa, you are getting *really* heavy," he declared, examining my chart through thick bifocals. I sat, paralyzed and transfixed by the bristly white hairs growing from his ears and nose. "You're getting to the age where boys and girls start dating. If you don't lose weight, no boy will ever want to take you out. You know, like on snowmobile rides and things like that."

Snowmobile rides???

I was far too mortified to do anything other than nod, but a few days later a switch flipped and I made a grim pledge. The fat had to go, and starvation was the quickest remedy. A ridiculous near-fast commenced—my fourteen-year-old brain totally convinced that the fastest way to produce serious weight loss was to quit eating. For two solid months,

I lived on apples, diet soda, and sugarless gum.

My Uncle Mark had three young daughters. Mom watched them occasionally on weekends so my aunt and uncle could have time alone.

"I picked up all of your favorite things," Mom chirped while stockpiling the kitchen full of junk convenience foods prior to the cousins' arrival. Her haul included Red Baron pepperoni pizza, Doritos, Fruit Roll-Ups, macaroni and cheese, and Pop-Tarts. Plus NEW COKE, my absolute favorite. Max Headroom, the futuristic Coke spokesman, was the latest 80's icon—and prior to the diet, I'd been forever conning Mom into bringing home twelve packs of the top-shelf stuff. Though the sweet carbonated syrup was pretty tempting, I vowed to stick to my plan.

Mom clucked her tongue in protest as I continued my food strike even in the presence of company. "Come on, Melissa. A little bit won't hurt. Just have one piece."

Seated at the table with everyone else, I ignored the high calorie spread and sliced an apple into tiny strips while secretly marveling at my own laser-focused self-control. Watching our guests happily gobble thick slabs of gooey pizza while I sipped Diet Shasta was quite painful, but the superhuman willpower it required also brought on a freakish feeling of supremacy.

"Dr. Reimer *said* I'm too fat," I insisted, nibbling the apple. Mom shut her mouth.

Connie Jones was the first to notice what soon became a twenty-five-pound weight loss. Her eyes raked over me in awe on the stairwell between classes.

"Have you lost weight?" she gasped.

My stomach flipped and I beamed. "Yes. I've lost about twenty pounds."

"Wow, you can really tell," this girl I barely knew gushed with admiration.

Connie's comments brought on an electrifying high and even more praise about my changing body. Down to 140 pounds, my Guess bibs sagged so much that I had to quit wearing them. Maintaining such a low-calorie regimen was tough though, and animal instincts took over sometimes. Intense cravings eventually drove me to polish off an entire box of Little Debbie oatmeal crème pies and a jumbo sack of Cool Ranch Doritos in the secret of the basement bedroom. The binges were never worth it, with the first few bites of glorious ecstasy slipping into revulsion and shame just minutes later.

During freshman year, I gave sports a whirl for the first time since Little League softball. Being immersed in Caribou Lake from May to September made the PHS swimming team a natural fit. Dad had been an expert in the water, so I figured it was in my genes. A spot on the junior varsity squad and the grueling practices that followed enabled free-range feeding without penalty, and the scale lodged at 120 pounds. Friends suggested that I was beginning to look gross from all the weight I'd lost, but I was secretly thrilled.

I'd known fellow teammate Carly Brand since kindergarten just like Amy—and most days before practice we'd indulge in forbidden junk food binges we'd later burn off in the pool. Little Debbies were always a huge hit—with a favorite pastime walking from the high school to a nearby grocery store to canvas the snack cake aisle. After scoring a box of Star Crunch or Nutty Bars, we'd camp out under the storefront mowing on goodies and chatting about the latest happenings. Carly was a great influence and swimming a healthy diversion that occupied a lot of time.

One day after practice, Carly and I slouched in a hard rubber seat on the bus sharing the headphones attached to her Walk-Man. My eyes roamed the aisle, eventually settling on a guy huddled in back. Though I willed him to look at me, he never did. He wasn't breathtaking—but seemed approachable. Slightly overweight with a mustache and scruffy sandy-colored facial hair, baseball hat, and satin jacket—his lower lip bowed out from what I guessed was a dip of Copenhagen. Chewing tobacco was sexy. Carly knew him—they'd shared the same bus route for years.

Though he was a senior, his unreliable, secondhand truck often tossed him back to the mode of transportation he hated. The guy was sure to be crowding eighteen, but I never once thought seniors were off-limits.

After the bus released us at her house, Carly and I grabbed some snacks from the pantry and then crashed in the rec room in front of a giant projection TV her dad had recently picked up. They had money, but Carly didn't flaunt it and never disparaged my humble home. As she flipped cable channels to a Madonna video, I remained preoccupied with Copenhagen Boy.

"Remember when we dressed up as Madonna for Halloween?" Carly laughed. "We were so basic."

My mind was off in a distant land. "The guy at the back of the bus? You know him? Put in a good word for me. You can look up his number too," I added.

"Seriously?" Incredulous Carly had never lowered her standards for anyone. She carefully returned the TV remote to an end table and stood brushing bright orange dust from her hands while watching me doubtfully.

"Well?" I demanded. "What do you know about him? Tell

me everything. You guys live less than a mile apart."

"What does that have to do with anything?" she scoffed. "Mitch is kind of a . . . how do I say it? A *slacker*."

"Come on!" I whined. "*I* think he's cute."

Finally, she agreed to find his number and call, and I crouched on the edge of the couch and giggled while she dialed.

"Mitch, it's Carly Brand. From your bus? My friend Melissa kind of likes you and wondered if you could talk sometime."

Carly was silent for a minute. "She was wearing a white sweatshirt. It said 'Party Chasers.' Yeah, that's one of the bars my dad owns. You want her number?" I gasped as she rattled off my digits. A minute later she hung up the phone. "You *owe* me. That was so embarrassing!"

We talked later in the week and although he wasn't too interested in academics or anything deep, Mitch was well acquainted with Duluth's most popular hard rock station, Ford trucks, and George Thorogood. Hours on the phone became a daily routine. On Tuesdays, his parents bowled on a league and we effortlessly weaseled into some unsupervised time.

My parents didn't investigate—they probably assumed that authority figures were around. After a little TV watching, inevitable couch groping followed. Mitch always smelled of Brut deodorant and Blistex lip balm—the sexiest, most alluring scents in my naïve world.

My cluelessness was startling; I knew about "making out" but had zero sex education. Mitch was ready to graduate and leave town for the military, but I was powerless to stop this thing we'd started.

My new love interest and his friends were an intriguing group of known partiers who squeaked by in school, and although my parents were passive-aggressively opposed to our age difference, they figured everything would fizzle out once he was gone.

With alarming impulsivity, Mitch became the centerpiece of my young life, and I embarked on a mission to sear myself into his heart forever and manipulate his capture. I was already a very good sweet talker. But our afternoon grope fests soon weren't going far enough, and he began to make elusive remarks about sex.

"Should I buy some condoms?" he asked one day out of nowhere.

"I don't think *that's* going to happen anytime in the near future," I responded, feeling the heat in my face from a sideways comment that seemed so illicit.

"Not now," Mitch insisted. "I'll just get some to have around."

Being a latchkey kid was beneficial now—my parents were never home after school. The *event* loomed between us, but resisting it made me terrified of losing him. Taking that monumental step could only serve to cement us together, I was sure.

6

I craved a Daddy who'd never leave, but the next best thing was someone nonthreatening and easy to take prisoner. Mitch was the first guy to return my attention, quickly forming my sudden, fervent, and suffocating fatal attraction. I briefly resisted his sexual advances but soon decided giving in wasn't a big deal. Mom was uncomfortable talking about sex—not a surprise considering her mother never went there, either. She was a teen who learned the hard way. I already planned to marry Mitch anyway, so why wait?

One night, my parents were still working, and the 1988 Winter Olympic Games droned on in the background. Mitch offered to stop—I said no. After some fumbling, at fifteen I entered an exclusive club only grown-ups were supposed to join.

Soul ties were nothing I'd ever heard of—the significance of the unplanned event ranked up there with watching movies carrying prohibited R ratings, or sneaking out of the house in the middle of the night. Going "all the way" seemed to seal my place in the adult world, and God's disappointment was the furthest thing from my mind. Sex was a sacred act Biblically reserved only for marriage between one man and one woman, but I never knew it.

Once the deed was done, my dependence to Mitch escalated on an epic scale. Sex is the tie that binds, and it would anchor Mitch to me emotionally for decades to come. Years later, I'd need heavy intercessory prayer to break the connection to him and all of the others who came later. The *world* didn't want me to know, but sex outside the confines of the marriage covenant would bring nothing but pain, hurt, and disappointment.

I couldn't wait to tell Carly. *Mitch and I did it. Sort of.* Wasn't it the thing to do, much like trumpeting the news of your first period or scoring a job at the mall? My close pal seemed disappointed, and our dynamic suddenly shifted. My parents had no clue what was going on, and as long as I behaved and made curfews I stayed under the radar.

Mitch was inexperienced with women, and though I had never asked, I guessed I was his first sexual encounter, too. This had to mean something very deep. *It just had to.* We were ultra-serious now, and sacrificing my body to him meant he wouldn't leave. This idea comforted me until his graduation day approached. But in late May of 1988 as I crouched in the dark high school auditorium watching a slide show commemorating Mitch's soon-to-be graduating class, reality struck. "Here I Go

Again" by Whitesnake was the anthem to a day I'd never forget. Mitch was leaving for the Army, and my attempts to convince him it was a mistake had failed. Boot camp was inevitable.

"We're getting married as soon as I graduate," I announced to my incredulous friends as we gathered in the lunchroom over taco salads. Desperately tethered to the future, I wanted to sleep through the next three years I viewed as nothing but a gaping hole: NO MITCH.

My fifteen-year-old friends were busy planning birthday parties and gymnastics camps and were awestruck about my pending nuptials. While Mitch and his clique closed the books on high school, I finished ninth grade in a rush to grow up.

Senior class status was the key to freedom. They had cars, fringed moccasin boots, and legal access to the smoking area. Independence seemed capable of healing my raging insecurity, and I despised everything related to youth.

I don't really know how I waited as long as I did to *really* start drinking. Alcohol was a faithful constant embedded throughout my family line, so it seemed natural I'd eventually start boozing alongside everyone else. I wanted a night of unlimited beer—and I'd been closing in on my goal for a while. My parents even let me sip wine coolers at family functions, and I was careful to walk and talk straight to prove I could hold my liquor.

Somehow I just knew I'd have a knack for drinking others under the table. And although I hadn't indulged yet—my brain was ready. Booze was timeless—patiently waiting to initiate me. Through it all, I never considered I could end up just like Dad.

Every family gathering involved heavy drinking. Grandpa (my mom's father) liked swilling brews, he worked hard, and golfed even harder. But Gramps also had an "off" switch, and lived into his mid-nineties.

Dad's side of the family didn't pussyfoot around the bottle—it was a rock-solid constant on every occasion, with Grandma June openly swilling Brandy Manhattans every Friday when we made our weekly visit to eat her overdone roasts and undercooked turnips. Alcohol did a number on Gram, demolishing her peppy demeanor into emotional ruin by the end of the night.

Dad had no problem putting away at least a six-pack most nights ("I spill more than that on my necktie" was one famous quip) and also supplemented with vodka and blackberry brandy, the hard alcohol growing heavier as the years passed. And every weekend, our lakefront house was the gathering spot for neighbors to drink adult beverages before a crackling outdoor fire.

Summer weekends my mother lounged by the lake with other neighborhood ladies, drinking vodka and pink lemonade from large plastic tumblers. Drying in the sun on a beach towel, I had no idea everyone was drunk; they just seemed to be having loads of fun. I was, too. Amy and I dove for clams and practiced handstands underwater, our plastic mask and flipper sets from K-Mart providing hours of entertainment. My mother was always very tired after these long days at the dock and would stumble into the living room and pass out while I ate brownies at the kitchen window and shook water from my ears. She'd wake up for a glass of cold water in a few hours, and I passed the time watching old reruns of *Laverne & Shirley*.

Freshman year closed and clips rolled across my mind's eye like a series of colorful computer thumbnails: laughter and silliness, relaxation and comfortably numb days on the dock, the sun-dappled waters of Caribou Lake and sounds of Tommy Roe's sweet little Sheila straining through the trees. Dad and his buddies chugged beer and flicked ashes into the fire, while the kids roasted marshmallows and chased fireflies. It was kind of idyllic.

The enemy had spent years patiently priming me for a night of unrestricted drinking, and one April evening, I got my chance. Mitch was on his way over, and soon we were barreling down Industrial Road in his repaired green pick-up with Guns N' Roses blaring.

"What is this band?" I asked timidly.

"This is GNR, the best frickin' rock 'n' roll band ever," was his cocky answer.

Appetite for Destruction became the soundtrack of the summer, with GNR catapulting me into a scary new world. The onset of the entire '80s hard rock scene ushered in a new, rebellious time that mirrored the genesis of my very own self-destruction. I ditched the popped collars and shaker sweaters of the previous year for various T-shirts featuring my favorite musical group, the most coveted of all depicting skull faces in the form of a cross.

The particle board walls of my basement room I'd returned to after Dave went away to college were now covered with heavy metal posters torn from *Circus* magazine, fake cobwebs, and a giant wall-sized hanging of the *Rocky Horror Picture Show*. A small altar with candles became another bold statement and was used to host amateur tarot card readings along with my old Parker Brothers Ouija board.

The new musical interests would quickly be joined by my soon-to-be closest confidante—booze. The synergy of the two delivered feelings of power and rebellion that speedily demolished any remaining foundation from my past exposure to Christian principles.

Blind to the words of the Apostle Paul and his letter to the Ephesians, I had no awareness of the demonic realm poised to strike: "For our struggle is not against flesh and blood, but against the rulers, against the authorities, against the powers of this dark world and against the spiritual forces of evil in the heavenly realms" (Ephesians 6:12, NIV).

The amateur spell casting I'd dabbled in seemed like kid games (Parker Brothers Ouija board? Come on . . .) and the music inconsequential, but the tarot cards, garish T-shirts, and albums with parental advisories weren't harmless. These increasingly accepted tools of the adversary had flung doors open wide for demons to enter my life. Following the crowd had started so innocently, but eventually ushered in faceless, shapeless beings with the real ability to destroy. Though I couldn't see the dark supernatural realm, its presence loomed heavily, ready to escort me into the spirit world of intoxication. I was about to access a dimension of false power, a gateway to the dark side.

Heavy metal and alcohol addiction might not manifest demonic entities for everyone. Listen, *I get it,* people are freaked out by this sort of thing. Obviously, my parents thought nothing of demons when they were allowing me to binge on Freddy Krueger movies and channel entities with my trusty Ouija board when I was barely twelve years old. They just didn't know any better. I've since learned the kingdom of darkness is very real, and if someone is not filled with the presence of God and taught how to take authority over dark forces, they are ripe for evil oppression. God had graciously provided positive role models like Marge and Harold and the modeling of my brother, but the pull of sin was just too tempting and my connection to the Lord too weak. The compelling draw of intoxication presented itself in a beautiful, alluring light. Alcoholic beverages aren't called *spirits* for nothing.

The mild spring night was ripe with possibilities, and our next stop brought us to a small clapboard house. The front door swung into the twilight, and a tiny blonde pixie bounded out, skipped down the sidewalk, and hiked herself into the truck.

"Hey Mitch," she chirped like an impish fairy. "Brad's waiting for us at his mom's."

Mitch introduced her as Tricia, the girlfriend of his best friend Brad. I was determined to smash the possibility of being viewed a tag-along freshman kiddie, and prepared to gulp alcohol with the best of them. After collecting Brad, the four of us rolled down the driveway and into the night.

"Let's catch a buzz," Mitch said easily, edging the truck onto Grand Avenue toward the Gary-New Duluth bar district.

Something was already swirling inside my head; its depleted dopamine system ready to lap up booze like a parched sponge. The far-reaching impact of this night was veiled from my eyes. No one cared, least of all me back in 1988.

Silent and uncertain, I stared straight ahead as Mitch drove. Our next stop was a liquor mart featuring an obtuse ceramic buffalo in the parking lot. Mitch screeched to a halt and disappeared into the store, but was back a few minutes later, empty-handed. Brad's shoulders slumped.

"It wasn't the old guy working," Mitch grumbled as he fired up the engine. My stomach tensed into a painful knot. Feeling stiff and out of place sandwiched between Mitch and Tricia, I prayed for beer. Tonight was the night. Mitch soldiered on with determination, still assured his facial hair made him appear at least twenty-five.

A second liquor outlet awaited just down the street, and Mitch soon sauntered out hauling a case of Pabst Blue Ribbon. The mood in the truck lifted, and I silently rejoiced. I was going to get drunk! I didn't yet realize I was about to experience the answer to every problem my fifteen-year-old self had ever faced.

After tossing the beer into the truck bed, we merged back onto the highway as I brimmed with nervous energy. Mild spring air billowed through the open windows, and as cattails and swamp reeds flooded by, I struggled to remain calm. A few miles outside of town, we came to a secluded rest area. There, I downed my first full can of beer.

Mitch's green truck held everything I needed—unlimited beer, an easy-going guy who reciprocated when I said, "I love you," and plenty of '80s rock. The music made the moments rich, with the perfect party playlist serving endless tracks from Dokken, GNR, and the Scorpions.

Some people don't remember their first experience with intoxication. But my encounter was life-changing. After I'd easily swilled two cans of Pabst, a pleasant numbness descended, and the answer to my anxiety, panic, and insecurity came to life. For the first time ever, I was totally relaxed and completely at peace—I now held the key to a pain-free existence. Insecurity and fear of people was replaced with soaring confidence, and the euphoria I felt was simply incredible.

"Bartender? You hooking us up? C'mon. Make it snappy. They'll want me home sooner or later."

Mitch smirked. "You sure? I think you're starting to get lit up. Don't you, guys?" he looked over at Brad and Tricia with a chuckle. Tricia was now anchored on Brad's lap, head tilted back, lips in lockstep with her beer as she slurped off the last drop.

"We can't drop her off in a puddle," she shrugged.

But I was ready to plead my case. "No, no. I can handle more. I'm fine. Really. My parents go to bed at like, nine! They won't even *see* me when I get home."

I folded my hands and placed them in my lap, attempting to look stoic and nun-like. "I hardly feel anything."

Mitch shrugged and passed me another beer, and I didn't waste any time popping the top and greedily knocking back half the can. The booze left behind an intense burn, fortifying my blood with a strange and powerful potion. The rest of the night flew by.

Two hours later, we were still parked and cracking into the last of our stash. The party in the truck cab had evaporated into nothing—hours spent chattering about nonsense and committing *Appetite for Destruction* to memory—but as we left without incident, I was blind to the den of demons I'd just disrupted. My first serious initiation to the wonderful world of beer ended in a seemingly harmless mirage of fragmentary blackouts.

The night in Mitch's truck with that case of Pabst was the catalyst for a major life decision: *get drunk again as soon possible!* Alcohol's power had been unleashed, I'd experienced *the remedy*, and now I'd need its services to survive. To cope.

My parents were asleep when I stumbled to my room, and the following day dawned with my first official hangover. Quietly suffering through the day, I carried the private party as my own special secret.

With weekend drinking now my main objective, parties, blackouts, and drunk driving were normal. Ninth grade ended, and after much begging, my parents allowed me to take the road test for my permit. Gram had financed the driver's education after accepting my lackluster promise of repayment through various odd jobs at her Proctor house.

The exam was a breeze, and I soon held the precious yellow paper documenting my ability to take the wheel with a licensed driver.

"I passed!" I screeched, fanning the test results as Mitch rolled up in his truck.

"You need a ride?" he called, and I couldn't jump in fast enough. The afternoon was already shaping up nicely, and I happened to have a beer in my backpack.

With excitement way beyond what was deserving of shiny aluminum, I gazed lovingly at the jumbo golden can. I'd hoarded the relic from a party my folks had hosted a while back for the perfect occasion. Today was that day.

"Mind if I drink?"

Half the beer disappeared in a single swig as Mitch chuckled in disbelief.

"Not sure that's so smart. Your parents are coming home later, right?"

Too busy noticing the vibrant colors of the muggy day, I kept sipping while contemplating a long summer ahead stretching from one party to the next. Mitch would leave for the military around mid-July, but that didn't worry me right then. Many drinking opportunities were on the docket first.

"They won't be home until after six. We've got plenty of time."

I'd never been drunk in the afternoon before, and that single giant beer torched my brain with an electrifying buzz.

Fifteen minutes later we were at my driveway, the beer was gone, and I was laser-focused on scoring more. *More, more, more.* Beer always tasted like *more.* Marching down the sidewalk, my pressured speech ran wild as I approached the liquor stash. Mom and Dad were downtown working and wouldn't be home for another three hours—plenty of time to raid the cupboards.

The Caribou Lake cabin house lacked a legit *liquor cabinet*, though we did have a metal cupboard that incidentally stored alcohol right next to other hazardous materials—household kitchen products like bleach and Pine-Sol.

"Let's have a cocktail," I suggested, rattling through the bottles like it was the most normal thing in the world.

The aging inventory made it likely I could snag something without the parents noticing. After I'd considered the rum, vodka, and brandy—I stumbled upon a bottle of amaretto way in back. The ancient purple liquor hadn't been touched for years; it was doubtful anyone would miss it.

Through my impairment, I decided it was safe to knock off the remaining dregs. Not yet sixteen, I had dieted down to 118 pounds, and blackouts came on fast and hard. Wasting no time, I dumped the syrupy liquid into a couple of glasses.

"You sure about this?"

"It's all good. Why so tense? You look, I don't know—*constipated*." I giggled. "Loosen up."

After passing Mitch a strong one, I downed mine in a gulp and poured another.

My last memory of that afternoon was sometime around four o'clock, perched on the edge of a crushed blue velvet sofa once belonging to Gram. She called it the *davenport*. Indescribable euphoria filled me, and I couldn't stop talking. Babbling incessantly, I held Mitch captive over our future.

"I can't wait for us to get married," I chattered drunkenly. "Where do you think we will live? It could be Turkey, Arabia, whatever . . . I don't care. Where do you think the military will send us?"

I can still see myself perched on the edge of the couch crammed next to Mitch, and the distant satisfaction I felt staring at the bones of my kneecaps, the hazy light of the darkening day drifting through my mother's window sheers. Then the curtains closed.

My next memory formed three hours later. Mom loomed overhead, screaming like a maniac.

"GET UP! Why are you sleeping? Why won't you wake up?"

Although I heard screams in the distance, I felt like I was struggling to ascend from the depths of a pool as water pressure pushed me back down to the bottom.

Slowly the ceiling came into focus. Particle board. Naked burning bulb. My mother's face.

"You're drunk! Get out of bed!"

Extremely confused and disoriented, I tilted my head to the side. My hair was wet and matted into the sleeve of my Benetton sweatshirt, now soaked with greenish-gray vomit. Twisting uncomfortably, I realized I had also wet the bed. *Red, red, wet the bed. Wipe it up with gingerbread.*

"Get up! Go take a shower!"

As Mom lost it, Dad started down the stairs.

"Sue, let me handle this," he offered, like they were deciding who should address the rotten report card.

Bypassing Dad, I crawled off the bed, grabbed some clean clothes, and stumbled up to the bathroom. Upstairs in the shower, it was impossible to form a coherent thought, it took all the energy I could muster to stand motionless under the hot water.

Afterward, I returned to face Dad, hoping distractedly that my mother had simmered down. No such luck; she was pacing the floor as Dad casually sipped a beer from my desk chair.

"What's the matter with you?" Mom erupted. "You were passed out in your own *vomit*. At six in the evening. What the hell is *happening*?"

Dad set his beer aside as though it was time to get down to business. "Sue, let us talk. You go relax and get into your robe."

Mom stomped upstairs in a huff. Seated at my desk chair, Blatz can close at hand, Dad was not threatening. His eyes followed me as I plunked down on my box spring (Mom had furiously torn away the pee-stained mattress) like I was a new species he wanted to investigate.

Drawing my knees to my chest, I leaned my wet head back and slowly banged it against the wall.

"I . . . am . . . so . . . drunk," I mumbled.

Dad was almost amused. "What happened?"

"Mitch and I had a couple of drinks after school." I shrugged it off as normal teenage behavior.

"Big surprise. You spilled vodka and orange juice all over the kitchen floor. You weren't too sneaky."

This was news to me. I had no recollection of helping myself to my mother's booze. Tears leaked from the corners of my eyes at my father's information, breaking into the vodka stash was no joke. No wonder Mom was furious!

"I don't know why we did it!" I sobbed. "We just wanted to *try* it. It wasn't Mitch's fault. It was all my idea."

"Learn from this," Dad advised. "Having hangovers is no fun. I'll work on your mother."

Mom never forgot that fateful day, and years later described her intense fear over what she'd seen in my eyes; the blackness—the vacancy. She'd witnessed the demonic possession that took place when I drank and knew instantly that alcohol and I were a deadly mix.

7

I wasn't punished for my drunken episode; everyone just seemed relieved I wasn't dead. Mitch and I caught up in the hall at school the next day—only a week stood between us and summer vacation, but being on house arrest and facing a month-long grounding put a damper on my excitement.

"Wow, you're still alive," he chuckled.

"Guess that giant beer wasn't so smart," I managed with a forced laugh. "Just got me started, I suppose."

Aching to reclaim the night and knowing he held the key—at the same time I feared the answers. "So, why'd you leave last night?"

Obviously, I had passed out—but I was about to learn *the*

rest of the story. Mitch adjusted his baseball hat and scanned the hall helplessly.

"I didn't *want* to leave, but it was my bowling night, and I needed to get over to the lanes. I couldn't get you to stop drinking, so after we did it, I dressed you and put you to bed. I thought you'd just sleep it off. Was that wrong?"

Dumbfounded, my mouth went dry as I stood anchored to my spot on the floor. *After we did it???*

"We *did* it?" I finally whispered in disbelief. I had no memory of anything sexual. Absolutely none.

"Yeah," Mitch mumbled, looking uncomfortable and perhaps realizing I had not been present in my body for what he considered a consensual romantic tryst.

"You were real aggressive. Don't you remember?"

I stared a hole through the floor, cheeks flaming.

"No."

My blackout default. Primal, impulsive, and totally irrational—no morals or ability to make proper choices. The harrowing result of functioning with a shutdown brain.

Shortly after his death, I watched a clip of Robin Williams performing a standup bit on alcoholism and blackouts. Although the piece was very profane, I understood its meaning all too well:

"Blackouts are your brain's way of protecting itself. Your prefrontal cortex says, 'You're about to (expletive) a troll. I'm outta here.'"

Devastated and riddled with shame, I couldn't reconcile how an innocent afternoon that started with excitement after passing my permit test had ended in a terrifying blackout and bed-wetting session. How much had I had to drink? At least a half bottle of amaretto, along with an unknown quantity of vodka. I'd nearly been poisoned, trapped in a drunken stupor for hours. Choking to death was a very real possibility, and I knew it.

Mitch didn't know I was mentally vacant and simply went along with my quest to get him into bed. The shame, remorse, and humiliation were hideous side effects I couldn't shake—but despite the near-death nightmare, all I could think about was drinking again.

The next fifteen years would be peppered with similar events—empty, maddening, guilt-ridden mornings of guess-work. Oh, I didn't always sleep with my accomplices, but the self-imposed prisons following a blackout were inescapable unless I could muster the courage to approach the witnesses.

The only saving grace of this madness was yet hidden from my fifteen-year-old self. My self-induced horror would even-tually be used for the Lord's work, but not before the enemy unleashed his demonic power—and having no awareness of any alternatives, I fell for it repeatedly. God either causes things, or He allows them—(he doesn't miss a *THING* so don't get it twisted) but once we submit to Him he can take what the enemy meant for evil and *turn it for good*. Romans 8:28 is one of the most incredible Biblical promises.

The devil had pegged alcohol as my ticket to destruction, with accidents, car crashes, or overdose the most likely means to the end. But Jesus had a back-up plan for every single drunken mistake and near-death nightmare.

My God-given gifts sat unused like fancy chocolates too pretty to eat. Books, performing, motivational speaking in the mirror, theatrics, writing, and swimming—were swiftly replaced by booze and boys, music with destructive lyrics, and promiscuity.

The devil had fine-tuned his plan for a long time by securing various strongholds in my mind, and presently he seemed to be winning. Methodically capitalizing on my weaknesses, the enemy exploited my neediness, low self-worth, and the holes in my soul. One of Satan's favorite tricks was to place directionless men into my path. I swallowed his lie that sex and emotional dependency would offer security, and it landed like a sugar cube lodged in my throat.

The enemy's master plan wouldn't work without compulsive drinking and plenty of vacant men who lacked spiritual direction. Mitch was just the first in a long string of guys who served as pawns for the devil's work. They reinforced what I already believed: alcohol and men were *the most important things*. They were helpful. They fixed me.

My blissfully clueless parents were preoccupied with their own addictions, financial problems, and baggage from the past. They did their best—bringing the family to church occasionally and insisting we do our time completing Christian curriculum. My empty display of devoted study in confirmation class only earned a worthless certificate void of any real relationship with Jesus Christ.

The day following the drunken King Can and vomit episode, Mitch still ruled me—the golden ticket to rationalizing the night away. Surely, he wanted to clear himself, too. After all, he *was* my boyfriend, and didn't intend any harm the afternoon I tapped into the aging amaretto.

"Don't worry about it. We all overdo it from time to time. No big thing."

He had already moved on, but the horror of that afternoon and my brush with death continued to haunt me. I *could have* choked, like so many rock stars I'd heard about. I made a silent pledge to control myself.

But rather than curb my budding drinking career, the

disturbing pee and vomit incident became the catalyst for many wild summer nights. Mitch held a part-time job at a golf course, and the beautiful greens were the perfect place to meet up. My parents thought I was "visiting" Mitch at work, and I easily fooled them into believing my trips to the driving range were completely wholesome.

One summer afternoon, I conned my mother into believing I was headed to Carly's for a sleepover. Funny to think I had once been a moral and dutiful child who admonished lies and was wracked with guilt anytime I tried to tell one. Alcohol had changed all of that—deception now dripped from my tongue like water rolling off a duck's back. Mom dropped me off following her usual weekend day of cocktails—lately she'd seemed suspicious of my proposed activities, but the faint smell of vodka on her breath made lying to her face effortless.

"Behave," Mom called as she backed out of Carly's driveway.

Carly wasn't happy about being dragged into my ruse, but Mitch was top priority, and groveling to my closest friend was worth capturing a stolen night with him.

Twenty minutes after my mother's taillights disappeared up the road, I stood at Mitch's door, panting from the brisk walk and anticipation. His parents were gone for the night, and the evening slipped away with beer and the sounds of the Scorpions.

"'No One Like You?' Is this a new song?" I asked.

Mitch chuckled. "No. It's old. The Scorpions have been around forever."

Sometimes our age difference was obvious. Mitch could drive, vote, and buy cigarettes—while I had barely secured my driving permit. I was fifteen. FIFTEEN! The night was soon swallowed up by dawn as I drifted into a drunken sleep.

Jolting awake terror-stricken, every vehicle rumbling down the road in front of Mitch's house sounded like Dad's painting truck. I was convinced he would eventually burst into Mitch's bedroom and find his fifteen-year-old daughter wearing nothing but skimpy underwear.

The con job was a success, encouraging me to push my limits a little more. The following weekend brought more lies.

Friday night, the golf course beckoned with a cooler waiting to be tapped. Mitch's friends crowded in the parking lot like a pack of stray dogs: Darren, Bryce, Brad, and Mitch were inseparable through high school—underachieving, beer-swilling all-stars who'd earned top honors in gravel-pit drinking and dirt-track spectator sports. Definitely a wonder any of them graduated, but they all managed to somehow.

Darren was alluring with his lanky, string bean body and quick wit. With delicious unpredictability, he kept me on my toes and greedily devouring the sparse quips slipping from his mouth. I labored for his attention, very drawn to the mental challenge Mitch didn't even know he was lacking.

The late afternoon sun grazed the greens, and leaf patterns dappled the hood of Darren's car as I reclined swilling beer and wine coolers. Days like these seemed to stretch forever, the party's end a distant, far-off nag. I checked my watch routinely, reassured by the many hours before I was expected home. I was double-fisting it, and my curfew seemed light-years away.

Mitch headed off on the golf cart, leaving Darren and me in a secluded parking lot concealed by heavy vegetation over-looking a deep ravine. Edging closer, I drank him in. Dark and mysterious, a little dirty. An opportunity void of watchful eyes felt tempting and luxurious.

Mitch wasn't bright enough to sense my attraction to Darren. Affable and assured his buddies would always have his back, Darren was an opportunist when it came to women and Mitch was trusting and clueless.

After crushing an empty can under the heel of his palm, Darren faced me with piercing eyes just a shade from black. "I'm going into town to get some more beer. You wanna tag along?"

I was sliding off the hood within seconds.

"Let's go."

Darren piloted his beat-up old Cutlass with a terrifying death wish. We headed down Skyline Parkway, a winding and scenic drive high above the city of Duluth. The large rocks hugging the shoulder offered little protection from the steep embankment just inches from the pavement. Sucking in my breath as we careened around hellishly sharp bends in the road, I expected to catapult off the cliff at any moment.

Darren eyed me clutching the door handle with fright and chuckled. Reaching under his seat, he pulled out a plastic two-liter bottle and shoved it toward me.

"Relax. Have a drink."

I accepted the offering, captivated by his long snaky fingers raking deliberately over mine. Struggling mightily to be coy, I cautiously took a guarded whiff of Darren's death potion.

"Hmmm. Potent."

I didn't turn the bottle away; that was the last thing I ever did. Though it radiated a nasty odor, being pampered by fruity wine coolers or frothy daiquiris wasn't necessary in my world. Whiskey would work.

Darren was tiptoeing lightly because I was his *best friend's girlfriend*, and this undeniable current of tension made him extra enticing. With a shrug, I took a mighty gulp from the two-liter, wincing as the cheap booze blazed a path down my esophagus. Darren smirked.

"You like it? It's Coke, with a twist."

I will never forget those powerful words. How I loved the bad boys.

Several liquor stores later we scored more provisions for the night, then Darren pulled into the parking lot of a K-Mart and headed for the camping department. Passively scanning the music aisle, for no premeditated reason at all, I decided to swipe something. I plucked the Scorpion's *Savage Amusement* and a couple of other selections from the rack and slid the long plastic cases inside my shirt.

Moving down the aisle, my sandals clacked on the linoleum, quicker—my only focus was the great outdoors where I'd be home free. Darren stood at the checkout as I walked straight by with tunnel vision.

My breath erupted in a forced gasp as I passed through the front doors, right by a worn-out ceramic horse kids could ride for a quarter. *Just keep going.* Darren's Cutlass was up ahead beckoning safety. Still a little drunk but managing to walk straight, my pace slowed and I relaxed to adjust the plastic tape case pinching inside my armpit.

"Stop immediately!"

Three security guards bolted toward me.

Sprinting around a row of vehicles, I chucked the tapes under a parked car. A burly security cop closed in and grabbed my wrist.

"Let go!" I screamed. "Get your hands off me!"

Darren appeared with a new Styrofoam beer cooler and meandered toward his car like we'd never met.

"Darrrrrrennnnnn!" I wailed with psychopathic intensity. "Don't leave me!"

Without a word or backward glance, he fired up the engine as I stared in shock.

After being dragged back to the store, I was led to a sterile interrogation room and forced to view the surveillance video. I begged and pleaded for a pardon, but instead was cited for shoplifting and resisting arrest. While viewing the video footage, it was strange to see myself walk the aisles and slide the merchandise up my shirt. It was right there on film. The police report later described me as a *thin, white female*, and I took distracted comfort in this detail.

My mother arrived an hour later, looking like an elf peering over the dashboard of Dad's junky green F-150, possibly drunk and very emotional. I'd sobered up nicely by then, and no one suspected I'd slammed four beers and a 2-liter of wine coolers before the arrest. Mom cried all the way home while I shrugged and joined in her weeping.

"I don't know why I did it," I sobbed. "I just feel *lost*."

She looked at me helplessly.

For the next few days, I sulked in my room and evaluated my month-long grounding, the only reprieve from the prison of my musty basement bedroom a few stolen phone calls with Mitch. Though he tried to console me with promises of our future together, I was painfully jealous to find out he, Darren, and Brad bought concert tickets to see George Thorogood. I had been overlooked because I was on house arrest.

Dad accompanied me to my court date for the shoplifting incident and watched silently while the judge ordered forty-eight hours of community service.

"Stay out of the system, Melis," was all he said on the way home.

Though I hoped the day would never come, Mitch left town mid-summer. His family had already moved to another Minnesota town two hours away and I was not included in the sendoff. The pain of being abandoned again—left again—was excruciating, and my brain instantly scrambled for something, anything—to fill his void. The only coping method available was frantic clinging to high school graduation and the promise of marriage. Three years of waiting felt like an eternity.

But a wedding down the road wasn't enough to satisfy the festering sore inside me that demanded to be swaddled. Less than a month later, I'd found a replacement.

"I'm going for a bike ride," I called to Mom, then headed off to split a bottle of malt liquor with the new guy, having decided that "just kissing" was harmless. A fresh male diversion blotted out the lonely cavern throbbing inside me like an abscessed tooth.

"Mitch and I have an open relationship," I assured the substitute as we stood tipsy and romantic under a mottled August sky. Distraction boy soon fizzled out like the bottles of flat Mello Yello stowed around my room for hungover mornings, but another empty male vessel was always close by.

Maintaining the façade of a flawless long-term love affair meant writing heartfelt letters, sending pictures, and placing pricey phone calls. And when Mitch made his annual visit back to Minnesota, I promptly returned full devotion. My loyalty wasn't a concern, and I found it easy to justify my side interests.

Mitch had been gone two months when my dearest cousin Michele married. Dave and I joined the wedding party—having been very close to Michele and her family (her father was Dad's only brother—a minister who pastored various churches across the Upper Midwest).

Although their family moved around a lot, as first cousins, Michele and I remained very tight. The coolest person I knew growing up—she was always glammed up with perfectly feathered hair, Jordache jeans, and turquoise jewelry. After much wheedling and pleading, I was allowed to attend my first rock concert with her at twelve. Michele facilitated one of the most thrilling experiences of my life, and I was very honored to be part of her wedding day.

My bridesmaid dress was a beautiful shade of teal with a sweetheart neckline and satin shoes dyed to match. Mom snapped dozens of pictures in front of the Caribou Lake house. Excited for the wedding, I smiled and joked around while posing for the shots. In my satin dress, I was grown-up and pretty, beautiful, and good. Not a single thought about alcohol had surfaced; I was the perfect, model daughter just hours before the disastrous night to come.

Michele's husband-to-be was a member of the Air National Guard, and the reception was held at the local armory. After arriving with the rest of the wedding party, I stood stiff and jittery in my elegant formal dress while scoping out the impressively transformed gym—the once cavernous room now dripped with teal streamers and pink balloons. Gleaming green bottles of champagne beckoned from every table. No one was looking, so I poured a tiny glass and sipped it as if I were royalty.

Mom drifted off to chat, and Dad was occupied by the keg. My brother was chatting with a few friends. A little celebratory champagne for someone just about sixteen didn't seem like a capital crime. Wandering around with my fake crystal glass, I smiled and wondered if I passed for twenty-one. That little taste had helped so much; my anxiety was gone, and I was blissfully relaxed.

What might the kitchen have to offer? Cases of booze. While eyeing up the evening liquor selections, someone tapped my shoulder. I turned with surprise, and my body flooded with euphoria.

Darren. I hadn't spoken to him since the night of my shoplifting arrest when he left me high and dry at K-Mart. Now Mitch was filed away in the military and temporarily out of the picture.

"Nice dress," he drawled, intense amaretto-colored eyes raking over me. The blush on my cheeks intensified as he indicated his approval. With that, I drained my glass in one brisk movement.

"Thanks. What are you doing here? How do you know Michele? What are you drinking?"

A battery of questions rolled out of my mouth as the champagne pulsed through my head. A golden cascade of bliss built inside as Darren raised his drink.

"Screwdriver. I make the best. You want one?"

Glancing through the serving window, I spotted Mom standing in a group of people, laughing and gesturing. A gifted storyteller, she was fully occupied with her audience. Wanting to intensify the exquisite feeling slowly building, more booze was just the ticket.

"Set me up, bartender."

Plastic cup in hand, I cemented myself to Darren like a fungus, forfeited my coveted spot at the head table, and instead was thrilled to hover over him in the bleak armory kitchen. By the time the dance started, I was trashed, my dress crumpled and stained with champagne and orange juice. Though I prayed the dark gym would swallow me, it was obvious even to my inebriated self that I couldn't hide my condition. Some fresh air might help.

Where is my mother? Pushing blindly through a doorway in the corner of the gym hoping it led outside—I tumbled into a storage closet instead, knocking over a stack of chairs in a noisy crash. Sharp metal from somewhere in the pile snagged the hem of my dress, leaving a teal ribbon behind. Scrambling to my feet, my leg dripped beads of blood through deep scratches.

Fumbling for an exit within the pitch-black space, I flailed around like a fish flopping on a dock. There wasn't a snowball's chance in hell I'd regained any functionality, but somehow found the way out. Staggering back into the gym, I quickly replaced my mother as the new center of attention. The little circle of people who'd been listening with rapt attention to her stories now stared at me with horror.

"My childhood was terrible. I can't help it; I drink to forget." I slurred to a captive audience.

Mom jerked me aside, eyes wide and face twisted with rage. "We're leaving, *now*. You are *so* grounded, little girl. You won't see the light of day for months!"

Her words were terrifying—and birthed a deep drive to keep the party going somehow. Wrenching away, I slipped into the crowd and out into the night, the sight of Darren getting into his car an irresistible beacon of desire. Tearing across the driveway on uneven gravel, I yelped as rocks slipped into my lovely teal pumps.

"Darren! Wait! *WAIT!* They're coming for me!"

Flying up to the passenger door, I jerked furiously on the handle while he watched with curiosity and a touch of disbelief.

"Aren't you going to get in trouble? There's your mom," he gestured toward the armory entrance.

My mother's silhouette was framed in the streetlight, escaping her capture a ruthless and exhilarating game. Sliding into the car, I linked Darren's hand triumphantly, no worries anymore beyond a bad boy and his undivided attention.

"DRIVE!" I commanded.

On the highway with Mom in the dust and on the brink of a blackout, my demeanor shifted to something sweet, flirtatious, and possessed.

"Let's get married."

Perched on the console between the seats, I poured myself all over Darren, eyes glittering crazily in the rearview mirror. His reaction was passive interest blended with slight distaste.

"Married?" he scoffed with a half-smile.

"We could do it now, go to Vegas. I don't even think you need your parents' permission there. No, you don't."

Darren shook his head and kept driving.

Soon we arrived at a strange house party in a dumpy trailer. I wandered inside, eyes searching greedily for more alcohol. The guys living there had a bit of leftover beer but blacked-out-me shifted from finding booze—to getting Darren into bed.

The next day, I had a faint recollection of just that—in a dark, cluttered room in the back of the trailer. I guess I was a willing participant? I wasn't fighting him off—because I did have a couple of snapshot memories. "What took you so long?" CLICK. "Be quiet." CLICK. A millisecond of recall—but I fell right back into the black hole, and then morning was breaking.

As sunlight streamed through the cheap nylon curtains, Darren was silent while I searched for my clothes in misery. The bruises covering my legs would take weeks to fade and screamed my worst fears, and the once-lovely teal dress discarded in the corner was another ugly reminder. Darren barely looked at me as I begged for a ride home.

"I don't have any gas," he said flatly.

Overflowing with shame and cowering in the rumpled dress now stiff with dried champagne and screwdrivers, a panicky impulse to run far away took over as the frat house boys eyed me like a ghetto slut.

"May I use your bathroom?"

Degraded beyond recognition, I had no choice but to weasel my way home in Darren's Cutlass. We didn't speak one word all the way back to Caribou Lake.

8

Landing Liquor was a staple for winos in one of the seediest parts of Duluth. "Wino" is not a politically correct word, but I learned it from my mother and didn't know another way to describe people who passed out on sidewalks. Mom regularly had drunks and other undesirables imbibing in front of her office door on First Street in downtown Duluth, forcing unpleasant interactions to start the workday.

As the clock approached eight, bums gathered outside the Landing, too, awaiting the blessed jingling of keys that signaled relief from alcohol withdrawal. Heads low, they'd shuffle to the back cooler holding the bargain basement wine and the cheapest 40s my dad called bunny pee. After rationing out change, they'd slip outside to crouch by the dumpster, tossing golden caps into the bushes and sipping magic elixir.

Bums didn't frighten me—really, we weren't all that different—each had something the other desperately wanted. Their *age* would supply my rations for the weekend, and they yearned for the tips I banked as a server at the Ponderosa Steakhouse. Our arrangement worked out just fine, it only took a little grit on my part. Weekly, I'd head down to the Landing and pull into the back alley, waiting for the right prospect.

"Want to make a few bucks?"

A gangly, rough-looking guy with bright orange hair and a garish gap-toothed smile had stepped from the back door of an adjacent bar, now shuffling across the cracked pavement, eyes fixed on the ground and muttering something inexplicable. He didn't seem crazy, just focused his closeness to my age making him more approachable somehow.

"What can I do for ya?" he grinned as I approached cautiously, casting nervous glances around. Each time I steeled myself to proposition a random person, I was well aware my subject might disappear with the money AND the booze.

But the combination of beer and strawberry schnapps was enticing enough to take the risk. I'd inherited Gram's old car, an enormous saddle-tan Chrysler New Yorker, and my parents had no idea I was driving to one of the largest slums in the U.S. to score provisions. Being inconspicuous was next to impossible in that huge tank, but it enabled me the freedom to do as I pleased. While the gap-toothed guy shopped, I pulled further back near the dumpsters, then slunk down below the dash to wait.

When he stepped back into view a few minutes later, I was ready at the open trunk, tearing into the case and passing him a couple of beers as an extra tip for doing business.

"Thanks. I'm Tim—by the way. In between jobs, so this helps. See ya around," he called, cracking the beer as he sauntered off down the alley.

My new buddy was a regular at the Landing, and I'd sometimes deposit him back at his filthy tenement in the infamously shady Central Hillside. A few girlfriends joined me there to party sometimes, and Tim and his buddies loved a houseful of teens breathing life into the stinky, flea-infested hell hole. The slum should've been condemned—a total dump reeking of cat urine—but it was an alright place to drink as long as your shoes stayed on. Tim never pulled any fast moves on me but did enjoy hitting on my friends.

This unfortunate dude kept me fully stocked with strawberry schnapps, and empty bottles of it soon shared space with warm beer and wolf spiders in my bedroom closet. Though I papered my room with Top Gun movie posters and images of other popular heartthrobs, it was a pointless attempt to seem normal. To outsiders, my bedroom walls represented those of any other sixteen-year-old dreaming of a date with Tom Cruise, Sebastian Bach, or Bret Michaels. The colorful pictures of big-haired men with spandex pants and blinding white teeth didn't tell the real truth of my life, though. The actual story was me driving to the 'hood and propositioning bums every weekend.

Still holing up in the basement for most hours of the day, my parents rarely bothered me ("teenagers just like to sleep a lot")— and on hungover mornings, I'd creep blindly into the adjacent laundry room for generic popsicles stowed in the chest freezer to quench my raging thirst. Old and borderline moldy, they didn't taste great but saved me a trip upstairs to access the kitchen faucet.

Mom sometimes pointed out how thirsty I was following the late nights of stumbling down the basement steps—but never investigated beyond her passive-aggressive comments.

Dave once addressed my partying and made it clear he didn't approve. My boyfriends were also never liked or respected by anyone in the family.

"You starve yourself all week long and then drink all weekend! It's not sustainable!"

My distant brother feeling the need to have a "come-to-Jesus" intervention should have been a wake-up call, but I ignored his concerns. Soon, Dad's health became the family focus.

Dad took another nosedive around 1989—my junior year of high school marked by buckets of bloody vomit and seizures brought on by alcohol withdrawal.

A loud thud often signaled an episode—Dad would be frothing at the mouth and Mom in a sheer panic. With his medical situation rapidly declining, she finally insisted he seek help. The serious conversation held between the medical team and my parents didn't include me. Barely seventeen, I was sheltered from Dad's condition.

"Dan, you are very lucky to be alive," Dr. Sayler stressed.

Dad wasn't fazed. "Beats the hell out of the alternative, huh?" he quipped, with a wan smile and inappropriately dry wit.

The doctor didn't laugh as he calmly informed my father his liver was failing fast. He'd developed a very serious sign of organ death—esophageal varices.

In true Dad fashion, he wasn't the slightest bit distressed by all this medical mumbo jumbo. After a few days in the hospital, he went through a painful procedure to stop the bleeding in his throat like a champ. Per doctor's orders, it was then straight to

Miller Dwan Treatment Center for twenty-eight days.

Though he'd visited AA meetings in the past (it was never really his thing), Miller-Dwan was the first official treatment program he completed. Mom and I visited weekly, played games in the commons area, and practiced avoiding deep topics. Dad adamantly refused to participate in the family program.

"This is my problem to deal with. It's no one else's beeswax."

He executed a superb performance during our visits, leading us to believe his little problem was being handily treated.

"Things are going great," he insisted one Saturday halfway through his stay. "I've replaced my beer gut with all of this fattening hospital food!"

He *was* gaining weight and looked a bit healthier, but a steady diet of Butterfingers and Mountain Dew couldn't be the solution.

"I'm learning a lot about my condition," Dad assured anyone who would listen. "I've been telling you all these years, Sue, that it's a *disease*. It's a *malady*. I can't control it."

Mom smiled brightly, her happy-go-lucky, codependent self just dying to believe Dad's BS. She didn't realize her addiction to caretaking was as powerful as his was to booze—she'd lived that way for more than three decades.

Mom's parents had modeled such a dynamic over four decades of marriage, years she'd spent learning an enduring lesson of loyalty and standing by your man.

Bored and anxious to leave, I gulped Dixie cups of water from the cooler in silence as they rattled on—frustratingly aware I had no voice in Dad's attempted recovery.

Dad viewed the whole treatment process as a spa retreat or some great reset. Envisioning him without a beer in his hand was out of the question, and an enduring conversion to sobriety seemed about as likely as me making the hockey cheerleading squad or A honor roll.

To show her support, Mom was even shelving her after-work cocktail ritual. I found her sweeping patio bricks one afternoon during the last days of Dad's hiatus, gulping Diet Coke and dabbing her sweaty face with a paper towel. Peculiar behavior indeed, it was usually vodka sours once the workday was done.

"I'm trying too," she said sheepishly when I asked what was up with the soda.

Dad methodically ticked off the days leading up to his release from the "joint."

"Hey! Hon-reee!" Dad called to a tall guy with jet-black hair puffing a Marlboro across the room. His acne-scarred face made me want to look away.

"Danno." The guy wandered over and slapped Dad on the back.

"Melissa, Sue. This is Henry."

Dad beamed at his new friend as if he'd spared him from slaughter. "We're here in the crowbar hotel, huh bud?"

Leaning across the table, Dad stage-whispered, "Hank has *done it*. He's found out a way to *beat the system*."

Grinning, Dad eyed Hank like a revered prophet while his sketchy buddy shrugged and casually blew smoke at the ceiling. My sense of unease was growing—I knew on some distant level it wasn't right for Dad to gloat about his rehab pals conning their way through treatment.

Visiting hours wrapped up shortly after Hank made his grand entrance. As Mom and I prepared to go, he shook my hand, then held it out dramatically while he scanned me up and down. "What a lovely daughter, Dan. How old are you?"

I gritted my teeth. "Seventeen." *Creep!*

Dad successfully completed his stint at Miller-Dwan a week later, and Mom picked him up on a Friday. They were scarcely on the road before Dad's thoughts shifted to beer. Mom wanted to keep temptation as low as possible and had stocked the refrigerator with Coca-Cola and V-8 juice in anticipation of his return. But he wasn't interested in the options waiting at home.

"Why don't you swing by the liquor store?" was out of his mouth before they'd made it a block. Noting Mom's alarmed look, he urged her to relax.

"I don't mean *booze*. Just some near-beer. It's nonalcoholic. Harmless. I really miss the taste."

Mom dutifully made a detour to Hermantown Liquor and collected a twelve-pack of O'Doul's while Dad rested in the car. Once home, his irritation grew, he struggled to fill time, and a week later was back on the real stuff.

One night after my shift at the Ponderosa Steakhouse, I walked into the Caribou Lake cabin house to the sound of a boom box blaring Randy Travis tunes, my father and his superstar rehab buddy Hon-ree completely inebriated and polishing off a bottle of Silver Fox vodka.

"Wow, there she is," Hank slurred, staggering toward me. He slung his arm over my shoulders. "I need to ask you something, you pretty young thing," he mumbled, breathing vodka fumes that made my eyes water. "Are you still a virgin?"

Dad's ears perked up in protest. "What the hell, Hank? Sit your drunk ass down."

Hank obliged and tipped his hat. "It was just a simple question," he chortled. "Is ya or ain't ya?"

I glared. "You are a pig, Hank."

"She sure is purty though, Danno," Hank chortled as I retreated to the dark chambers of the basement.

I needed an escape. Dave's independent life had begun years ago, and sharing space with my parents had become an excruciating experience. Dad hadn't held a job in years, his life was completely directionless, and his constant presence drove me batty. I couldn't count on him being gone *ever*—he was proverbially lodged in the threadbare recliner he'd dubbed "Daddy's Chair" with a beer or cocktail, watching reruns of *Starsky and Hutch* or *Magnum P.I.* Some action and distraction were desperately needed.

A new man was just what the doctor ordered. The next victim on my dating agenda was an imposing dude who ran the cash register at a local convenience store. After several slightly flirtatious exchanges, the familiar magnetism of a new challenge gained unstoppable momentum. Drake stood poised to swallow up my world, becoming the necessary diversion to temporarily heal my discontented brain.

I knew I wasn't his caliber, yet some dogged determination to fake otherwise propelled me forward. Drake's plentiful offerings seemed just out of reach—looks, athletic ability, and intellect—he seemed so *solid*. Plus, he was a local college football star, lived with his parents to save cash (but did a lot for them and was not just seeking a free lunch), and worked two jobs. The idea of being with Drake became an inescapable compulsion. Soon, I grew addicted to pointless convenience store runs to pick up stuff I didn't really need, dressed up in pretty sandals and cute outfits to pump gas, well aware Drake was watching from the register.

One night, I entered the store after downing a six pack of

wine coolers and asked Drake out on a date. He looked flattered, flushed, and tempted.

"How old are you?" he coyly asked. "I'm twenty-two. Not sure if you knew that."

"Well, I'm *almost* eighteen," I hedged, as defeat sagged over me like a wet blanket.

My senior year was starting soon, but since I was still a few months away from legal age, Drake was even more hesitant to reciprocate the advances I threw out like playing cards. Heaping on the charm worked, and soon we were canvassing the back dirt roads of my youth, listening to loud music and sipping beer from the glove box.

"The deal with my girlfriend is a college thing that's dragged on way too long," Drake admitted. "But there's no harm in us hanging out I suppose."

Summer nights prior to senior year were not spent planning my wedding to Mitch and anticipating his return. Instead, my new boy toy was consuming every shred of time and energy.

Just when I thought I had closed the deal with Drake, he decided to give his sagging relationship another shot. The walls closed in, and panic ramped up as he patiently explained their long history. The next few weeks were spent stumbling around the house shedding bitter tears of teenage anguish.

The identity I'd scavenged from television sitcoms bit the dust as I sat despondently at my school desk, scribbling Drake's name despondently in round, girly flourishes. First-period English class was a sorrowful time, most mornings spent carving his initials into the wall as my favorite teacher Mrs. Otos admonished the temptation of using CliffsNotes as a substitute for actually reading *Jane Eyre*.

Eventually, Drake experienced a change of heart, and I was beyond euphoric. *I had won. She* was gone for good, and we resumed our nights of cruising down dark and winding Moccasin Mike Road along Wisconsin Point, drinking fruity malt beverages that tasted like sparkling water but got you drunk in a jiffy. Somehow though, our escapades weren't quite as exciting with the other girl out of the picture. For the record, our relationship was completely platonic until he ended things with her.

Drake and I quickly became a serious item, and soon I abandoned everyone to accommodate him. Family, friends, and the thin sliver of identity I'd somehow scraped together evaporated like a translucent mirage on the walls of my deserted heart. Just shy of my eighteenth birthday, my mind shifted to a lifetime with my new man, and I executed plans to evacuate the Caribou Lake cabin basement.

Next stop: Drake's house. He'd remain with his parents until his upcoming college graduation the following spring, so it was just a temporary arrangement. Having earned the respect of his family, I was accepted as part of the package now. Our arrangement began innocently enough: "We were watching a movie and fell asleep," *à la* "Wake Up Little Susie," and progressed along with my childhood like a train going off the tracks. With a basket of clothes in his room and the rest of my necessities in the trunk of my car, I had everything I thought I needed.

Still a senior in high school, but I was tantalizingly close to official adulthood and resistance to my insistent independence was weak. Ponderosa Steakhouse continued to fund gas for my car and other essentials— even $300 for the dream gown I wore to my senior prom with Drake.

Christy Olson and I also crossed paths that summer—and she became my new partner in crime. Brash and blonde with an infectious laugh and up-for-anything personality, we were soon inseparable best drinking buddies—partying, working, and donating plasma downtown for drinking money. One year older, she was attending a local community college and living in an apartment with her young daughter and a roommate. That apartment became a second home where rules did not exist. As long as I didn't flunk out of school, no red flags were raised.

Senior year was my ticket to complete freedom. Without a high school diploma, I'd remain reliant on others. I pulled together an ideal schedule of English, Modern Novel, marketing, and science—class until noon, mostly easy A's, and credit for after-school work. The second job I later picked up at a nearby convenience store offered great perks for employees like free car washes, fountain soda, and fast food including stale popcorn and overcooked hot dogs.

The night I'd obsessively anticipated for years finally arrived—my eighteenth birthday. I was *a legal adult.* Christy whipped up a surprise birthday party with several Ponderosa work buddies.

"Come over, and we'll watch movies and drink beer," she had suggested, as a way of luring me to her apartment. Ascending the trashy back steps leading to her West End duplex, black windows stared back, and I peered through the glass, wondering if I was being punked. Tentatively I rapped on the door anyway, and Christy flung it open wide.

"SURPRISE!"

A crew of work friends and Drake jumped out of the shadows, hooting and throwing confetti. Christy had baked me a special birthday cake with little candy pieces forming the number 18 and had amassed an endless supply of alcohol.

Oh, what a night! We mowed through the cases of beer in no time, then cracked into a quart of root beer schnapps. Who knows how many shots I downed . . . seven? Eight? My final memory of the night was loud and drunken singing to the Steve Miller Band.

Christy had an enormous water bed in her wood-paneled back bedroom, so monstrous that it was difficult to squeeze between the padded side railings and the wall. I don't remember going to sleep that night but came to from a beer and schnapps death grip—Drake and Christy passed out beside me. The fact that all three of us were fully clothed was a good sign. But, wait. I was wet. I wet the bed. Oh crap. What if Drake knows? My life was becoming a constant parade of blackouts, bedwetting, and shame.

How the hell did THIS happen?

Another night, another near-fatal overdose. Heart pounding, I fixed my eyes on the ceiling and quietly had a panic attack as alcohol withdrawal flooded my system, my brain scrambling to make sense of the morning.

9

Drake's parents served as my surrogate family throughout senior year. Poor Mom was fully occupied with Dad's raging alcoholism and frequent drunk-driving arrests. Everyone doubted courtship with Drake would last, but I didn't give two flying figs. People-pleasing and a helpful attitude would eventually captivate them all. Soon, I rode reluctant shotgun with Drake's mother for many football road trips to cheer on the boy-man she'd begrudgingly agreed to share.

Drake drank beer occasionally, but it lacked the compulsive allure it held for me and never ran his life. His identity was found in football, and any activity that could jeopardize the sport was off the table. That meant no drinking before any game and reliable service as a designated driver. His imposing size was a welcome diversion that helped me slip into bars unchecked.

"Melissa, I think you have a drinking problem. You're an alcoholic," Drake insisted one night as we bickered on the long drive back to Superior from the Kro-Bar in Brule, Wisconsin.

"Just like my dad, you're saying? I guess we can't all have the *Leave it to Beaver* family like you do." Chuckling hollowly, I lowered the window an inch to flick a cigarette butt out as Drake's grip tightened angrily on the steering wheel. He despised smoking, especially in his prized truck, but the alcohol allowed me to swallow his disdain without fear of reproach.

Unwilling to drop the conversation, I wanted to revisit his accusation until he felt the full gravity of its absurdity. "So, I have a few beers, and now I'm instantly a drunk? Eighteen-year-olds can't be alcoholics!" I railed.

Drake was done talking, but his hostile comment had already taken up space in my soul. His cutting words reinforced the ugly truth I'd known deeply since my first drunk. *I wasn't like other people*—like other *drinkers*—no matter how much I wanted to believe otherwise. I wasn't wired for booze, though I refused to surrender.

Christy was a faithful adjunct to keep the party going when Drake was occupied—we had a blast toting innocent-looking thermoses of booze to his football games, and rooting for a team that struggled to pull off even one win, our cheering escalating to drunken howling by halftime. Proud to be Drake's girlfriend, I paraded around in his black and orange UWS team windbreaker. The football number stitched on the upper arm identified me as his property, and I was fine with that. Whenever he did something cool, like tackle someone, I went nuts. His amazing skills couldn't carry the whole floundering crew though, and after a big loss he was withdrawn and pouty.

When Drake was depressed about football or cramping my style, Christy filled in the gaps. Fast and blunt, her bleached-blonde hair was eye-catching, and guys loved her—almost making me cooler by association. *I don't remember driving home that night. I hate it when that happens!* was a constant we accepted as part of the package. Sailing in the same sinking alcohol ship, there were no judgments about blackouts, empty wallets, or strings of vacant boyfriends entering the picture who were big on promises but short on follow-through.

An evil twin holding the same carefree attitude about endless nights of blackout drinking helped to dismiss the memory-barren mornings where I "came to," wondering what the hell had happened.

"I'm a *heavy drinker*," Christy giggled after one of these blowouts where we found ourselves crashed out in the living room of her dingy duplex—a litany of Busch Light cans cluttering the scarred coffee table, some unknown guy in a foam trucker hat sleeping in the recliner. "Not an *alcoholic*. They changed it now. The criteria or whatever."

Commiserating over drinking antics, our atrocious hangovers, and the stupid things we'd done helped to normalize things. We were two peas in a pod, enabling each other's life-threatening chaos.

Drake hated my side hustle with Christy, strongly preferring I stay home with his parents, watching TV in his tiny boyhood bedroom and anxiously awaiting his return. Urges to control were neatly hidden for a while, but his flaring temper didn't stay hidden forever. Our exclusive relationship continued in spite of my growing pushback—I was nineteen and trapped between shedding my chrysalis to seek new adventures and staying in the cocoon with Drake and his parents. The pull was painful—I hungered for independence, my own apartment, and the freedom to nibble Chinese food from take-out cartons, not *needing* anyone but myself. But a more insistent piece lurking deep inside whispered other things—*You can't be alone. You won't make it. You'll go crazy.*

I needed a host, a warm body, to survive.

Graduation day arrived in June of 1991, and Drake and I celebrated a huge milestone by leaving his family home and settling into our very own apartment. His mother wept, but we were resolved. After scraping together $550 for the first month's rent and security deposit, we happily wrangled our tired collaboration of possessions to the second floor of a battle worn but somehow hopeful building overlooking Kari Toyota in a gray and industrial part of town. The tiny, one-bedroom efficiency lurked in a shady area of Superior's North End—but was handily plopped right across the street from a dive bar called Mama's Place that sold me carry-out provisions without so much as batting an eyelash.

Free, clear, and living with a loyal and responsible man the day I graduated, this stability cocktail should have produced the happiness I'd chased for years, but instead, I was falling apart.

Alone in the apartment, antsy and riddled with unease, I paced the floor and watched game shows while Drake worked, eventually cracking open a bag of tortilla chips we'd bought during our latest grocery run. He'd be mad if I ate too many, so I measured out a serving of fourteen chips and then secured the sack with a chunk of Magic tape.

"I'm starving," Drake announced, barging through the door just after midnight. "Make me some mac and cheese? And can you bring me some chips? I've barely eaten all day."

Rising from my post by the cheap metal fan that had been a fixture in Drake's family for years—(they called it "Frigid" after its brand name), one of Drake's goofy habits was to crouch down in front of it while it sputtered and choked and whisper *Frigid jam, Frigid jam . . .* to coax the tired machinery into working one more time—but now Frigid was slowly dying and doing nothing to cool down the ninety-degree apartment. I wasn't looking forward to standing over a boiling pot—but reluctantly rummaged through the pantry, wishing I could go to bed and stop the rising panic. I needed to tell Drake something before the acid of the dirty secret ate me alive.

Fetching the chips, I couldn't miss Drake's frown as I passed them over.

"You started eating them?"

"Well, yeah. I had a few. What's the big deal?"

Drake slipped out of his gas station smock and threw it over a chair while eyeing the snacks I'd violated.

"We shopped for all this stuff, it cost a lot, I thought we'd just eat it together."

I turned my back and rolled my eyes. He even wanted to control my chip consumption.

"So how was work?" I ventured, changing the subject.

"Dillon had three drive-offs," Drake offered, chuckling snidely. "I swear, that guy has something missing upstairs. I'm going to get my butt chewed by the boss next week for letting that happen."

Dillon. Dillon delivered a sudden gut punch. It seemed serendipitous he'd been mentioned, like a sign from God.

*Jenny had suggested going to the old reliable frat house on
Fourth Street since gravel pit parties weren't happening. This was
our last resort; it was in the 'hood, and the guys were much older.
College. Momentary apprehension melted away drinking kamikaze shots from plastic cups. Sitting on the edge of a disintegrating
futon, I chatted with a guy with sidewinder black hair and jeans
with worn knees. In and out of fragmentary blackouts, I sensed
sloshing in a waterbed, bonking into the headboard but unable
to do anything about it. Awkward parting and I searched for my
green cowl-neck sweater, the one I'd worn in my graduation pictures.
What was your name again? Dillon.*

"There's something I have to tell you," I managed, as panic
thundered through my heart.

Drake stopped stirring the pot of macaroni while I pulled
out a kitchen chair, knowing I had to act fast.

"I had a thing with Dillon."

Sitting at the table weeping, any boundaries I'd ever had
completely collapsed as I disclosed every dirty secret from my
past to Drake's disbelieving and incredulous ears.

"WHAT? You told me you'd been with, like—three people!"

"I know, I'm sorry," I sobbed. "But it feels so good to tell
you everything! I'll never hide anything again."

Disclosing every shred of myself felt like a requirement, a
test to gauge his loyalty, and now we had a clean slate. Drake
agreed to forgive me and wasn't going to leave.

We started over, settled into our apartment, and Dad soon
embarked on a beer and boredom-fueled cleaning rampage.

"Come and get your stuff," he demanded. "We're trying to
get rid of things. I have nowhere to store my *musical equipment*.
We might start having jam sessions in the basement again."

As if. He hadn't played guitar in years.

"Dad, we don't have room for it," I complained. "Our apartment is like the size of a storage room."

"I wouldn't know, you haven't invited me and your mother over yet," Dad griped. "I'll include your old junk in my next trip to the dump, then."

No way would he ever do that, but to get him off my back I downed a six-pack for motivation and headed out to Caribou Lake the next day. Buried in the basement closet of my youth, Mom appeared at the top of the stairs with the yellow wall phone lodged between her shoulder and ear.

"Melissa, it's Mitch for you." I stood frozen as she gestured wildly, *get your butt up here.*

What were the odds? My eyes widened, and I was a child again, buried in shame and cardboard Busch beer containers tucked in the back of the closet. Mitch? He hadn't called for a year.

"Mitch? I haven't heard from you in so long!" I managed, trying to sound excited.

"Guess what? I'm coming home!"

My discarded military man was in the dark about the new and exclusive relationship I'd forged with Drake, convinced I was patiently pining away for his return. I stood, head anesthetized and unable to think.

"That's great," I managed, my shocked brain moving again like stalled machinery seeking a new and less arduous destination.

I had to make Mitch go away, so I eagerly wrote a letter— a long, gushing, plaintive narrative—to rationalize what I'd done—blaming it all on how we'd drifted apart. My boyfriend of old was essentially a stranger now—I was detached, simply seeing myself perform a necessary but somewhat shifty task—like canceling an appointment or ditching work when I wasn't really sick.

Mitch took it hard—but maintained his usual predictable presentation just the same.

"Well, I don't know what I'll do with the ring now. Guess I'll sell it."

He didn't simply go away afterwards as I'd hoped and continued to mail long and detailed letters to my parents' house. The carefully written messages filled me with guilt. *It makes me feel pretty bad when I look at your picture, which still hangs in my military locker. My mother loves the color of your hair.*

Brushing the shame aside, I returned to Drake. My saving grace was to focus on the splintering delusion I'd managed to harness happiness by stealing Drake from his old girlfriend and securing an efficiency apartment and $200 junk car. The hatchback came from a Caribou Lake neighbor who drank beer in his front yard during the transaction, insisting I'd cause a crash through my roadside habit of laying out in the sun. I guess it was a compliment, but the guy was crowding forty.

The boyfriend, apartment, and discarded vehicle were threadbare delusions I collected like pocket change that helped to plug the soul holes. I decided that no explanation was required on the Mitch front   Drake had easily dismissed him as an old high school sweetheart who'd disappeared from my life years ago, which was pretty accurate.

Inside, I frantically rationalized, not wanting to vomit any more of my past into Drake's lap. *He doesn't need to know the details. Mitch and I were basically broken up. He was thousands of miles away.*

Life with Drake continued for another year, but the tourniquet restricting Mitch's memory eventually began to loosen. My usual intoxicating pursuit of a courtship had turned inside out, complacency crept in, and I searched compulsively for external things to fix my growing discomfort.

Fighting over quirks that had initially drawn us together became a regular occurrence with Drake. My once-cute rebellion and spending habits were now despised. Diet Coke, Fig Newtons, and trips to Target for clothes were not allowed.

"Where's your tax return?" he exploded, when I returned late one afternoon, loaded with Target bags. "Show me where you spent it. Is all that money *GONE* already?!"

I cried as I packed up my new clothes, though Drake stopped short of forcing a return trip to the store.

Now I was on restriction—with poor money management bringing a strict budget imposed by Drake. I was a caged rat, discontent and impending doom my constant companions.

Needing some refreshment, I quit both part-time jobs and landed a new gig at a Spur convenience store near our apartment. The novel duties and change of scenery rebooted my restless brain, but the focus soon shifted to my stagnant relationship. I needed a ring and a proposal, stat.

"What would you think about getting engaged?" I asked brightly.

Drake shrugged. "Someday."

I wanted *now*. Pondering ways to accelerate the process, I circled some engagement ring pictures in the JCPenney catalog and instructed my mother to point them out to Drake. Wedded bliss was my mission, but his nonchalant attitude persisted.

At first, fellow Spur employee Seth Walker was just a guy

who worked the graveyard shift whose time card lived in the slot next to mine. For months, he was like a vampire who only came out under the cover of night, long gone when I punched the clock. But after a while, our shifts began to overlap. We became fast friends, and I discovered he cared little about sports or displays of physical strength and had a captivating intellectual side. Before long, hours spent manning the store flew by as we bantered through friendly debates about everything from politics to the sleazy tactics of the paparazzi. Seth was almost like a budding professor, seeming to share my desire for a meaningful connection.

Ephedrine became the next drug in my medicine cabinet. Meth hadn't really hit the scene yet, but chemically, the two are very similar. Seth used the cheap over-the-counter form of speed to stay awake during his graveyard shifts, and I quickly learned the magic pills were like confidence in a bottle.

"I'm exhausted," I complained one Saturday after the duties on the clipboard had been checked off and I was ready to clock out.

"These help me stay up," Seth offered, gesturing to a locked plastic case behind the cash register.

Mini-thins became the antidote to lethargy, weight gain, and procrastination. The initial effects were electrifying—just a few in the morning provided incredible energy, floods of ideas, and superhuman confidence. Soon I was gulping handfuls of white cross with fountain soda, even rotating stores to build my supply. Frequenting a little trap line of gas stations kept me stocked up, and I found incredible energy to drink all night long by mixing pills with alcohol. Before long, I developed an enormous tolerance that required thirty tablets a day.

Seth wasn't interested in popping tabs outside of his night shifts, and I pretended I didn't take them often, either. Tucked into a secret purse pocket, my new favorite friend was hidden away, though my body started to suspect I was poisoning it. Sometimes after I swallowed my usual handful of bitter, chalky tablets, my system rebelled, and I'd begin pouring rivers of sweat. I often gulped the pills while driving, sometimes causing excruciating pain and the fear my stomach was about to explode. Mind reeling, I'd entertain crazy thoughts of dying behind the wheel and someone eventually stumbling upon my bloated dead body.

One weekend in March, Drake dropped by while Seth and I manned the store. As though wanting to mark his territory, he leaned over the magazine rack and delivered a terrifically awkward kiss.

"Who was that?" Seth asked once Drake left. "Are you dating that guy?"

"Yeah, that's Drake. My boyfriend."

Seth seemed dejected and enforced new boundaries; he was friendly yet brief, and our long, soul-searching talks ground to a halt.

That summer, Drake prepared to leave town for the wedding of a college friend.

"I wish you could come," he griped, zipping his dress clothes into a garment bag. "Can't you ever take days off?"

"It wasn't enough notice," I lied.

The possibilities of another drunken night zoomed into focus as my shift ended. Drake was miles away, I was free, and a case of beer waited in the trunk of my car. Drinking buddies were needed though, so I dialed up Christy.

"What's going on tonight? You have plans?"

My best drinking buddy was on a mission to round up a babysitter for her three-year-old. I rushed through shift change, anxious to get the party started.

Seth's red Blazer rolled into the parking lot as I was clocking out, and a pump of adrenaline surged through me as he sauntered into the store, passing a hand over his perfectly gelled shock of coffee-colored hair.

Whipping to the register with an embarrassed look, he grabbed some Big Red from the candy rack as I stood contemplating whether he really *needed* a pack of gum or was just pulling a bogus store visit like I used to in the early days with Drake. As he fumbled for bills, I considered something I knew wasn't a good idea.

"I'm having a little get-together tonight. Want to stop by?"

Seth looked uncomfortable but interested. "I'm heading over to a buddy's house now, but maybe later?"

"Yeah, whatever works," I offered as though I had a ton of options. We'll be around."

The change I handed back from his purchase defied me though, the coins damp from sweaty palms and desperation.

Christy and I had no problem entertaining ourselves alone, I'd almost forgotten Seth's halfhearted pledge to stop by. Swilling beer and playing makeshift DJ, I reveled in my favorite alternate universe where drunkenness brought about my deepest desires.

Our second 12-pack was running low when we heard a timid knock. Seth stood in the doorway, looking shy and harboring a new addition to the liquor supply.

"You drink beer, right?"

I laughed like he needed to have his head examined.

"Of course! Come on in!"

The night rolled on with our extremely welcomed bonus guest, and I flowed with unbelievable charm until incoherence set in. Eight beers had wiped away any residual anxiety, and Christy and I cut loose and broke into an impressive dance party for Seth. Eventually she passed out, and it was time for me to make my move.

"I've wanted to do that since we met," I breathed, after delivering to Seth my most mind-blowing kiss.

Morning dawned with awkwardness and a painful hangover. My guests lingered around to watch a movie before heading off, and I hung blankets all over the windows to block the sun in a subconscious effort to keep things hidden.

Cleaning up the apartment and rehearsing a dialogue for Drake offered needed distraction. Being a good liar would have come in handy, but my weak boundaries made fudging the truth extremely difficult.

You guys didn't really do anything. It was harmless. Everyone was drunk.

When Drake returned, I continued mindless activities to snuff out the thoughts that could easily spiral into a panic attack. The most elaborate dish I could manage—spaghetti— was on the menu. Juggling cooking pots, draining noodles and browning hamburger occupied me as I listened politely to a summary of the wedding.

"It was a low-key night," Drake finished. "I only had two beers. Do you believe that?"

"Sounds pretty lame," I managed with a fake laugh.

Life resumed, my guilt faded, and visits with Seth during his graveyard shifts at the convenience store again became a habit. By now we had advanced to make-out sessions in the soda cooler. A little bell chimed when a customer walked in the door, so I waited in the dark and chilly recesses until Seth took care of business, giggling and vowing our secret activities would never go *too* far.

Drake's gas station was a thirty-minute drive from Superior, and he always worked weekends. One warm June morning after he'd left for the day, the phone rang. It was Seth calling from the Spur station.

"What, did someone not show up? You need me to come in?"

"Nope. I'm just clocking out, but it's such a beautiful day I can't bear to waste it sleeping. Want to go for a ride with me?"

Two friends on an innocent little drive. Seemed legit.

A secluded place on Wisconsin Point awaited, and a cooler of beer kept us occupied for a few hours. When our supply ran dry, we headed back to town to a store that sold to underage customers only to find one of Drake's football buddies manning the cash register. Seeing me with Seth made him do a double-take, but my alcoholic haze blunted any concerns. After collecting another case, we returned to our deserted lakefront spot and drank into the night.

The hours melted away as we lounged on a remote beach, hidden away from the world and thrilled with each other's company. Inspecting sun-bleached sticks of driftwood reminded me of art projects I had made in Vacation Bible School where discarded Lake Superior wood was the canvas, pussy willows, rocks and shells handcrafted adornments. Tunes from Seth's tinny radio kept the party going. Drake was probably home by now. I'd just tell him I'd been out with Christy.

Seth and I went too far that night, and the thing I swore

wouldn't happen—did. The night was fuzzy, my memory as secure as a slab of deteriorating Swiss cheese, but there was no question that I'd done *the thing* I vowed I wouldn't.

Heading home drunk in the dark was a confusing mess. We conducted a massive recovery mission for my underwear (which seemed funny in the moment), and my socks were later found stuffed into my pockets.

Seth deposited me at my apartment and I stumbled inside to find every light in the place blazing and Drake looming large in the kitchen. He slammed the telephone receiver down hard as I entered.

"Where have you been?" he exploded, eyes filled with rage and lower lip trembling. "That was Todd, from the liquor store. Have you been out with Seth all this time? What the *hell* have you been doing?"

I stared at the floor.

"Yes. We went too far."

Drake collapsed to the floor as angry tears blazed a path down his stubbly face.

10

Drake spent most of the night begging for assurance my betrayal was a one-time situation. Leaning close to my face, he softly sang an old Meatloaf song like some plaintive lullaby from the 1970s, the one about pleading someone in a highly codependent way to offer undying love. Cold and unresponsive, I insisted I couldn't promise anything. The whole deal just seemed like a huge inconvenience.

Morning dawned with a raging headache and vague memories of an evening I would've loved to erase and rewind to the days of harmless make-out sessions in the soda cooler. Now I had crossed a line, and Drake was irreparably hurt.

His desperation was precisely what I craved—a man willing to put up with my shenanigans and still stick around. Believing that Drake would accept just about anything allowed me to express a startling level of detachment, the one I'd learned as a small child.

"You have to stop seeing him," he implored again as soon as the sun cracked the horizon. Fourteen hours of solid drinking the day before had produced a traumatized brain, and I couldn't bear his intensity. I just wanted to sleep.

"It was a mistake. It won't happen again. Can we talk later? Please?"

I was a straight-up cheater, and somewhere deep inside knew I should be ashamed, but my hangover blunted the severity of the situation.

Halfheartedly wanting to work things out, I struggled to squash the feelings of straight infatuation I still harbored for Seth while salvaging my two-year investment with Drake. I had formed another soul tie, which made me emotionally connected to two separate people, and I didn't even know it.

Swapping out tills in the back room of the convenience store a few days later, Seth and I were finally alone. I had to level with him.

"I need to give it another shot with Drake. I just can't throw away all this time with the guy."

Seth silently completed his money exchange and slammed the safe.

"I understand," he said simply, and walked out.

Once I recommitted to our relationship, Drake no longer demanded control of my money or time. Bar junkets with Christy were now welcomed and even encouraged, and knowing my love of it—he joined me for nights of drinking at her apartment.

Crammed face-to-face on her well-worn sofa with beer flowing freely, undying devotion was easy. My emphatic vow to adore him forever made his eyes glisten with tears, and Drake finally popped the question I'd craved so many years.

"I don't want to wait anymore. Will you marry me?"

"Do you mean it? I will make you the best wife ever!"

Swept up in the rapture of the moment, we embraced—and at just nineteen, I believed I'd been spared a life of loneliness and abandonment.

The exquisite feeling lasted a few weeks while I showed off the new engagement ring Drake and I had selected together, but it wasn't long before the novelty wore off.

Delicately subtle in the beginning, the reality crept in as the chill of autumn does when daylight shrinks into winter's gaping mouth. The thing nibbling the far reaches of my brain was like the hazy deception of a distant mirage, something I could discern but not identify. Restlessness. I'd soon need more chaos in order to survive.

Christy and I ramped up our drinking escapades—the night always finishing off with a drive by the gas station that had become a beacon of temptation. So far, I'd managed to sail by on autopilot, but like an addict passing a favorite watering hole, I weakened a little every time. One night, I crumbled beneath the impulsive urge to pull into the parking lot. Seth stood behind the counter of the empty store.

"I can't do this anymore," I sobbed. "I want to be with you."

Our secret meetings reignited, and I scrambled to initiate mindless arguments with Drake for another month but soon resorted to flat-out lying.

One afternoon I claimed to be running an errand. Minutes

after I reached my destination, Drake's truck squealed into the parking lot, tires burning with angry anticipation.

"What the hell?" he yelled, charging inside. "I knew it!"

Intrigued by the whole dramatic showdown and two guys fighting over me, I stood with silent curiosity as Drake and Seth exchanged insults and profanities.

Jumping to my defense, Seth faced the brawny beast who towered a good six inches above him.

"Man, you're pathetic. Can't you see she doesn't want you?"

Drake's eyes brimmed with rage and anguish.

"Is that true?" he asked incredulously, after turning to face me.

I paused for emphasis. "Yes."

Drake didn't ransack the store as I'd expected. He just turned and stormed out.

Seth was speechless for several minutes, then chose the most exquisite words to break the long silence.

"So, you're all mine now?"

Smiling with what I hoped was true radiance, I envisioned I had scored the lead role on *The Young & the Restless*.

Returning to the apartment I shared with Drake was clearly not an option, so I crashed on Christy's couch for a few nights. It was kind of fun being homeless, mostly because I knew I really wasn't. Christy was having trouble taking my current situation seriously and loved ribbing me about all the hair gel and cologne Seth used.

Flying under the radar was impossible when I was on stage manning the store though. Drake soon stopped by to deliver a sharp and public warning: "Your stuff will be dumped into the middle of Tower Avenue if you don't come get it by the end of tomorrow."

"Please don't," I begged. "Can I just pack things up while you're at work?"

"Forget it," he sneered. "I don't want you alone in *my house*. Come over when I'm off work. Take it or leave it."

Nervous and panicky (probably because I was sober), I arrived at the appointed time to find my belongings crammed carelessly into sagging boxes on the front porch. Drake followed me as I conducted a quick walk-through of the bathroom and bedroom.

"I can just imagine the two of you together," he marveled. "I can *picture* you cheating on me. I hope it was worth it. I really thought I *knew you*, Melissa."

Flee. Flee. It was the only answer. I had to get far away from this feeling. *Was I making a mistake?*

"Please don't hate me," I begged, tossing out the Minnesota Nice card in a last-ditch effort to save face.

Drake wasn't softened by my empty pleading. "Hurry up and get your crap out."

I'd lost my home through self-imposed chaos, and I'd soon wear out my welcome on Christy's couch. With another roommate and a child, she had no space for a third tenant.

Memories of Drake constantly haunted me from the background, but it was too late to turn back time. Unable to create space to process my broken pieces, subconsciously I knew where to find relief. Alcohol, and a new man.

Meanwhile, Seth and his buddy had executed their own rental search and had just signed a lease on a large upper duplex in Superior's East End. Even though it was *way* too soon to shack up with another guy, he made the idea seem easy and reasonable.

"It's perfect!" he insisted, as I toured the old Victorian

mansion, already imagining where my possessions would go. I'd quickly fallen in love with the bay windows and enormous walk-in closets.

"With the rent split three ways, it will be dirt cheap. Seriously, it's so huge, we probably won't even bump into each other much. My dad's going to make us a bed, too. A bed frame I mean," he grinned.

That old thought of asserting myself, getting my own apartment—surfaced again. Maybe a small efficiency? The idea made my stomach heave and churn like the gales of November. *Could I? Could I be alone?*

Slipping into Seth's place was so warm and comfortable though, and a pocket of belonging opened before me as he smiled eagerly over the idea of us taking things to the next level. So much better than a cold, lonely efficiency or a room above the Rose Hotel near the North End dive bars, probably the only thing I'd ever afford. *I can't do that.*

So I relented and joined Seth's moving party in July of 1992 along with his buddy Piker, and the excitement of a brand-new adventure fortified me once again. His dad did make us that bed, it looked like something out of a knight's castle, with Seth and I selecting gorgeous sheers and fabric to hang from the top. Seth had once aspired to be an interior designer, and had some mad skills. I finally had the canopy bed I'd always wanted.

"We can't let Randy know," I insisted, after we'd been living together a few weeks.

Randy was our manager from the Spur station and also a good friend of Drake's. He hadn't agreed with my decision to dump Drake and delivered stern warnings about the absurdity of jumping into a new relationship right away. Randy was like a father figure in some odd way, and I loathed disappointing him.

"Who cares what Randy says?" Seth shrugged. "You're my girlfriend, we live together. So what?"

Party, party, party. The three of us ran the consummate frat house, the huge, four-bedroom duplex the site of many crazy gatherings including an epic Halloween blow out with a hundred or so superficial friends. Seth, Piker, and I managed a never-ending supply of booze in spite of our humble jobs, and our doors were always open to anyone wanting to drink and crash. Weekends were spent at the Superior bars, and enduring the early morning gas station shifts was brutal. So many nights I drank until 4 a.m., slept two hours, then woke up under a hot shower that revived me enough for the 7 a.m. cashier shift. I was even promoted to assistant manager of the store. Copious amounts of Visine and mouthwash didn't do much to cover me, and the only saving grace was the abundance of leftover booze waiting after work.

The good times mostly outweighed any negative consequences, though I did survey the house in tears after that massive Halloween party that left the stately old mansion trashed. So many had paraded through, guzzling from free kegs and burning holes into countertops.

The morning after, Seth and Piker played video games and drank leftover beer while I plunged toilets and mopped layers of dried mud from the worn-out hardwood floors, crying over the disgusting bathroom conditions and lack of help.

Christy moved into the legal world of alcohol consumption that fall, and Seth followed just a few months later. I burned with jealousy—a year behind them all and suddenly at a strong disadvantage. How could I find a loophole into the nightlife I craved?

Superior, Wisconsin, was (and still is) well-known for its abundant watering holes: twelve glorious blocks of clubs, pubs, and mom-and-pop joints. Their squat profiles were absolutely beautiful to me, dominating the desolate industrial sweep from Fifteenth Street, across the railroad tracks, and all the way down to Fifth.

Knowing each one on an intimate basis became my personal mission—bartenders, clientele, entertainment schedule, and specials. A fake I.D. would handily solve my underage problem, and fortunately Christy donated her expired license to my cause after her birthday. We soon put it to the test.

The Odyssey night club was a bright blue eyesore on the east side of Tower Avenue, and I'd long awaited the chance to experience the debauchery I'd so far only seen through the glass. The scantily clad girls, pulsating dance floor, and elevated DJ booth made it well-known as a meat market, but to me, it was screamingly close to the Garden of Eden.

Pumped full of liquid courage, Christy and I pulled into the back parking lot, her huge blue eyes glittering in the streetlight as she leaned close to the rearview mirror and applied lip gloss.

"You go through the side door, I'll take the front," she barked as though we were conducting a police investigation. "I'll order first. Wait a few minutes, and then come in. They have three bartenders on duty, so we should have no problem."

Seconds later, I crept inside to meet a dead and mundane bar—nothing close to what I'd witnessed on my Friday night drive-bys. A few people crowded on barstools hunched over glasses of tap beer, and a couple of old guys shot pool. The DJ booth was silent and empty.

Smoking and chugging a beer, Christy was already settled in and right at home. Walking over confidently, I flashed my most charming smile as the bartender approached.

"Large tap beer, if you would please."

"I.D. please," she responded flatly.

Fully expecting this, I reached into my purse and retrieved the laminated card I was convinced held the keys to life itself. Scanning it briefly, the bartender's eyes moved from Christy to me with a smirk.

"I'm calling the cops."

Her declaration spurred immediate action. Christy and I scrambled outside and jumped into my car but didn't make it more than a block. Through my haze, I saw cherries flashing behind me, so I obeyed and pulled over, where I was cuffed and hauled into the back of the squad car. As the officer put his hand on my head and guided me into the back, I slid over the hard plastic bench seat, surprised by the lack of upholstery. Christy looked on from the sidewalk. She wasn't in trouble.

The officers led me into the station and issued citations for minor frequenting and misrepresenting age. My first arrest at the age of twenty, I managed to escape the DWI I certainly deserved, but was slapped with an additional ticket for resisting arrest. This was just the beginning of my altercations with Superior law enforcement.

Forced to hail a cab back to the apartment and still in booze-induced tears, Seth was sleeping and completely oblivious to what I'd done. His scolding was minimal; he was more exasperated about being awakened in the middle of the night than anything. I passed out beside him with my once-pretty face streaked with mascara and bitter, underage tears over the loss of my precious I.D.

11

As our relationship progressed, I talked marriage, ditched my birth control pills, and relentlessly pushed Seth for a commitment. I added a new job at a mall jewelry store, and we moved in with my parents in a lame effort to save money. My new position involved endless hours perusing the new diamond and bridal inventory, and before long I conned Seth into a shopping expedition. What began as a harmless trip to the Miller Hill Mall ended with a line of credit in my name and a half-carat engagement ring.

He'd make his marriage hesitancy obvious through various comments over the coming months ("Don't you ever get nervous about spending the rest of your life with just one person?"

should've been a red flag), but his cold feet didn't deter me. Subconsciously, I figured a pregnancy on the front side of the wedding would just add another dimension to our bond. Seth was aware I'd abandoned my birth control over fears of weight gain, but was apathetic about it. We weren't seeking a baby, nor were we preventing one.

Six short weeks after I'd decided that oral contraception was sure to make me grossly obese, I felt seasick in my college classes and cradled my spinning head while the professors lectured. The weeks passed, and the monthly sign I'd been praying to see had dried up like a potsherd.

Time for a pregnancy test, but only to ease my mind. After chatting with the nurse briefly and providing a urine sample, an excruciating ten-minute wait followed.

She was back with a flourish. "Your result was positive. You are pregnant."

Stunned, I stumbled out to my car in shock, then drove aimlessly down I-35 halfway to the Twin Cities in a daze before stopping in Hinckley for a drive-thru fish sandwich and fries. And since I was now growing a baby, I requested a much-hated carton of milk at the last minute. My mother once told me I gave up milk at six weeks of age.

Seth was lounging in our little living space (the site of my musty childhood bedroom) smoking a cigarette when I returned hours later. We'd tried to spruce the area up to look like a small apartment with a separated sleeping and living area—but the fact that it was still a moldy basement was obvious.

"I'm pregnant," I blurted, the second our eyes met.

Dragging from his cigarette, Seth blew smoke rings at the ceiling.

"What are we going to do? You want to keep it, right?"

Without hesitation, Seth pulled me into a tight hug. "Of course."

Things changed dramatically in that pivotal moment—and my rituals of drinking and partying evaporated. Alcohol was no longer an option, the thought of chugging a beer alongside a growing fetus was repulsive and hideous. Seth still indulged in after-work drinks with his buddies prompted by his need to relax. With mounting resentment, I attempted to kill my wedding day fantasy of partying, doing shots, and ending the night dancing in a short cocktail version of my actual wedding dress. No booze for me now—though the keg would likely be the focal point for everyone else.

Along with the baby bombshell and wedding planning, Seth and I made another huge life decision. Given his strong affinity for Kansas—his parents' home state—I was easily swept up in the tales about his parents' humble beginnings and convinced that a move to the heartland was the ticket to happiness.

With our wedding day approaching fast, I pondered strategies to make Superior, Wisconsin, fade into the backdrop. Seth and I hit the Odyssey to play pool with some friends one night.

"I've always wanted to leave this hell hole," he declared as the group retrieved their drinks. My ears perked up, since any Superior-bashing was a welcomed topic. As the liquor flowed, splitting town became a done deal, and we finalized plans to move six hundred miles south to Kansas City right after our wedding.

Seth, loose and jovial after several cocktails, sketched out our life plan on a bar napkin. "We're two halves of a whole," he declared, while explaining the roadmap for our next few years.

That memory sustained me for a very long time—providing shaky assurance of his love.

Supercharged by the rapid succession of life-changing events, I recycled the possibilities as we closed down the bar: marriage, moving, great jobs, our sweet little baby—a beautiful life of domestic bliss was taking shape.

Wandering out at closing, I passed by a row of empty stools, and my twenty-first birthday just four months earlier flashed to mind. I'd been so drunk I ended the night tumbling from my bar stool and slamming my cheek into the linoleum floor. The patterned tile in grays and tans was barely in focus as I scrambled up before too many witnessed my fall from grace. Later my friends had shared their fear for me: "It was like your eyes just went black, and then you fell backwards." I had just lurched off my stool, as though some other power propelled me. I figured it was typical for a big birthday bash.

My dad was locked up—serving a sentence for his most recent DWI at the *work farm*, the place that used to terrify me as a kid. He'd become a serial drunken driver no longer eligible for a slap on the wrist as penance. I'd since learned the minimum-security prison camp he was confined to was no Fort Knox, just a low-key collection of buildings for drug and alcohol offenders located in a surprisingly serene and peaceful wooded setting—right across the lake from my old cabin house.

Dad's presence for my wedding day seemed unlikely. Though I insisted it didn't matter, his probation officer granted him permission to walk me down the aisle.

May 28, 1994, dawned bright and breezy. Mom and I enjoyed a quiet breakfast together at the local Pike Lake diner.

"I am so proud of you," she gushed, eyes welling with tears.

"You'll make a beautiful bride. I just wish you weren't moving so far away. Are you sure it's the right thing?"

I looked out the window at the sagging sign pointing entry to the aging diner that had been a staple of my childhood, scrambling to change the subject. Sunny optimism was tough, but I pushed forward without much thought. I was twenty-one years old—about to be a wife and mother all in the span of a few short months. The whirlwind of it all was overwhelming, and the pancakes I struggled to choke down tasted more like a plate of panic.

Seth and I shared a lovely and uneventful wedding day—our crowd of just one hundred swallowed up in the cavernous interior of Seth's family cathedral. My childhood pastor also took part in our ecumenical ceremony. Seth had insisted we avoid telling his priest we were living together and made sure separate addresses were noted on our applications. All the Catholic traditions seemed stuffy, archaic, and antiquated—but I went along with Seth's desire to give his mother a proper church wedding. After the short service, we took a few pictures on the grand cement steps facing Belknap Street while my new husband and his groomsmen scammed a few sips from their engraved flasks, but everyone behaved themselves. My ivory veil flapped in the stiff wind off Lake Superior, shrouding my troubled expression.

My brother was also part of our wedding party; he'd spent the past several summers in Wyoming working as a whitewater rafting guide. Always respectful, he stayed out of the drinking shenanigans awaiting that night but enjoyed reconnecting with old friends.

Dave and his fiancé Jenn were in the process of planning their own wedding and would exchange vows in September.

Although my brother possibly had strong opinions about Seth and me, he never shared them.

After the reception dinner wrapped up, Seth escaped with the bridesmaids for the traditional "steal the groom" nonsense while Piker and the boys slipped a blindfold over my eyes and shuffled me next door to a neighborhood bar where I stiffly sipped an O'Doul's, yearning for the real thing.

Mindful of the clock, we returned to the hall half an hour later, but Seth and the rest of the wedding party hadn't returned. Another hour passed—still no groom or bridesmaids. The guests became restless as I anxiously watched the parking lot. Soon, people began to leave.

In tears now, I summoned the best man for help and together we called every bar in town in an effort to track down the gang. Just as we finished going through the entire list, Christy ducked in the side door looking obstinate. I shot her a death stare. My best drinking buddy and I would remain estranged for a very long time.

They were all hammered. I jerked Seth aside.

"Half the guests left the party!" I yelled, unable to control my voice.

Seth was drunk and in a charitable mood as he placed his fingers gently over my lips, took my hand, and stroked it.

"Honey, I'm so sorry. It wasn't my fault. They kept taking me to different bars. Honestly! I couldn't help it. Let's start the party. I will *NOT* have my bride crying on her special day."

Drying my tears and smiling, he claimed to be the luckiest man in the world.

Seth led me to the dance floor where I sobbed onto his shoulder during the entire first song, wondering if our guests figured I was just overcome by the reality of my new marriage to a living Ken doll. With my face tucked into his shoulder, I wept for reasons unknown to the crowd. I knew I was making a huge mistake.

After the first dance, I spent much of the night holed up in the bathroom, avoiding the drunk wedding party and checking the clock a thousand times. Dave caught me in the hall after I'd executed another great escape.

"How's everything going? Great party you've got going here, sister."

My smile was fake and my voice forced, but I'm not sure he noticed.

"It's fun, isn't it? Have you met my work friends? You really need to talk to Edward. The guy is super hilarious, you would *love* his jokes." I gestured toward the bar.

"That guy isn't your friend," Dave replied quietly.

"What are you talking about?"

"Melis, I overheard him talking about you. I'm not going to share what he said, I'm just going to tell you he's *NOT* your friend."

Jenn appeared. "What's up, guys? Dave, why are you stealing all of Melissa's attention? Lots of people want to dance with her!"

Though I begged him to give up the details about Edward, he wouldn't budge.

Finally, I forced another troubled smile. "Fine. Ed's a d-bag. I get it. Whatever. I better get back to my guests. Thanks again for driving all this way for the wedding."

Back on the dance floor, I stared at Ed slamming shots of whiskey. Dave never revealed his words, but I trusted my brother on a deep level. My good buddy was apparently a snake.

By midnight Seth was a happy drunk dying to extend the party; I couldn't wait to leave. He grabbed the DJ's mic at the end of the dance and announced we were off to consummate our marriage. Classy.

The next morning, Kansas City was our destination. After packing our humble belongings into a small U-Haul, Seth somehow managed to secure it to the trailer hitch of his Chevy Blazer in spite of his severe lack of mechanical skills. I followed in my car with the rest of our possessions. Dad was still incarcerated at the work farm; Mom had passed our little convoy on her way home from visiting him at the place we'd dubbed "Camp Walkaway" (due to the weak security) and cried all the way back to the Caribou Lake cabin house, knowing I would soon be six hundred miles away.

Leaving Mom was brutal, and I drove on the verge of tears with a mounting urge to scrap the entire plan. The miles down I-35 were endless, each one driving a deeper valley between me and the only life I had ever known.

Kansas City loomed at dusk; a bustling urban metro appearing so much more daunting than Minneapolis—which, for the record, I'd never actually driven through by myself. My concept of "life in the fast lane" had been only a few trips south to a popular Minnesota amusement park west of the Twin Cities. The traffic and unfamiliar surroundings were harrowing—generating countless anxiety attacks as I white-knuckled it through the bustling downtown and crazy maze of freeway interchanges. Sweeping the nearby scene, I took in riverboat casinos crawling with people out for the night, clubs, beautiful fountains, and world-famous BBQs—this was my new home.

Well, the downtown was certainly cool—but we were headed out west to where the wheatfields blew. I soon learned sunflowers and agriculture were the defining features of Kansas, and I should get used to seeing a whole lot of both. A complete KC novice, I'd only visited the area once the year before—a short weekend trip spent boozing and bar hopping with Seth and his cousins, totally unaware of the tiny seed I was carrying.

Nope, I didn't know squat about the Sunflower State but still had hallucinated that moving hundreds of miles away was the perfect escape from everything that threatened to derail my life goals. *This would mean I had made it.* Our wedding announcement appeared in the local paper the week before, making our relocation official. "The newlyweds reside in Clearview City, Kansas," it read. The bold newspaper statement proved we'd elevated beyond our hometowns. Backing out now would be stupid and immature.

The rent in Kansas City and its associated ritzy suburbs was out of our league, but Seth's cousin had secured a place for us twenty miles outside of town in a tiny village that sounded so quaint on paper. "Clearview City is mostly farms. There's not much there," Seth's mother responded with a puzzled look when we told her about our destination. The exact location didn't really matter to me, as long as it served the purpose of removing Seth from interference: meaning friends, women, distractions, and bars.

We headed west on highway 10 for about twenty miles, then made a left turn near a green highway sign that read SUNFLOWER AMMUNITION PLANT. Lodged halfway between Kansas City and Lawrence on the desolate highway, our new home awaited. Gently rolling hills led to an expanse of squat-looking brick buildings cropping up over the hillside. The twilight sky was all-encompassing, wrapping around so snugly that it hurt my brain to make sense of all the empty space. Wheat fields blew in the distance as a surge of fright and raw loneliness overtook me. *What have I done?*

The ammunition plant had ceased production years ago, but once housed its employees and their families in sturdy brick duplexes lining neat and orderly streets marked by letters. Our apartment was a simple and tidy unit at the end of Lane P. I followed Seth into our assigned parking area and spotted his cousin's car idling nearby.

"You made it!"

Lexy was waiting to help us unload and bounded out of her Hyundai with excitement.

"You're here!" she screeched, hopping on one foot with excitement while pulling back her cocoa-colored hair in one mighty tug for emphasis. Her exquisite joy over our arrival snuffed out my panic-riddled thoughts, so I returned her warm hug and made small talk about the long drive while dragging boxes out of my hatchback. My car was loaded with bins and plastic crates; the U-Haul carried our other worldly possessions. Three pieces of living room furniture—a cheap sofa, loveseat, and a chair—plus a TV and stereo financed by a tax return—that was it.

Lexi clutched our apartment keys and raced to open the front door. "I can't wait to see what you think of it!" she shrieked. Following inside, I surveyed the small space with pleasant surprise. It was cute, and the hand-me-down table passed along Seth's family for ages would fit perfectly under the window opposite the tiny kitchenette featuring compact but relatively new appliances. Still too young to acquire anything high quality or matching, Seth and I owned no bedroom furniture, just a mattress and box spring sitting on that fantastic wooden frame Seth's dad had built for us when we first moved in together. We'd stripped off the canopy and grand fabric drapes, and decided that reassembling them was too much work. The tiny bathroom space was passable—just the basics and a shower stall covered by a slightly moldy peach curtain.

"You guys live like paupers," Lexi laughed, once we had our possessions organized by room. "I thought you were actually going to put me to work!"

Returning to her car, she was back a minute later with a cardboard Domino's box and deposited it in the center of the living room floor. Her chatter and exuberance kept the moving party going and my panic at bay. "Eat, eat," she chortled. "Andy gets unlimited free pizza!"

Lexi's boyfriend was a delivery driver for Domino's, and we'd share many complimentary pizzas in the coming months. The food wasn't agreeing with me at all though, and when I sat down on the floor to enjoy a slice, my current circumstances came crashing in, and I was blindsided by a terrible wave of panic. *I am six hundred miles from home* recycled through my mind like an exasperating commercial jingle I couldn't squash. Suddenly the pizza turned to sawdust in my mouth, and my stomach recoiled. No appetite always meant something terrible, and suddenly I felt far from home. My heart raced. *You're alone. What are you going to do?*

I escaped to the bathroom and examined my pasty white face in the mirror while clamoring for an anchor. I felt faint. *Stop it. You'll be fine.*

Seth and I both found work our first week in Kansas, and

staying busy helped to ease my raging homesickness. Seth was excited to land a job driving a tow truck for a service station, and I waitressed at a Denny's restaurant fifteen minutes south in Olathe, Kansas, where I soon bored my coworkers with my mournful tales about being ripped from Minnesota (subtracting the part about my full-on investment in the moving plans). Waiting tables was punishing on my expanding body, but the tips were okay, and I didn't have other skills to bring in decent money.

By July, I was five months pregnant and cursing the sweltering heat. Performing the simplest of tasks was a major chore, and adulting felt like a punishment I didn't deserve. I wanted to give the baby the best start possible though, so I didn't shirk the importance of prenatal care. The weigh-ins made every visit dreadful, and I hated being evaluated by the metal nemesis that had determined my worth since age nine.

My obsession with fatness was in hiding because I was *pregnant*, and everyone insisted it was healthy to gain weight. The rules relaxed, and I enjoyed pancakes and peanut butter, ravioli and chocolate. I swallowed my vitamins religiously, but still, I worried. *What if people can't tell I'm having a baby and just assume I'm fat?*

My fears were bluntly validated by a coworker. One evening as we closed out our shifts rolling silverware, Jolene stood beside me smoking long menthol cigarettes and yapping about her grandkids. After finishing up another epic tale, she regarded my belly and laughed.

"My husband saw you working one day, and do you know what that jack wagon said? *Wow,* that girl has got one big gut—and an even bigger butt! I told *him*, 'She's *pregnant*, you idiot!' *MEN!*"

After tossing a final silverware roll into the bin, Jolene ground out her cigarette and walked away chuckling.

I was devastated. No, no, no! I couldn't be mistaken as *fat*.

"Seth, Jolene's husband thinks I'm fat!" I sobbed into the phone. Seth didn't know what to say. I hung up, ran into the bathroom, and had a meltdown. While I collected myself, my manager ranted up a storm about the Grand Slam breakfasts growing cold under the heat lamps.

Aside from my occasional hormone-induced breakdowns, Denny's wasn't that bad. Seth seemed to enjoy his job too, and we settled into a comfortable evening routine of dinner, TV, and bed at the same time. I decided I liked our lifestyle.

12

A month later, my beautiful new life showed serious signs of decay when Seth survived a horrible car wreck with his tow truck. He escaped serious injury but was fired because his employer could no longer afford to insure him.

"Don't worry, you'll find something else," I soothed, but he was in no mood for my cheerleading. Dejected and gloomy, Seth avoided me for days.

"Won't you just tell me what I can do to help?" I begged, but was met with more silence. I grew frantic.

A week later, I returned from my shift at Denny's to find Seth poring over paperwork at the kitchen table.

"I'm going to bartending school!" he announced.

I felt like I was choking. "What do you mean? This is the first I've heard of you wanting to bartend. It costs a lot to take one of those courses, doesn't it?"

"My grandfather loaned me the money," Seth answered. "I'll pay him back when I get my first check. I've wanted this for the longest time. You know the moves they do, like in *Cocktail?*"

Grabbing a candlestick from the table, he flipped it up in the air and caught it behind his back.

"I'm a natural, see?"

He was so stoked about his new career that I couldn't argue, but inside I was a mess of ugly emotions. Bars meant *other women*, drinking, and *possibilities . . .* as well as less opportunity for supervision. What would happen once he rejoined the life I so desperately wanted to restrict?

After Seth completed a two-week bartending course, he scored a job at a trendy night spot forty miles north of Kansas City in Leavenworth. Late-night shifts didn't exactly promote a family lifestyle.

"I wasn't *DRINKING*," he insisted, as he rolled in just before sunrise one morning. "I had *ONE* drink after my shift, and then we went out for breakfast. I have to unwind. I can't just come home and jump into bed."

"Were there girls with you?" I pressed, unconvinced.

"Yeah, of course. Girls work there. What do you think?" Seth untied his shoes with a flourish and threw them in the corner. "What are you getting at? Why do I feel like I'm on trial or something? Forget it. I'm going to bed."

I quizzed him endlessly about the unknown women I was convinced were on a mission to get him into the sack.

"What do they look like? Are they single? Do they ever hit on you?"

Seth stomped away from my interrogations, the remainder of the evening spent in stony silence. As his bar shifts increased, I dreaded the lonely hours I'd face. My grip was slipping, and I knew it.

My brother's wedding took place three months later at a rustic dude ranch in Cody, Wyoming—the serendipitous spot he'd met his future wife. Seth and I made the long drive from Clearview City to Cody and slept in the car to save money, using our government-issued food coupons to purchase Pop-Tarts and orange juice.

Relatives and old friends converged on Cody to celebrate my brother's nuptials—we shared a picnic-style rehearsal dinner the night before the wedding, along with sightseeing, storytelling, and lots of laughs. Reconnecting with family and friends ignited powerful emotions though, and I dreaded the inevitable return to the state of Kansas.

By mid-November 1994, I was gripped by intense home sickness and an overwhelming urge to do something, and *fast*. Living in Kansas after I gave birth seemed unbearable, so I blindsided Seth with an impassioned plea.

"I want to move back to Minnesota. What will we do when the baby gets here? We need help."

Annoyed by my hysterics, Seth pushed back. "Are you crazy? We've hardly been here six months! You haven't even given it a chance."

His words were hollow and carried no impact. Recapturing the old life could beam us back to the times of partying with Piker. I was certain we could recreate that carefree lifestyle, the bassinet and baby stuff would just be a side dish. Our northern roots just had to be the salve to save us from impending disaster.

"Kansas is the problem," I insisted. "We're always fighting. We have no support system. We need our parents' help!"

Seth offered one final statement before shutting down.

"We're broke. It's *not* going to happen."

He retreated to the bedroom and slammed the door, but I continued yelling through the paper-thin walls.

Determined to make something happen, I worked seven days a week and searched for a second job. Meantime, I propositioned Gram. She had been diagnosed with lymphoma at seventy-six and had already made it five years, but was not long for this world.

"Gram? I know I've borrowed lots of money in the past and didn't pay it back, but this time it's different."

She was silent and all too familiar with my con jobs.

"I want you to be able to see the baby grow up. Can you please send us $1,000 so we can move home?"

Since I'd effectively spun my tale, Gram obliged and withdrew cash from her burial fund. I never made good on the debt before she passed away the following year, though she often told me how much it had meant to spend her final six months with her great-granddaughter.

Once I had the money Seth moved out of my way—I was resolved, and he was defeated. Escaping Superior—town of the dive bars—had been his lifelong dream, and I'd crushed it to smithereens. Feeling triumphant for a brief time, I didn't realize then that our marriage wouldn't survive another huge adjustment.

November 15 was my twenty-second birthday. Now three days past due and eager to meet our child, the wait would soon be over. A few days later, my Braxton-Hicks pains transitioned to real labor, and our baby girl came into the world shortly after we squealed into the Shawnee Mission Medical Center.

The eight-pound bundle we christened Hope Amanda was a perfect, beautiful creature, and I couldn't take my eyes off her sweet little face, tiny perfect nose, and buttercup ears. Seth should've been jumping up and down like Richard Dawson on *Family Feud*, but he was a reserved guy, and that wasn't his style.

"I might have to go back to work tonight," he casually mentioned after Hope was taken to the nursery.

"You're kidding, right?" I bolted upright as he raised his hands in a peacemaking gesture.

"Hang on. I have to call my boss. I'll see what I can do."

Though he ended up staying, his actions left me feeling very unsettled.

Studying Hope, I wondered how on earth my flawed vessel had served to birth such a beautiful creature. The awe of her arrival was coupled with terrible dread though, my own inadequacy and immaturity generating an overpowering fear I would ultimately fail the overwhelming task of motherhood.

"It's like I'm worried something will happen, and I won't be able to handle it," I tried to explain to Seth the following day, but he just nodded distractedly like I was a fly he wished would sail into a pest strip. As we moved through the hospital room packing up, I watched Hope—wrapped securely by the adept nurses and tucked into a plastic bassinet. Once we checked out, I'd be on my own.

Mom and Dad reached Kansas City the day of Hope's release from the hospital.

"Oh, beautiful baby!" Mom cooed. Dad was equally enamored

with our sweet little package from heaven. Mom later shared details of the harrowing six hundred mile road trip. Dad's legs were painfully swollen from excessive alcohol use, liver failure, and unmanaged diabetes. His useless liver was causing ammonia to build up in his body, making him seem drunk all the time. Doing all the driving, making frequent stops, and dealing with Dad's medical issues had made Mom a nervous wreck.

As soon as we got home to Lane P, my mind shifted to the bathroom scale. My weight had almost hit 180 just before Hope's birth, but I was hopeful I'd magically shed at least thirty pounds in delivery. Stripped naked to face my atrocious jelly belly, I took note of the angry red stretch marks I hadn't noticed before. Taking a deep breath, I gingerly stepped onto the scale and saw 166, which was *not* what I had expected. I had a lot of work to do.

Mom and I enjoyed showing Hope off the week before we returned to Minnesota. We made several shopping trips, explored local restaurants, and drove around the city. I adored carrying my sleeping child close to my chest, and it was nice having Mom nearby when I needed an extra hand. Before I knew it, reality was back, we were loading a U-Haul again, and I was saddled with a sickening feeling.

With every stick of furniture packed away, Seth and I camped out on the floor that final night in Kansas. I woke just before dawn, shaking violently from a delayed reaction to the anesthesia I'd received during labor. With Seth curled up halfway across the room, we were definitely strangers in the night.

"I'm so cold. Will you hold me?"

His reluctance spoke volumes, and suddenly a moment of clarity and a deep knowing blindsided me: *Our marriage won't survive the move.*

At six the next morning, we left Clearview City for good. Mom insisted on taking Hope in her car though I argued.

"How hard is it to hold a bottle and drive?"

"Harder than you think, Mom insisted.

Sounded like a Grandma June demand, but I was too beaten down to fight.

So it was just the Ford Probe and me—riding on a donut pillow provided by the hospital—making the six hundred mile trek. Ten hours alone was an eternity to ponder what was too late to undo, and the sad songs on the radio triggered overpowering grief. "Because You Loved Me" by Celine Dion was the catalyst for a violent round of tears. Never before had I experienced depression so crushing and intense that it almost left me breathless. The stitches I'd earned in Hope's delivery were barely healed, and I was suffering through a solitary road trip I had no one to blame for but myself.

The familiar lights of the Twin Ports glimmered around twilight after a long, draining drive. Seth's dad and a few others waited at our new apartment to help us unload, and I faced the same people who'd just moved us out not six months ago.

The small and narrow duplex was nothing impressive, and directly above an older couple I'd learn were nosy neighbors with too much time on their hands. After the crew of five had everything hauled up the back stairs, I cornered Seth's mother.

"Do you think Hope could stay over at your house tonight so we can get settled? We might go out for a little bit, too."

Giggling awkwardly, I sensed the audacity of seeking a sitter for my week-old baby, and I didn't miss her fleeting look of disapproval.

I worked my way into a pair of black stretch pants (one of

the few garments I could still squeeze on) and Seth and I headed off for the dive bars. I imagined the few friends we ran into later gossiping about my post-baby body.

Seth didn't seem excited to be out together, or to glow about his new infant as I'd hoped. We wandered through several establishments and sipped beer in front of TVs blaring sporting events but barely spoke. My mind wandered to Hope repeatedly with pangs of shame, but I reminded myself Seth didn't have an issue with our pub crawl, either.

A blinding night of booze ensued, and excessive drinking could not squelch the constant companion of rejection. I had a man, alcohol, and a brand-new baby—everything I thought I wanted and needed, but I was beside myself. I couldn't re-create the old days, and nothing had changed with the bar scene. Same old people occupying cracked stools, backs turned, glassy eyes locked with screens.

Teary, guilty, and full of dread the next morning—I certainly was not an attentive parent. Hope slept in her baby swing near the bed while I napped off a head-splitting hangover. The once-reliable alcohol remedy now carried an escalating price tag—crippling anxiety, terrible depression, and extreme hopelessness.

Seated before my former boss from Gordon's Jewelers in the mall food court a month later, I had somehow squeezed into a pair of tailored pants while wondering if I was regaining my post-baby body to fit the world's timelines. Marilyn rehired me, and I felt triumphant for a moment thinking I'd scored an essential piece of the nostalgia puzzle.

Seth quickly landed a bartending gig. Though I didn't approve, I had to pick my battles. At least Chi-Chi's restaurant wasn't a nightclub and seemed to attract a tamer crowd. An ideal arrangement for Seth—my day shift at Gordon's ended just in time for us to swap parenting duties and he'd head off to work in his Mexican shirt, hair slicked with gel and cologne trailing behind him.

The lonely nights and lack of help were miserable, but I stayed up fueled by adrenaline and television. While Hope slept, I studied obsessively for the night courses I was taking to finish college, again hoping an official degree would be the missing link to the family life my battered heart craved.

"I'm done working, but I'm going to have one with the crew," became a nightly refrain from Seth. Lying awake at night, I strained for the sound of his Blazer while a popular Pearl Jam song about someone who'd fallen out of love tumbled through my mind. Seth didn't want me anymore and probably never did. I'd duped him into marriage. *But it wasn't ALL my fault, was it?*

One night after Seth returned home in the wee hours, I ransacked his wallet while he was in the bathroom. Unsure of exactly why, something foreboding was brewing, and I needed confirmation. Folded tightly into a secret pocket was a Post-It note. *Kendra.* Along with a phone number.

"WHAT IS THIS?"

Flying into a sheer panic, I completely lost it. Seth was angry and defensive.

"It's nothing, Melissa. Nothing. You met Kendra when you visited me at work that one time, remember? She just wanted to stay in touch after we moved."

Of course I remembered the night I went with Seth to Club 2010, eight months pregnant. He decided it was a good idea to see how many shots of Goldschlager he could consume (for the record, it was seven), and I drove him home with one hand over his chest to ensure he was still breathing.

Kendra had given me a certain look that night, a resignation, a challenge. Her words made me uneasy:

You have a beautiful wife, Seth.

His word against mine, though, I couldn't prove anything. I dismissed the hidden Post-It, but it still reinforced a belief that anything to do with *the bar* was bad news.

Resentment over our work arrangement was building, and I couldn't shake the idea of finding a job to match his schedule. One night, I decided that a position in a night club might be the solution, so I began scouring the want ads.

"How's that going to work?" Seth demanded. "Who'll watch Hope?"

"Don't worry about it! I'll figure it out. *I always do.*"

My snarky comment kicked off another huge argument that left me sobbing in the bathroom. My attempts to be tough always resulted in deep regret and self-doubt.

"Seth, do you love me?" I wheedled after emerging from my crying jag.

He stared at the television, entranced by his Sega game.

"*Do you?*"

"*Yes*, Melissa. *I love you.* Now leave me alone."

13

Seth and I were back in the Superior routine a few short months when the Keyport Lounge became the center of my universe. A popular mid-1990s entertainment hot spot, the neat brick building greeted motorists at the foot of the bridge into Superior. Soon, I'd spend as much time as possible within the comfort of its walls. Two bars, a restaurant, and a liquor store in one handy location—it appealed to a variety of ages and was not seedy like some of the dives on the North End. My new position seemed poised to heal my failing marriage.

Cocktail server suggested glamour, sexiness, and intrigue. Feeling like Dorothy stepping into the Emerald City, my first day on the job included a few greasy guys emerging from the back kitchen to give me the once-over, providing assurance that I fit the mold of "Keyport Girl."

Hope was three months old, and though I was working hard at dropping weight, I'd plateaued at 150. The Mini-Thins I'd shelved when I found out I was pregnant returned and provided more ammunition for dieting, swallowed with a healthy dose of coffee and saccharine.

Suddenly a frequent shopper at the nearby GNC, I befriended employees who schooled me on new products promising fast weight loss and energy. The pill bottles cluttering my medicine cabinet contained pseudoephedrine just like my beloved gas station speed—and soon I was again heavily dependent on the cheap and easily accessible weight loss aids.

The bottle's label promised energy, alertness, and fat burning: certainly not the adrenal fatigue, metabolic derangement, and addiction that was actually happening. I didn't know then how dangerous the unregulated supplement would prove to be; it was later banned from the market after being linked to 155 deaths. Had I known this information back then, I'd probably use it anyway. The scale was finally my friend—and I removed it from seclusion to step on in front of Seth. Parading around in skimpy nighties, I begged for attention. *Notice anything?*

"Do I look any skinnier to you?"

Seth looked up briefly from his video game to flick his eyes over me.

"No, not really."

The number on the scale represented acceptance and was all-consuming. Long and lonely hours without Seth were spent focusing on my body and vainly believing my gritty investment would eventually pay off. Seth usually left for his bartending shift around three in the afternoon and rarely made it home before dawn. Fourteen hours alone was an eternity for Hope and me. We took long walks in the stroller, went to the park, and made trips to the grocery store for whatever weird fruits and vegetables I was allowing myself to eat.

A friend from the bar had given me an old Stairmaster his sister had planned to donate to Goodwill, and I wore it out with endless cardio routines after Hope was asleep. Twenty-five pounds disappeared within four months, as I sweated my way toward a physical prize Seth couldn't refuse. I was thinner than ever, but the coveted scale number didn't change anything at all in my life—in fact, it made my mental health worse.

My weekdays were focused on Hope, and I tried to be engaged and interactive. But once Friday night rolled around, it was party mode where epic cocktailing shifts yielded a hundred bucks in cash. Working at a bar was hardly like *work* at all; after logging a few hours serving people, I'd earn my reward in free cocktails. Seth and I became ships passing in the night. With both of us seeking weekend shifts with abundant tips, we ended up shuffling Hope between grandparents.

A year passed, and our second wedding anniversary approached. A night off together was rare, and I'd hoped for a cozy evening on the couch or maybe even a sitter for Hope. Seth had other ideas.

"My boss wants me to play darts with him and some other guys. They need someone to sub on their league. It's not like I can say no," he shrugged when I proposed a date night.

My demeanor switched from hopefully expectant to steely and angry, as I considered the likely course of the evening—Seth would drink too much, end up crashing at his boss's place, and never make it home. With building hysteria, I watched as he mixed a stiff White Russian.

"Nice. Do we really need to drink every night of the week?"

"Right," he responded contemptuously. "Like you don't get wasted any chance *you* get."

Well, he certainly had a point.

Plopping down on the pine green pleather sectional we'd recently blown our tax return on, Seth shut me neatly out of his world, picked up the remote, and settled in on ESPN. Eyes fixed on the television screen, I was tuned out with a flick of a button.

Having reached my breaking point, I lunged across the couch and grabbed his coveted controls. "The frickin' TV is more important than our marriage!" I screamed.

Seth faced me with firmly set eyes.

"I want a divorce."

Wait, WHAT? We hadn't even crossed the two-year mark!

"What do you mean?" I squeaked, pivoting from anger to pitiful desperation. "You can't be serious! We can work things out!"

On his feet now, Seth was moving around the apartment with terrifying resolve.

"I *want out*. I've been thinking about this for a long time."

He grabbed his jacket and slammed the door in my horrified face.

Snatching the phone, I dialed hysterically. "Sandi?" I sobbed. "Seth just walked out on me!"

My best friend from the bar rushed over with a 12-pack of beer. We took opposite ends of the sectional and stared blankly at late-night infomercials. Desperate for something to relieve my panic, I dialed the Psychic Friends Network and babbled so long that my "consultant" eventually hung up.

"Your husband has a chemical imbalance," the woman on the other end of the line droned before abruptly ending the call. "Have him tested."

I racked up a $300 bill for this stellar piece of advice.

Sandi left near dawn, and I fell into a jagged sleep. After a couple of hours spent tossing and turning, I summoned Seth's brother to come over and watch Hope so I could lay in bed and cry.

Despondent for an entire week; my head wouldn't stop spinning as I clamored for a way to turn back time. Caring for my baby daughter was a struggle, and she didn't understand why I was crying all day.

A total basket case for six long days, I trudged around work like a zombie, held Seth's mother hostage at the kitchen table for advice, and consulted with various friends from the bar for pearls of wisdom. Nothing really helped.

The evening of day six, I was still wrecked. Though I wracked my brain for a solution, nothing came, and I couldn't sleep. Suddenly I had an urge to pray. *Please help me accept this.* God hadn't been on my radar for a very long time, and for once I wasn't seeking a magical escape hatch from my present pain. I just wanted peace.

I drifted off, and hours later Sunday morning broke. Hope and I still shared Seth's parents' house while we attempted to sublease our now-empty apartment right across the street. Rested and oddly calm, I watched the early light of dawn color the gauzy window coverings. *Something had happened.*

I felt completely different, like a massive shift had taken place. I wasn't just imagining it.

Crawling off the bed with something resembling excitement, I ducked into the bathroom to examine myself in the mirror, then moved to the small room at the end of the hall where my sweet Hope was tucked into a small portable crib. Tears welled up in my eyes as I watched her sleep. Something within my spirit told me we were going to make it.

14

The rental options in Superior were depressing. After a thorough combing of the classifieds, my search had only resulted in a few efficiency apartments in shady areas of town.

"Stay with us as long as you like," Seth's mother offered. Her kitchen table hosted many tearful conversations, and she patiently discussed her own marriage trials and hardships.

"Just be strong and hold out for what you really want. Marriage is tough, and you have to be willing to do the work."

I wanted to keep hope alive, but a nagging thought persisted. I'd forced the union with Seth through my own stubborn will. Would God salvage something He hadn't authored?

My Creator and I had no real relationship then, yet I

somehow knew that consequences must exist for imposing my own timeline on something as important as marriage. Now I was paying the price for my obstinance, and the weight of the past several years flattened me like a ton of bricks. My current reality blazed into painful focus—I was twenty-three years old with a toddler who would grow up shuffled back and forth between her parents. I sat feeling cheated of important information I wished I'd known. Sex, marriage, major moves—countless huge life decisions I had made relying on self-will and my own harebrained intuition.

The blocks that bordered the University of Wisconsin Superior offered slightly shabby but affordable housing, and I managed to unearth a passable duplex a few weeks later. The location lacked parking, and the price that had first hooked me wasn't quite so compelling when I realized that none of the utilities were included. Seth continued couch surfing, and I tried not to care.

Filled with gloom and pensiveness, my dear Mom tried to help by hosting a shopping trip for household items. The awareness of living without a man for the very first time had left me tentative and anxious.

"Let's see," she said cheerily as we browsed through Walmart. "You need a toaster, don't you?" I nodded listlessly, and she tossed one into the cart. My new residence was dubbed "the Alamo" and had a strange southwest stucco exterior, but inside I found the hardwood floors and charming woodwork comforting. The building was probably decent in its day, and the thick green shag carpeting remained plush in low-traffic areas.

My dad and a neighbor buddy wrestled my few pieces of furniture inside (I'd acquired the green pleather couch in the separation) while polishing off a case of beer. As they worked, I busily pasted up a border of sunflowers in the kitchen while struggling to ignore the inevitable emptiness that was coming when night fell. The small room off the kitchen would be Hope's, and I managed to paint a passable depiction of Curious George hanging in a tree over the plaster-cracked wall.

I'm going to be better, not drink so much. Do more Mom stuff.

Still unsettled by the thought of being there *alone*, I had to get used to it. The joint custody agreement between Seth and me left three childless days every week, and I wasted no time filling them with drinking. Although I struggled to make ends meet, I never lacked wads of abundant tip dollars.

My worst fear was harming Hope, and I tried to keep the booze under wraps while she was home. Just like the old high school days when I juggled good girl with kegger queen, I now struggled to balance competing identities of doting mom and saucy bar entertainer. My conscience sometimes won in its efforts to reveal my depravity, even compelling me to quit drinking for a full week. Hope and I bonded over art projects, and I threw my best effort into mixing papier-mâché—and although our attempted masks ended up looking pretty sad, Hope didn't seem to mind. Enchanting bead art soon hung from the archway between the living and dining rooms like a medium's lair, and Hope loved the tinkling noise the plastic beads made when we moved from room to room. Shunning convenience foods, I cooked a meatloaf dinner, complete with homemade mashed potatoes.

When Seth's parenting time came, I found short-lived euphoria in new body art: a vine of sunflowers around my belly button etched into my skin by the artists at Superior Tattoo.

Feeling amazing, I jogged down Tower Avenue in a sports bra, past all the bars I'd given up.

Working in a nightclub made the straight-edge lifestyle hard to sustain though. On the seventh day, I broke down and picked up a 12-pack.

You quit for a whole entire week! That's great! What seemed to be willpower assured me I probably *could* control it.

Though not legally divorced, I was single by everyone else's definition. My closet was packed with Keyport clothes, with each new addition to the wardrobe smaller and tighter. My friend Sandi and I spent hours combing through clearance deals at TJ Maxx with gritty determination, thrilled to score tiny sizes at discount prices. "If it was easy, everyone would do it!" Sandi would howl when we lamented over the work involved in canvassing the tightly packed racks. Was there anything better than a flashy new outfit to draw better tips?

The Keyport underworld soon morphed into a new drug, with affirmation from the regulars my empty sustenance. The scale plunged to 113 pounds thanks to handfuls of ephedrine, pots of coffee, and dehydrating alcohol on my highly anticipated nights of binge drinking. I hit my lowest adult weight ever.

My morning trips to the scale were now a joy, I'd succeeded in crafting a concave twenty-four-inch waist, but the new figure quickly disappeared as my body rebelled against the punishing regimes and loads of stimulants. To my absolute horror, the scale started to creep up again.

My boss approached me after I'd been bartending a few months. "We've been watching you, and you're really good with the customers. Would you be interested in training to run the karaoke system?"

His words inflated my ego to disastrous heights, and the new position offered more opportunities to drink on the job. The rules for the karaoke DJs were more relaxed, and a bottle of beer fit neatly below the mixing board. My musical background and desire to perform easily revealed a knack for reading the crowd, and my own drinking only added life to the party.

15

HOT RED HEAD. 5'5", 125 lbs.
MUST LOVE CHILDREN.

The newspaper classified ad was circled in red and centered smack in the middle of my DJ mixing board where I couldn't miss it. A quick search of the lounge didn't produce any helpful clues to reveal its origins.

Three union workers, dusty with drywall powder and fresh off the clock, gathered over whiskey sours, and a few stools farther down an eccentric couple sipped beer and brandy on the rocks. The woman was heavily made up with Mary Kay cosmetics and wrapped in an ivory fur, always requesting her beer served in a wine glass. I guess drinking it from the bottle cheapened the experience.

The long green hallway just past my sound booth connected the lounge to the liquor store, where endless rows of anything a drinker's heart could desire beckoned. Although the booze outlet was technically part of the complex, its employees were removed from the social scene in the adjacent bar, and our contact was limited. The workers were cordial when I sometimes served their after-work drinks, but most did their cocktailing elsewhere.

I craved some excitement. My bar crowd wasn't offering any; they were placidly sipping drinks to an old 80's rock disc and making an actual live DJ presence pointless. Stepping out of the booth, I strode purposefully down the hall, pretending to be on an important mission. Maybe I'd score a pack of cigarettes to pass the time.

The liquor store was empty—not a worker or customer in sight. I busied myself by perusing the selection of smokes near the cash register before getting sidetracked by a colorful array of schnapps—fruity flavors in plastic fishbowls for less than a buck in neon-colored airplane bottles. They looked tasty, so I tossed a few next to a pack of Marlboro Lights. I'd later down the schnapps in a bathroom stall during my DJ shift.

The guy manning the store was fairly new to the Keyport arena; our previous contact had only been a few passing exchanges. He appeared from the back beer cooler pushing a dolly loaded with Franzia wine into a silent center aisle. As I busied myself building a pyramid of schnapps, I discreetly conducted a more detailed assessment of him. He was a *younger man*, which was *bad*. I'd be twenty-four soon—the liquor store worker who'd caught my eye was barely of legal drinking age. I also had a child, which changed the dating dynamic considerably. You just never knew how men were going to react to this news.

As he fussed with the wine, I took him in. Tall and lanky with a pair of smart wire-rimmed glasses and a brown windowpane sweater, he methodically finished stocking a shelf as I watched with amusement.

"Mel." He stepped behind the counter with a smile, regarding me like a shiny object that might hold promise, something he'd seen before but hadn't fully investigated.

"We haven't officially met, have we? I'm Brady. I just started in the liquor store a few weeks ago, but I feel like I *know* you." A mysterious little smirk curled his lips. "Were you at Frankie's Bar? Maybe a couple of weeks ago? You've got a great voice. You do Reba?"

Oh yes.

"Fancy," I offered, blushing. "Questionable lyrics, you know? I mean, was Fancy a call girl, or a maid? No one really knows for sure." I prattled on out of nervousness while Brady stood patiently, a faint smile pulling the corner of his mouth.

"Either way, I love the chorus. Infectious, right? Not sure I can pull Reba off, but I keep trying."

I clamped my mouth shut, awaiting his response and hoping my gushing was endearing somehow.

"Fancy" was a secret weapon, and privately I wanted to believe I was a real superstar on that number. I even won second place with it once in a singing contest at a Canal Park bar.

I extended my hand, hoping the quality of my voice would set me apart from the other girls undoubtedly seeking his attention. As his hand grazed mine, a current of electricity traveled up my arm. His neat goatee, ice-blue eyes, and mischievous grin already had me hooked.

Brady punched the cash register as I stood soaking him up.

"Bet these will liven up your night," he winked, stuffing the little airplane bottles into a sack.

I felt light and airy, an instant connection already forming.

"Nice to meet you," I managed as I turned to go.

Brady called after me. "Did you find the want ad I left at your booth? Sounds a lot like what I've been looking for. By the way, I love redheads."

He didn't know I'd started dying my hair and was not a natural redhead.

Like magic, two nights later Brady and I were anchored on bar stools together, sharing cocktails and war stories. As the drinks flowed, our connection deepened, and before long I was loose enough to begin drawing lightly on his arm. He got the message.

Friday night, I chose a form-fitting black and gray button-down dress and high-heeled boots with Brady in mind. My delight was in overdrive when he parked himself on a stool and stuck around nursing a White Russian until the wee hours, somehow knowing my "last call" announcement wasn't meant for him. Once the final stragglers were out, I wasted no time pouring myself a stiff rum and Coke.

"You don't have to go home, but you can't stay here," I quipped, stacking clean ashtrays in a spiral under the beer taps.

"Why don't you just sit down and enjoy your drink?" Brady's eyes locked with mine and my stomach flipped.

"You've been busting your butt, I'd say. I've been watching you for hours."

My next step was a systematic process of heavy flirtation and seduction tactics: Brady my sole target. Alone in the dark with just the lights under the bar offering a faint glow, we had to be discreet—Wisconsin law required everyone—including employees—out by 3 a.m. My intimidating boss was an absolute stickler about this rule, but the synergy of male attention and booze was worth the possible wrath.

Until the break of day, Brady and I passed notes on bar napkins. Bossman would have had a stroke if he'd driven by and found us having *drinks on him* until six in the morning.

Brady: Do you have a boyfriend?

Me: Not that I know of . . .

Brady: Do you want one?

Me: Depends on who's applying for the job.

Brady: This guy is a really good kisser.

Me: Let me be the judge of that.

Not exactly how I envisioned our first kiss—making out on swiveling stools in the empty lounge. I wonder if the cameras recorded it.

Five weeks of euphoria erupted—each day with Brady offering incredible exhilaration and inexpressible joy. Parading through the bar on his arm was a dream come true, our connection showing coworkers and regulars alike that I was now *off limits*.

No longer needing the attention of wayward customers, Brady was my sole drug of choice. We drank a lot together, too—Long Island teas, White Russians, and endless taps. This new flavor of the month was not even close to settling down, but seemed to enjoy swilling cocktails together. Meantime, I tried to reign in my intense drive to tame him. Could he sense my desperation? Some say men can smell it, like dogs. Most of our interactions took place on a Keyport bar stool or cruising around in his car listening to Van Halen—there was little substance to construct a long-term commitment.

Distance grew after one short month, and I sensed things moving in the wrong direction. As the holidays closed in, I wanted Brady to commit to family gatherings that could show-case our growing bond, but he remained frustratingly sketchy.

"I'm not sure what's going on for Christmas, I might be going to my parents' house, but who knows," he shrugged.

Dead silence. Subconsciously, my mind scrambled for a way to keep his interest.

"Are you just going home now?"

Trailing behind Brady through the empty parking lot, I wished he'd invite me over to his house (I'd partied there a couple of times) or even better—out for a drink where people could see us together. But he seemed anxious to ditch me.

"What's the matter?" I pressed. "You don't seem like your-self tonight."

"It's nothing, really. I'm kind of tired. I've got an early day tomorrow. My brother and I are going hunting."

My eyes narrowed with jealousy over the brother I hadn't even met, stealing Brady's time away.

He fumbled with his keys, before deciding to continue. "I just want to do *whatever*, you know? Not be with just one person."

My quickly eroding self-esteem took a final nosedive. *Was I getting dumped?* Before I could respond, Brady jumped into his car, fired it up, and cranked Sammy Hagar.

"Night, night," he called, peeling out of the parking lot.

I drove away in furious disbelief. *Night night?* Was he freaking kidding? He'd been keeping pace with me just fine—even professing his love for Hope and desire to adopt her someday.

The evening was one huge red flag failing to quench my relentless pursuit of the trophy fish struggling to get away. A few days later, I weaseled Brady into joining my Uncle Mark's Christmas Eve get-together, hopeful his eventual agreement *had* to mean something. A liquor store run on the way yielded a couple of 40-ounce beers to get the party going and a bottle of Brut champagne for the gathering.

The gala was already petering out when we arrived; it was late and many had already left. The anticipated annual get-together was far from the good old days of years past. I'd hoped for a Christmas miracle and a pledge of Brady's love, but my reality was simply more screaming desperation to con a man into submission.

Anchored on his lap as if my placement solidified our couple status to the world, I swilled cocktails, babbled, and sang. Trapped and possibly reluctant to ruin my Christmas Eve, Brady let me pretend he was my boyfriend one final night.

After the last stragglers disappeared, the cocktails had run dry, and we'd worn out our welcome. Hope was spending Christmas Eve with Seth and his parents, and I was expected to arrive for present opening early the next day. After thanking my family for hosting, I walked as straight as possible out to my car and drove drunk back to Superior. As I turned into the Keyport parking lot next to Brady's car, the darkness was laced with something foreboding, a heaviness between us that we were both drunk enough to face.

"I don't think we should see each other anymore," Brady

managed. "Things just moved too fast, you know?"

After brushing away a small tear, he was gone. The end.

I squealed out of the parking lot and made the six blocks to my empty apartment where I crumpled onto the living room floor and continued my hysterical crying. Pathetically prone on the threadbare carpet of the Alamo that countless cats had probably used as a toilet, I was eye level with the paltry tabletop Christmas tree I'd thrown together to represent the holidays for Hope. It twinkled like a promise I was much too thick-skulled to comprehend, imparting a faint idea of Christmas and its true meaning into my disabled heart.

Immanuel—God with us, the promised Savior coming to Earth to save the world, the day He put on flesh and moved into the neighborhood. I'd known this story since 1982 when I committed John 3:16 to memory, but had a very hard time believing it still applied.

A single strand of lights about two feet long covered the fake evergreen, and this bleak representation of such a beautiful holiday flattened me. I was wasted on Christmas Eve, sobbing on the floor over a young party boy I'd dated just five weeks.

Might as well check my weight and compound the misery. The old bathroom scale under the sink revealed I'd gained twenty pounds since my all-time post-divorce low of 113. My body was fighting the excessive amounts of gas station speed and diet pills, struggling to rebound to its set point. My weight was still pretty normal, but I felt grotesquely fat.

Huddled on the floor in the dark, I fought desperately to understand how I could be gaining on handfuls of white cross pills. My system was so saturated with stimulants they'd become totally ineffective.

Fully convinced that Brady had dumped me because I was a porker, I mixed myself stronger drinks to stow behind the karaoke booth and ushered in an exclusive playlist of man-hater songs. My personal favorite—"Dreams" by Stevie Nicks—was reserved exclusively for Brady's after-work visits. I'd belt out the second line of the chorus very loudly, emphasizing the PLAYERS part and making it clear that my angry anthem was dedicated to him.

One night, a group of high school friends I hadn't seen in years wandered into the bar.

"I didn't know you worked here!" a guy named Jake yelled across the lounge when he spotted me behind the mixing board.

Jake had some DJ experience and wanted to check out the Keyport sound system. Perfect. A stand-in offered the opportunity to wander around, schmooze, and swill free drinks.

Denny, a long-time regular, plunked a shot of Jager down.

"Ya on break?" he laughed. Denny's teeth were tobacco-stained, and his half-shut eyes indicated he'd been there since late morning, which wasn't a rarity for him.

"I am now," I responded, pounding the shot with a wince.

Next, I moved on to a Long Island iced tea financed by some stranger, but the drink I swilled was not even close to being my first of the night. My prework routine had involved a stop at Tony's apartment, another liquor store worker whose refrigerator was always stocked to the hilt with every kind of booze imaginable—free promos of Bacardí Limón, Leinie's Honey Weiss, and beautiful collector bottles of Jägermeister. Any Keyport employee was welcome to stop by before or after work to get primed.

As a frequent visitor to Tony's pad, I'd guzzled obscene amounts of rum and lime Kool-Aid to kick-start my karaoke shift. I was already hammered once I rolled in—really drunk—not just tipsy. Happily allowing Jake to run the sound system, I wandered the bar helping myself to long slugs from customers' drinks. Sucking down a stranger's margarita was my last dim memory—the whole night was like a lucid dream.

Guilty and paranoid the following day, I agonized over vindictive witnesses eager to report my bad behavior to the boss. I was so hungover I could barely crawl out of bed for work, but I prayed I'd slipped under the radar.

My Sunday shifts were always easy—the slower night and more relaxed crowd of regulars afforded some serious drinking with the abundant "mistakes" I made (pours of the wrong liquor) along with drinks sent back because of dirty glasses. Not only that, customers were constantly supplying provisions I didn't bother waiting til after hours to enjoy. The din of the lounge gang was smooth and low maintenance—just enough to squash complete inebriation—but not so challenging that it got in the way of shift-long sipping.

Near closing, throwing a drink into a mouthy customer's face seemed like a good idea. My cocktail waitress shook her head in disbelief as I insisted the sassy patron deserved it. That was my last memory—I'd later have no recollection of leaving the bar in a very orderly fashion, counting down the till, or driving home. Everything was done on autopilot.

The following Wednesday I worked a dayshift tending bar until five, then punched out and settled myself on the opposite side where I seamlessly blended in with what appeared to be my first beer. But I could no longer work without drinking. I seemed to be getting away with it, but dragged around a disturbing feeling that my dirty little secret wouldn't stay hidden forever.

16

"I'm still your *wife*," I often reminded Seth. Eight months had passed since we separated, and no divorce had been filed. We avoided the entire excruciating subject, as we had every other conflict. Each weekend when I brought Hope over, the wound that was again ripped open made the bar a necessary destination.

"Guess I'll see you on Sunday then," I managed from the doorway after I'd kissed our daughter goodbye.

Seth hesitated. "Can we talk for a minute? I've been thinking about my priorities. Do you think we could get together on Sunday night?"

After several speechless minutes, I nodded in agreement.

Sunday came with a bundle of nerves. Drinking hadn't been part of my original plan, but I changed my mind after deciding I'd be too stiff without some chemical help. Seth and I met at Grizzly's restaurant and chatted easily over a few beers—effortless as long as we stuck to surface stuff—sports, news, the quality of the beer, the server's nose ring.

Hours later, my mood skyrocketed as we approached oblivion. Giggly and buzzed, my nerves had dissolved with the abundant supply of strong Guinness tap beers our prominently pierced waitress faithfully delivered. After closing Grizzly's down, we moved on to the Keyport, where I happily re-introduced Seth to my puzzled friends. Everyone assumed I was divorced—they'd seen me with Brady not long ago, and Seth had been out of the picture for months.

"We're working things out," I whispered to Sandi when Seth was out of earshot. As I drank, the fierce determination to salvage our marriage came raging back.

When the bar closed, we had no intention of calling it a night and headed over to my apartment to continue the party. Drunk enough to face possible rejection, I delivered the question that had plagued me since the first beer we'd shared.

"What does this mean?"

Seth knelt at my feet and took my hands.

"I was a fool to ever leave you. Give me another chance, and I will never hurt you again."

His pleading eyes filled me with elation.

Without much discussion, we resumed our life together, and Seth joined the upper duplex haven that had helped me develop a thin sense of identity. The codependent waters were still warm though, and I easily slipped back into the pool. Holding my ground just a little meant insisting we follow through with counseling sessions.

For the next month, I wrestled to force the honeymoon we never had while orchestrating family activities and bonding time. Seth was wonderfully attentive for a while and struggled to take an active part in Hope's young life, but the therapy sessions were surface-level and mediocre. Though I desperately wanted to expose the reasons for our marital collapse, the problematic binge drinking was locked in a vault of secrets. One night, booze activated us in some angry old way, and I abruptly decided to leave.

"I'm done for the night," I declared, as Seth and I followed a group of friends for one final drink. "Do we really need last call?"

He was still in the mood to party.

"Why can't you just finish off the night with us? Drop me off and go if you want to go home so bad," he answered dismissively.

With blazing eyes, my rationality switch shorted out and I demanded he choose. "Pick me or pick your friends! *Right NOW!*"

To my shock, Seth climbed out of the car, flicked his cigarette into the gutter, and strode into the Pacific Club.

Oh, hell no!

Wanting to be tough, I squealed away hoping to convey a colossal "screw you," then drove around the block in mortified anger. Drunk and crying, I rehashed the scene until I decided I'd made a grave mistake. *I shouldn't have asked him to choose between his wife and his friends.*

Compelled to repair the situation at any cost, I marched my sorry self back into the bar to find Seth bellied up, mesmerized by sports highlights.

"Last call?" I waved the bartender over. Seth flicked his eyes over me in brief acknowledgment but didn't say a word.

Still not on speaking terms the next day, I prepared for our counseling appointment feeling ragged, defeated, and tired of nursing our floundering marriage.

"What's the point?" Seth argued when I reminded him about the session.

What a wasted hour. Aloof and guarded, Seth was in no mood for professional coaching.

I was desperate for guidance, however, and eagerly reenacted the previous night's dispute for the shrink. The therapist was hoping to bring clarity, but Seth remained chock full of excuses.

"It was my birthday. Everyone was drinking a lot, but it was a party, so what?"

The counselor jotted down some notes. "Seth, looking back on everything a day later, let's say you could do it all over. What would be different?"

Seth pondered the question for a few minutes as I silently hoped for an admission to repair the damage.

Slowly and deliberately, he responded, "I guess I wouldn't do anything differently."

That pivotal moment brought another moment of clarity, the most recent being our last night in Kansas when I had asked Seth to hold me in the night to ease my violent shaking. I suddenly knew our beautiful and promise-filled reconciliation was destined for failure, and it wasn't long before the same old pattern emerged. Seth withdrew, stayed out all night, and stonewalled me. Our third anniversary approached, and I made one last ditch effort. I wanted to renew our vows.

"I think it would be great to remember why we got married in the first place."

"Why, Melissa? Most people wait at least ten years to do that!"

Our foundation was built on the shifting sand of binge drinking and infatuation, not to mention my unfaithfulness to Drake had been our starting point. I was delusional to think God would bless such a gross display of free will and, well—unrepentant sin. A ritualistic public Band-Aid wasn't going to fix our deeply rooted damage, but I went ahead and planned a second wedding anyway.

The whole spectacle was an empty public display. I found a beautiful, ivory cocktail dress, reserved my childhood church, and told Seth to put on a suit. Afterward, we had the night to ourselves.

"I'll take Hope home so you guys can spend the evening together," Mom offered after the short ceremony concluded.

Dinner turned into a drunk fest, and the night I envisioned to be a special time for Seth and me to rekindle our love was just another pub crawl starring his friends.

Hours later, I was very drunk but coherent enough to realize my options: leave immediately or pass out on the floor. From the seclusion of a corner booth, I scanned the bar for Seth.

"I'm not feeling well," I slurred when I finally spotted him wandering over with a buddy. "Take me home. I don't think I should drive."

"Go on then," he responded. "You'll be fine."

Somehow I made it to the apartment in one piece and woke the next morning in an empty bed. I'd slept in my formal—the lovely, refresh-the-marriage, rekindle-the-love, Barbie doll dress. Had Seth even noticed it? Barbeque sauce was dried on the front now, and it was torn at the slit in the back.

The stain revealed a late-night trip to Hardee's I didn't

remember. When I got drunk my old habits reemerged. Big roast beef, curly fries, and a chocolate shake—running on autopilot.

Why had I bothered? My desperate efforts to redeem the marriage that should have never happened were becoming increasingly ridiculous. Seth had crashed at his friend's place, and things just worsened after the vow renewal intended to reboot our floundering relationship.

Father's Day came a month later, and I offered Seth *one* last chance. But I was sidelined before I could even propose anything.

"I'm taking off," he announced, rummaging in the hall closet crammed with miscellaneous sports equipment. "Golfing with the guys."

"Are you *kidding*? Father's Day is a day for dads to spend with their families! I thought the three of us could do something!"

"No, Father's Day means I get to do what I want," he shot back, slamming the closet door.

"It's always your friends. Or sports, or fantasy football, or video games. I don't even think I'm on the list."

"I'm not in the mood for another fight. I'll see you later."

Seth walked out once and for all on June 13, 1997.

Finally, letting go felt good. The Lord had prepared me well for this day, though I didn't realize it back then. He is so patient with His children and provided me with the peace and closure I desperately needed. The final six months spent with Seth revealed the truth—making a marriage work was not a one-way street. *God had something better for me.* Seth and I filed for divorce on September 4, 1997, a day Jesus would completely redeem seven years later.

17

I'd started college right out of high school in 1991, but my directionless approach to life and lack of identity resulted in many dead ends and failed starts. I switched majors more often than I changed underwear, and by the fall of 1998, I had returned to college to continue chasing a bachelor's degree. But my nonstop drinking had made completing anything worthwhile impossible.

Alone at the Alamo and feeling empty, I once again vowed to clean up my act. *No* more drinking on school nights. Shifting majors to mass communication seemed like a good idea and with a bit of studying, I produced respectable Bs.

Along with a few electives, two nagging class requirements stood in the way of my full-fledged degree: one of them the most-hated of all: math. I always went like gangbusters at the beginning of the semester, then fell off the map and withdrew from any failing courses at the last possible minute.

My illustrious bar life was always derailing my vows to be responsible and made reaching goals out of the question. Every night at the Keyport was an opportunity to party—an alternate reality where nine-to-five jobs, savings accounts, and responsibilities did not exist.

My liquor store coworker Tony was turning twenty-seven on a Wednesday night, the middle of the week for normal people with regular jobs. For me and the rest of the bar staff, it was just another opportunity to get wasted.

Sandi called that afternoon. "I can't wait to party tonight!" she squealed. "We're taking Tony out on the town. You're still coming, right?"

Drinking plans made me excited and manic.

"Yeah! Of course."

"Good. We're taking him to that real nasty strip club way down on Tower Avenue. It will blow his mind," she giggled.

It was a night I'd never forget, either.

"I'm bringing Jeff," I added. "I can't wait for you to meet him."

Jeff was my current boy toy and next-door neighbor, a transplant to Superior from Green Bay. He didn't belong in Soup Town at all, which led me to envision him as the special exception to my usual pattern of alcoholic, self-centered men. Jeff was a bodybuilding egomaniac and aspiring athletic trainer. At least he had goals.

"Great. I finally get to meet this dude you've been gushing over," Sandi laughed.

"You will like him. He's like, a *bodybuilder*," I proudly stressed.

Actually, he was pretty arrogant, but a trophy to parade around. Perhaps he'd make me better by osmosis. If *only* I could become a fitness fanatic, I was sure to have a relationship with Jeff in the bag.

Wanting Jeff to commit, I'd shown my loyalty by scoring a membership I couldn't afford at his exclusive gym. Toned and attractive was right up his alley. I was working on it—but excessive drinking, blacked-out trips to Hardee's, and handfuls of ephedrine derailed my efforts.

Jeff undoubtedly viewed our "thing"—which consisted of sipping a few beers and watching *The X-Files* at his apartment late at night when no one could see us together—harmless fun with no attachments. Mr. Meathead kept his distance, likely because no one halfway stable would ever *commit* to a girl like me. I acted too desperate and drank way too much.

I brought Hope to Seth's for her usual Wednesday night sleepover, and then my plans unraveled. Jeff had left a voice message while I was out.

"Mel . . . I have some bad news for you,"

My stomach sank. He was about to blow me off.

"I'm kinda sick . . . so, uh . . . I won't be able to come out with you guys tonight. Sorry."

Jamming the delete button, I cursed under my breath as my eyes teared. I *knew* it. Jeff's fading interest wasn't just in my head.

Pacing around the living room with fiery agitation, I wracked my brain for plan B. It was only five, and the gang wouldn't meet up until eight. My fridge lacked beer, and I needed something strong to quiet my angry emotions. From the sidewalk, I rummaged through the hatchback of the Probe in my stocking feet for the emergency rum I kept in the spare tire compartment. It was the perfect solution to dry DJ gigs like school dances and I usually saved it for desperate situations, but getting stood up at the last minute qualified. No good mixers in the fridge, but Kool-Aid would work.

As the clock moved closer to the magical bar time, the rum reinvigorated my body and soothed my rejected spirit. Jeff didn't matter much as I imagined the ease of going downtown and luring some other prospect away from the strip club. This couldn't happen alone, but alcohol—my faithful assistant—knew what to do, almost like a spirit guide.

Listening to music and methodically applying heavy coats of mascara in the living room calmed me, as did combing through my closet for evening attire like I had somewhere very important to be. Jeff's dismissal wasn't going to change that. Frowning at the many options no longer appropriate for my expanding frame, the role of ephedrine in my weight problem was unknown. Maxed out from too many pills, my metabolism was shot, and I was putting on pounds like crazy. Jeff surely thought I was fat, too. No wonder he lost interest, he saw the reality through the mask—I was not a sexy workout queen, I had love handles, and I got sloppy drunk on the regular. Plus I was painfully desperate, a major turn-off.

A short, zippered miniskirt I'd bought early on in the days after my divorce caught my eye, and I regarded it wistfully while realizing I didn't have a prayer of fitting into it now. Slinky Keyport cocktail dresses stretched to maximum capacity still worked, however, so I chose a spicy royal blue number paired with black tights to camouflage my thighs.

My rum-impaired vision created a much-improved version of me—I'd recaptured my ideal weight of 125 pounds as I sucked in my stomach and posed for the full-length mirror. Alcohol smoothed and fuzzed all the edges, like the filters for iPhones do now.

Heavily buzzed and sleazed up, liquid courage propelled me to Jeff's door. I marched out of my apartment, stepped around the corner, and rapped sharply on his window, taking in the brisk night air. Jeff appeared in the entryway, squinting into the darkness.

"Look what we have here! Jeff is *aliiiiive*!"

With a perplexed look, Jeff opened the door and moved aside so I could step through. Dressed in a white T-shirt with cut-off sleeves, his biceps strained against the torn fabric.

"Hello," he said, collecting himself and turning hospitable. "Come on in. I'm just playing video games."

Standing in disbelief, I wondered if he'd already forgotten his little tale of sickness. Sinking into a tattered chair, I crossed my legs and eyed him suspiciously while he and his roommate continued to crouch before the TV set, totally captivated by their video game controllers.

"So, you're feeling better?" I finally prompted after a long silence.

Jeff glanced up. "I suppose. Honestly, I didn't really want to go."

I rose without a word and bolted out the door.

Off to the bar, where that lonely male prospect watching the dancers with glassy eyes surely awaited. No one asked what had happened to Jeff, and that was the last time I'd see my bodybuilding trophy boy.

After making the rounds through the usual Tower Avenue haunts, we stormed into the sleaziest strip joint in town. My short blue dress had fit a lot better when I was thirty pounds lighter, but after several shots, I easily believed I could give any of the hired help a run for her money. I even joined my drunk friend in trying to convince the manager to let us "try out" on stage. Thank God he refused.

By nine, the blackout was in full force and at closing time, I apparently agreed to deliver Tony to his car in the Keyport lot. My next snapshot clip memory was of crashing my head into the Probe's windshield. The force of the impact shattered the glass, and someone at the scene called the police.

After convincing the responding officers that I was seriously hurt, I talked them into delivering me to the hospital. They agreed, but assured me that I'd have to provide a blood test upon arrival.

Once I was checked into a room and prepared for a CT scan, I realized my surroundings for the first time since the strip club. The night nurse disappeared for supplies as I combed through the recesses of my mind for clues. All business when she returned, a dreadful proposition awaited.

"Step up on the scale."

"Are you sure I have to? Why?"

"Yes. Step up." She was in no mood. Noticing I was beginning to annoy her, I shifted to people-pleaser mode and kicked off the black KISS army platform shoes that, just hours before, were showpieces of the dance club floor. Many had complimented my footwear that night.

The nurse leaned over and adjusted the slide on the doctor's scale until it parked at 157. *Even with my shoes off?* I gasped, having avoided the devil's platform for at least six months and obviously in serious denial about how much I had packed on. *What happened to the 130s around Christmas?* So much for that magical blue dress.

I drifted in and out of consciousness as the CT scan was performed, but I wasn't particularly distressed. The whole procedure of getting attention I didn't deserve was oddly reinforcing, seeming to prove I truly did have a legitimate medical problem.

Next, I was escorted to another room where I stared at the ceiling and slowly sobered up. Clips from the bar rolled back— Tony with a dollar bill resting on his face, me thinking the dancers at this seedy place weren't nearly as hideous as legend would suggest.

Time passed, but I couldn't track how much. Eventually, the nurse returned with the test results. "Here's where you hit your head," she said, pointing to the image. "You don't have a concussion though. You'll be fine."

After hesitating a moment, she went on. "Do you drink a lot? Your brain scan indicates a history of heavy drinking."

"No. Of course not, I only drink socially," I lied.

The nurse said nothing more, but her look of doubt did all the talking.

Morning broke with real awareness and a vicious hangover. The past night had been shadowy, but now the shame I'd masked with alcohol and immersion in a world of flesh, raunchiness, and debauchery spiraled in.

My first call was to Jeff, to feel him out and seek pity.

"I got arrested last night," I wailed, hoping he'd offer to rush over and pick me up.

"Bummer," he concluded, after a short pause. "Man, that

sucks. Listen, I gotta run. I hope everything works out for you. Take care, Mel."

Feeling even more pathetic and weepy, Tony was my second call.

"Oh dang, Mel, I'll be right there," he promised, after I shared my night of hell through broken sobs.

"Hi," I said meekly, sliding into his car a half hour later still clad in last night's dress and of course the renowned platform shoes. "Do you want to go out to eat?"

"Yeah, of course. I am so sorry this happened to you," Tony said as we pulled away from the dreadful clinic. "Totally my fault. I shouldn't have ever asked you for a ride."

We talked about the crazy night after settling in at Louis Café, a popular downtown Superior spot for farm breakfasts and late-night grease platters. Our conversation was just what I needed—comfortable, easy, and without judgment. My bar buddy drank a lot too and was not one to point fingers. While he also nursed a hangover, his was not complicated by a $2,000 hospital bill and a DWI.

"It's not your fault. I was stupid enough to do it."

The breakfast stretched on for hours, and I did everything possible to avoid going home alone to face what I'd done. Around lunchtime, Tony had to get going and deposited me at my car. The sporty Probe looked lonely in the last parking spot of the Spur station; my accident had happened just one block east of the store and the officers had blessed me by not impounding it. Leaning over the dash, I examined the windshield that now displayed a softball-sized spider web where I'd cracked my head. Everything seemed so long ago.

The Alamo was only a few blocks away, and I could safely

tuck my car in the back alley where it could again fall into obscurity. But my life of crime was gaining attention, and the authorities were well aware that I lacked a valid license to drive that sassy silver Probe.

As I rolled up behind the Alamo to hide by the trash cans in the alley, a police car was waiting for me, along with an officer eager to issue a ticket for my eighth driving after suspension offense. Beating the system was a thing of the past now.

By spring of 1999, I was still gaining incredible amounts of weight and my drinking was off the charts. Nothing slowed the gains—I even saw a doctor for a full physical and thyroid test but was assured that everything was normal.

"I'm going to start the Atkins diet," I announced proudly. "You know that high protein thing?"

The doc wasn't impressed and launched into a lecture about substituting low-fat products while assuring me Atkins was a fad.

Perhaps the scale shouldn't have been my primary concern. When the results from my hospital labs arrived in the mail, I discovered my blood alcohol level had been .30 the night of my arrest. Alarmed, I stuffed the frightening report way back into a kitchen drawer.

Low carb or not, as the scale numbers kept climbing I doubled the daily ephedrine dose, hoping it would produce weight loss as it had back in my early Keyport days. No such luck. My metabolism was bottomed out; liver heavily stressed from too much alcohol and unable to regulate fat storage because it was so polluted. The excessive speed just compounded my metabolic problems.

Each night of binge drinking eroded any resolve to lose weight, and I capped off the night at Hardee's—my fast-food joint of choice. Their 24-hour drive-thru was a big hit with drunks. Most of the time, I was so trashed I didn't remember my visit, and it was stunning that I didn't pass out while inching to the window. The long string of cars was an endless stream of other bar flies patiently waiting for a Thickburger or Big Roast Beef. Though blacked out, the evidence of my food escapades revealed itself the next day via greasy wrappers and stained clothes.

One night, I rear-ended someone while shuffling in line for my Big Roast Beef. I passed out and my foot slipped off the brake, the resulting accident snapping me to attention. *Oh no! I gotta get out of here!* I maneuvered around the car I'd just bonked and peeled away. Somehow, I made it back to the Alamo and lodged in the back alley.

Days later, the cops called, and a very puzzling exchange took place. Once the officer described my little fender-bender, my memory jolted and I grasped a very faint recollection. I'd been reported by the Hardee's drive-thru employee, but the authorities were powerless to do anything more than deliver a lecture. *We're on to you.* My reputation in the city of Superior was rapidly worsening.

Not only was my rep declining, but binge drinking had a way of facilitating extreme impulsivity and foolishness with money. Perpetually "in the moment," rent coming due in a few days or late car payments weren't pressing concerns when the party was going. As I dismissed important matters, I grew more desensitized to the mountains of debt I was accumulating. Soon I was six months behind with the snappy Probe's payments.

Thursday afternoon I manned the smaller of Keyport's two bars, the trendy haven for sports enthusiasts connected to the lounge. An uneventful night was taking shape—I'd probably rack up fifty bucks in tips serving pizzas and simple pitchers of beer—no demand for fancy, high-level cocktails requiring a shaker. Leaning over to wipe the far corner of the bar, I watched with curiosity as two guys in business suits entered through the side doors. Tossing a couple of cardboard coasters toward them, I smiled widely, hoping for a big tip from these out-of-towners.

"What'll it be, gentleman? We have five-dollar pitchers tonight during the game, or if you're feeling extra adventurous, the Texas tea is only six bucks. Five shots of liquor," I added.

The stockier of the two men cleared his throat. "We're not here to enjoy the amenities, though we do certainly appreciate your mastery of the specials," his wry smile made me wonder if sarcasm was underlying his words. "Actually, we are looking for an employee"—he consulted the stack of papers wedged in the crook of his arm—"Do you know a Melissa Ellefson?"

Almost dropping the tulip glass I'd been wiping with a dish towel, I immediately shifted to a hushed tone, instinctively edging the two investigators to the far corner of the bar, away from other customers.

"I'm Melissa." I stage-whispered. "What's going on? Is this something to do with my ex-husband?"

The pair exchanged a knowing glance, while the balding one flipped the paper stack and pushed it forward for my inspection.

"No, ma'am. We're here for business relating to your account with Ford Motor Credit. The silver 1991 Probe out front? Our client's records indicate you're $1,152 past due on your payments. We are here to collect the vehicle. So, if you can just sign here at the bottom—we'll take the car and you can get back to work."

Suddenly on the verge of vomiting, I flipped the papers face-down while reaching for my purse tucked under the bar.

"I have three hundred dollars," I managed in a voice barely

above a croak, "please, let me give it to you, and I'll pay the rest next week."

Stocky dude's lips stretched into a thin line as my heart pounded and blood rushed through my ears. "That's not going to work. You're *six months* past due. It's not like this just happened," he added severely, as if I didn't know. The other man waved a ballpoint pen three inches from my face. "Sign it."

Panicking, I felt the urge to pee, the world closing in as I struggled to grasp a solution. The bank reps eyed me like the latest convict from the local trailer park. *What about Hope? How will I get to work? I'll never get another car loan. I'm screwed.*

Denny, a faithful regular, sat quietly a few stools down, methodically sipping a screwdriver and appearing engrossed in the basketball game. He drained his glass and motioned me over.

"Not trying to be nosy, little lady. But I couldn't help but overhear. You having some financial troubles and repo man is at the door?" I nodded, glued to the floormat while Denny further processed matter as though planning to drop off a nugget of advice and forget the conversation ever happened.

"You don't gotta do it," he finally concluded. "You don't have to sign nothin'. If you do, it's all over. Tell them you're going to make arrangements. That's what I'd do."

Denny spoke his peace and then raised his voice to a normal level.

"Another drink when you get a chance. Watchin' all these athletics has brought on a powerful thirst," he winked.

Suddenly empowered, I realized I had options. Composing myself, I pushed the papers back toward the two men. "I'm going to call Ford Credit tomorrow, and I'll work something out," I said firmly.

The guys exchanged a glance, gathered their documents, and walked out without another word—while I stood savoring a flood of relief. Denny looked over with a smile, which I returned gratefully as I resumed my bartending duties. He never said another word about what had happened. Even in a bar, even when I was running from Him, God offered grace through Denny in that moment.

The coming week was packed with double shifts, a few DJ gigs, and collecting every last tip dollar to claw myself out of arrears. A couple of years later, I'd pay the Probe off entirely, and it would become the first vehicle the bank didn't own. The problem though, was that I never did anything proactively. I always insisted on waiting until my hair was on fire.

Forever on the prowl for the next job opportunity, I didn't plan to make bartending a lifelong career. Even my regulars warned me not to plunge too deep into the Superior nightlife.

"How old are you?" Wayne Eastman asked one night, out of nowhere. A rich businessman, Wayne owned several bars in town and stopped by regularly. Always dressed to the nines and impeccably groomed, he appeared to struggle mightily against the Superior, Wisconsin, stereotype of bar-owner-as-town-drunk. Still, there were nights I knew he was blacked out because he'd return the next day repeating the same stories. Distantly disturbed, I listened politely as if for the first time. Blackout drinkers made me uneasy, and I knew how to spot one.

That night he'd asked my age I proudly answered "Twenty-six" thinking of how young I really was—how many years away from thirty—so much time to escape the bar scene and do something really great with my life.

Wayne had regarded me wistfully. "Twenty-six. Wow. I

remember those days. I'm fifty-five and it went by in a blink. Don't let it slip away, okay? The years fly by fast, and before you know it, you're in too deep to get out."

Wayne drained his Jameson on the rocks and turned up the collar of his peacoat. "It's easier than you think for twenty years to disappear," he repeated, tipping his hat and heading off to check out the scene at his various establishments down on the strip.

His words stuck, always gnawing at the back of my psyche like an exasperated woodpecker. Something foreboding was wrapped in them, and deep down I knew my bar life was a road to nowhere.

Shortly after that conversation with Wayne—I found a lifeline to help escape the bar scene. Like a bright yellow beacon, GREAT OPPORTUNITY FOR STUDENT ROCK RADIO DJ blazed from my professor's office window. I scrawled down the digits and called Gail Biden later that day.

"We really need some help around here," she said, sounding frazzled. "What's your school schedule like?"

"I only have class on Monday and Wednesday," I said quickly, already wanting to sell her on my availability. "Plus the semester will be ending soon. I bartend a few times a week, but I'm free most days."

A radio job might offer the renewal I needed, and as we chatted my desperation intensified.

"I don't know how much we can pay you," Gail finally admitted. "We're running on a very limited budget. How about this . . . come down and see me Tuesday morning. Around nine? I can't promise anything, though."

Meeting day dawned, and I assembled the only

semi-professional outfit I could muster: black stretch pants from Walmart, K-Mart dress shoes, and a pink button-down shirt. I raced across the bridge to Central Avenue on expired license tabs, parked, and scampered through the side door of the Pioneer National Bank building right at the scratch of nine.

The glitzy radio studio I'd hoped to see once I hit the second floor was more like a construction zone. Old furniture was piled everywhere: desks, stacks of chairs, and bookcases lined the center aisles and rotting ceiling tiles hung precariously from above. Gail would later tell me, "They let us stay here because we're losers." Apparently the station's operations had spilled from the tiny studio they rented to the adjoining storage space. As I stood surveying the dismal conditions, I heard music and faint voices drifting from somewhere down the hall.

"I'm just *saying*, we need to target women more," the female voice implored. "They're buying the majority of our airtime."

"But the guys are going to be hitting up all our summer promotions," a male argued. "Guys, cars, bars, and motorcycles. They're a natural fit."

The source of the sounds came into view a few steps down the hall. A tiny brunette woman about forty was seated behind a desk littered with papers, CDs, envelopes, and advertising literature, and an imposing man wearing leather pants and a menacing beard slouched in a wing chair facing her desk. Large silver buckles glinted from his combat boots.

The woman looked up and smiled brightly. "You must be Melissa!"

The guy dragged from a cigarette and extended his hand.

"Jed Trampp. I'm the new program director here at Z Rock."

His greeting was somewhat lukewarm, but Gail was sweet as pie.

Stubbing out a cigarette, she beamed from behind her colossal desk.

"Gail Biden. My dad owns the station, and we're proud of our heritage. It's the last of the locals here in Duluth. We're doing what we can to keep the corporate guys away."

I liked her instantly and envisioned a place in the studio as she beamed proudly toward Jed.

"Dad and I just brought Jed on board. He's one of the best in the business, and he's really turning things around. I mean, the other guys wanted him—they were literally *salivating* over his talent! We have a big summer coming up and could use some extra help. Jed will be super busy amazing us with his programming skills and taking things to the next level." Gail gazed at Jed with admiration, who looked away and picked at his fingernails. Faintly uneasy, I sensed something was up with him.

Hmm . . . salivating. Jed must be the next Wolfman Jack, huh?

"Yeah, I've got a lot of ideas," Jed chimed in, forgetting his makeshift manicure to agree with Gail's praise report. "Can you get credits for working here or something?"

They don't want to pay me.

"The school does offer that, but internships are only awarded in the fall. I'm so excited to learn this business, though. I already do some DJing at a bar in Superior . . . I could help you guys out really cheap."

"There would be sales involved," Gail interrupted. "We desperately need people to sell the station. Do you have any experience?"

"Well, I worked in jewelry for a while. Retail. I guess you

could say I did well . . . I won a few awards from corporate. They called me a 'Selling Star,'" I added for good measure.

Gail seemed pleased, and as we wrapped up, she promised I'd hear from her soon.

Preoccupied with the promise of a new life in broadcasting, I waited for five excruciating days until finally, the phone rang.

"Hello?"

"Hi, Melissa, it's Gail Biden. We'd like to offer you a sales position. You might also get to fill some weekend shifts in the studio, but I can't promise anything."

"Awesome! I'll take it!"

The selling piece sucked, but I believed it was my ticket to radio fame, so I dealt with it. Gail served as coach and mentor, training me via appointments with local businesses. Jed approached one Friday afternoon after Gail and I wowed the SuperValu store management with Z Rock's advertising opportunities.

"Are you free tonight?"

I had planned to hit the bars, but was curious.

"I can be . . . why?"

"You want to go on the air tonight at six? The evening guy called in, and I need someone to cover."

The tavern would have to wait, my on-air debut was calling and I needed a stage name. Mel Del Greco was my first air handle, and I could hardly get over how cool it sounded: *Mel—Del.* Jed parked himself across the street at the Rustic and asked the bartender to tune in Z Rock. As I was signing off at midnight, Jed reappeared, jovial from five hours of tap beer.

"Great job," he commented. "I'm impressed!"

Successfully making it through my first on-air shift earned

enough credibility for a weekend slot. My ego adored telling people, "I'm on air at Z Rock now. Call me up and request something, I take requests all hour."

A fresh crew of boozers awaited, and I quickly gravitated toward Jed and the other heavy drinkers. Gail rarely indulged in more than two cocktails, but joined us at the bar to keep her new programming wizard under control. He seemed to have personal problems, and her preoccupation with his issues muted my own indiscretions. Soon, I was out on the town with the radio crowd several nights a week.

Jed was a hothead crowding forty who hadn't grown up yet—he lived on the edge fueled by chaos. Technically he was my superior, though his apparent lack of boundaries quickly revealed we lived in the same place with regard to alcohol, bad choices, and disorder. With a sketchy employment history and radio career, I was later shocked to learn Jed's poor credit had forced him to rent a room above one of the local strip joints.

One night after partying in Superior, his current lady friend left him stranded.

"Why don't we just head over to my place?" I offered. We were already in Superior, after all. "I've got booze."

Work sure wasn't happening in the morning. After stumbling into my apartment just before dawn, we cracked a couple of beers and uncapped the bottle of Jag I reserved for special occasions such as this. The radio station was the furthest thing from my mind until I jolted awake many hours later.

"Holy crap!" I yelled, jumping from my bed. I ran to the couch where Jed had crashed and shook him.

"We're late. Very late. We are so screwed!"

Jed shrugged. "Who cares? I'm the boss today. Gail's

probably out doing something with her kid. Thank God for automation, huh? The station's running itself."

Most days, I showed up for work still half-drunk, but Jed never breathed a word—he was probably in the same state of mind. Gail had family values and wanted to run a clean station, so I did what I could to assist her. Four-year old Hope attended the local Head Start program now and had to be on the bus bright and early, and I did my best to juggle it all. After seeing her off, I made it to the morning meeting at the station, then headed out on my business calls.

Once I made enough sales to show I'd done something for the day, it was time to head home for a little break. A power nap helped to ease my hangover, then I'd meet Hope's bus and bring her back to the station to wrap things up. Gail knew I had a young child the same age as hers and afforded me this flexibility. I had everyone fooled into believing I was a dedicated, hard-working single parent. In some ways, I was.

My drinking was tightly under wraps, but managing my growing addiction was a wearisome grind.

Sometimes I went too far. One night, I was so drunk I didn't have a prayer of waking up on time. I figured a drunken voice-mail delivered right before passing out might help the situation.

18

With no word from my boss the next day, heavy guilt burdened me. *Did I still have a job?* Gail finally called around six that evening as I sat eating sleeves of generic Pop-Tarts in an effort to ease my increasing apprehension.

"Hey Gail," I answered, trying to sound impaired by a swollen mouth.

"Melissa, this isn't working out."

"What do you mean? Is this about my dental appointment?"

With a heavy sigh, she told me I was unreliable.

"I need someone I can count on to be here *every* morning, bright and early, to go out and sell advertising for my station. You're not that person."

Oh, sweet Jesus.

With increasing panic, I restored to begging. "Gail, please. Give me one more chance. I can turn things around."

"I don't think so. Jed and I agree you aren't a good fit."

Jed? So now he was turning on me?

"Gail. Just *one* more chance. You know I'm a single mother. Just like you. I can't waste this opportunity."

It was the triple whammy I prayed would earn her grace: begging, pleading, *and* playing the single mother card. Gail was silent for a long time.

"*One* more chance. That's it. I'll see you tomorrow morning."

I breathed a sigh of relief as I hung up. I had somehow saved myself.

Soon, I realized I was extremely lucky Gail had given in, because a few days later my Keyport boss summoned me to his office. It wasn't to praise my performance.

"What's this all about? Am I in trouble?" I asked as I took a seat nervously.

My boss stabbed his glasses onto his nose. "I learned something that disturbs me."

I cleared my throat. "What is that?"

"You let a friend of yours run the karaoke booth a couple of months back. Not only that—you have been drinking behind the bar. This is serious."

His words hit like a sledgehammer, and a current of panic coursed through my body like a wheat field bracing for a tornado. I thought briefly of the night with Brady, drinking under the fluorescent lights until 6 a.m.

"Who told you that?" I managed.

"Customers," he responded shortly. "Good friends of mine.

I have no reason to doubt them."

Stunned, I sat unable to comprehend the audacity of such heartless betrayal by *my* customers, *my* patrons, the people I had busted my butt to entertain. Defending myself was pointless since I had no clue what had even happened that night.

"Listen, I only had a couple of beers! You *said* we could. Everyone else does." I sounded like a ten-year-old begging to have her ears pierced.

"*No one else is allowed to touch the equipment!*" Bossman boomed. His intimidating voice had me on the verge of wetting my pants, a usual reaction when faced with angry authority figures. "I trusted you with my system, and you *failed me.*"

Filled with shame, I continued my feeble attempts at self-defense. "My friend wasn't really *running* it. He just wanted to take a look. Come on, Bill! You can still trust me!"

"No. It's final. We're done here."

Sweet talk wouldn't work. Slinking out of his office, I walked a few paces to the lounge bar.

"I'll have a beer," I told my fellow bartender, Sandi. "And a Jag. You got any chilled back there?"

My good buddy would set me up. The growing reality of my problem was squelched as I sat gulping my drinks to forget the harsh reality—I'd just blown a very good gig. The karaoke position had been easy money, twenty dollars an hour.

"So what happened with Bill?" Sandi asked, shaking her gorgeous auburn tresses from a hair clip. "Was he pissed about something?"

"He just up and decided he wants to get rid of the karaoke! Out of nowhere. Claims he doesn't like the crowd. He's such a tool." With a shrug, I tossed her a hefty tip to illustrate I was washing my hands of the whole drunk singing scene. "I don't know how many more times I can handle hearing wasted people sing 'Friends in Low Places,' anyway," I snidely concluded, glancing around the bar. "Anyone want to go downtown?"

After gathering a few volunteers, we went off to drink ourselves into oblivion.

My latest consequence represented much more than just the loss of karaoke duties; it was now a skeleton busting through the closet of my soul.

I continued bartending by the skin of my teeth, although fear of another reprimand for drinking on the job hadn't impacted me enough to change my ways. Shifts were just too *boring* without booze, and forcing sober small talk with patrons made me squirm. A nagging feeling that the end was near hung on, but I couldn't muster up the motivation to take the necessary drastic measures.

A few weeks later, I was summoned back to the boss's office. Truly puzzled this time—thinking I'd been "pretty good" since our last heart-to-heart. The drinking was on the down-low. My customers were usually drunk, too, so what did it matter?

"You punched out ten minutes early last Sunday," Bossman reported. "Too much has happened. You're not reliable, and it's time to let you go."

The "not reliable" deal was becoming the defining theme of my life. With that, I was wiped from Keyport history. Sandi and I still talked occasionally, but I was too embarrassed to stay in touch with anyone else. My illustrious four years as a cocktail server, skilled bartender able to mix everything from a Rusty Nail to a Poor Man's Bloody Mary, and highly entertaining karaoke DJ screeched to a halt with no fanfare, no going away party, nothing.

Shifting focus to the radio station, I plunged into full-time sales and proved myself a reliable team player. Terrified that others would learn the truth about my relationship with booze, I tried to become a homebody, but it was next to impossible. Sitting alone was a torturous experience requiring constant numbing to stop the relentless thoughts.

Summer of 1999 was busy enough to distract from my growing drinking problem—chock-full of activities and outings for the radio station. Weekly on-air shifts, sales calls, and live broadcasts filled my days, the ideal deflection for a life slipping into quicksand. Forever behind on rent and other bills, my financial arrears never hampered my bar runs. The radio venture was dreamy for a drunk—endless live broadcasts and concerts held at bars or festivals with beer tents.

I tagged along as Jed's emcee for many rock shows featuring aging stars—lots of schmoozing, boozing, and wallowing in beer-soaked festivals. With free tickets and backstage passes to the annual Moondance Jam concert, Jed was unable to front the station that weekend, so I traveled alone to the three-day event held in the small town of Walker, Minnesota.

Roaming the grounds with a fat, laminated media pass, I adored watching people stare at my credentials even more than the free access to beer and top-shelf liquor. *I'm representing Z Rock.* The celebrity life was just out of reach—meet and greets with Kevin Cronin from REO Speedwagon, the band members of ELO (minus Jeff Lynne), Eddie Money, and Robin Zander of Cheap Trick kept me high on borrowed fame. Posing for pictures and inflating my piddly radio role, I had finally arrived.

During the downtime, I hit the slots, gambled at the casino, and pumped twenty-dollar bills into machines while chatting with random strangers. Fake assurance and the illusion of mystery breathed to life the familiar delusion that alcohol would magically manifest whatever I needed.

Letting it all hang out didn't even work. *They probably think I'm fat.* I'd lamented to Jed about my enormous weight gain earlier, and he didn't disagree. Pausing to catch my reflection in a mirrored row of slot games, I gasped at my girth. Mr. Scale had registered my highest weight ever that morning—185 pounds. I just drank more, hoping I could forget I'd cracked into the obese category.

Lynyrd Skynyrd hit the stage that night—but the band is famously private and shooed media away. Following an episode of highly irrational sobbing, I met a guy named Jared and conned him into hoisting me onto his shoulders to watch the show. Though he was a big, sturdy man, handling my hefty frame for a solid hour was still quite a feat.

"How much do you think I weigh?" I coyly asked after a while.

Sweat pouring from his forehead, he shrugged, "I dunno, 160?"

"NO! I'm 135!" I insisted.

It was extremely doubtful he was buying that. At the end of the concert, Jared invited me back to his hotel room. Something about him repelled my drunk self, and I refused, even though I was so wrecked I could barely walk and there wasn't a motel room for a hundred miles. Instead, I stumbled out to the Probe and crashed in the hatchback.

Hideously nauseated the next morning, I woke with the sun beating through the glass, pouring with sweat and in alcohol withdrawal. The liquor stores weren't open yet, but I somehow managed to make it to a nearby gas station for a quart of Strawberry Quik to settle my stomach. No plans to get drunk that early in the morning, but later on a six-pack of Mike's Cranberry Lemonade staved off the sickness so I could perform my radio duties.

The six short months I spent working at Z Rock led me to believe alcohol had helpfully aided with boosting my career into the stratosphere, but the high life would burn out faster than a set of batteries from the Dollar Store. Habitual drunkenness was glamorous, commonplace, and part and parcel of the radio DJ lifestyle—but my rock and roll debauchery would soon catch up with me.

Many nights after work, the station crew migrated to the Park Inn—a nearby bar with great drink specials and live bands.

"Want to shoot some pool?"

Jed loomed overhead. Bar games didn't interest me much, but unlimited glasses from random beer pitchers while we played sure did.

In between games, we wandered back to our stools for another round of drinks. A huge mirror above the bar reflected something familiar: Christy, my old drinking buddy. We'd been estranged since my wedding day five long years ago. Seth's departure with Christy and the bridesmaids that night had put a serious damper on the reception, but it was all water under the bridge now.

Our eyes locked: she wore the same sky-high, bleached blonde hair, her enormous eyes wide with expression like electric blue gumballs. Dragging from a cigarette as though it may offer inspiration for what was coming, she stabbed it into the ashtray and pushed her stool back excitedly.

"Melissa, it's been so long!" she thundered, erupting in her trademark cackle and crushing me in a huge bear hug. "Where the hell have you been?"

Our chance meeting bred desperate yearning for the old days—the fun shared when we were young and without responsibilities.

"Ah, you know, just around. Doing the DJ thing at Z Rock. Hope is almost five now, can you believe that? So, you moved away I heard?"

The demise of my marriage wasn't even mentioned. Christy had found out somewhere along the way that Seth and I had divorced.

"I was living in Montana for a while, but a drunk cowboy rear-ended me, and it sent me back here to Minnesota. Lost my insurance, needed some extra help from the family. Long story," she cackled.

Drinks and laughs kept the reunion going until bar close, and in our usual fashion we tried to weasel the bartender into an after-party. He declined, but graciously offered up a complimentary shot of tequila before showing us the door. Christy and I made plans to meet again the following night to finish what we had started.

The next afternoon, I canvassed my closet for something marginally cute. Could Christy see all the weight I had gained? I cursed every piece of clothing hanging in my wardrobe. The old Keyport clothes were still there, beckoning like a lost lover I knew I had no chance with.

A few beers helped my closet inspection along though, and a tired pair of nylon Nike shorts paired with a tie-dyed Z Rock T-shirt seemed acceptable. At least I could hold onto my local celebrity status as a way to deflect from my growing size.

Christy was always dressed to the nines with matching accessories, but having a unique or coveted style had never been my thing. Very troubled to find her much skinnier than me now, I thought back to our plasma selling days when I was dropping pounds and we'd both weighed in the 140s on the big doctor's scale at the donor center. But drinking worked to alleviate my feelings about the body I didn't want to live in. Hell, the more I consumed, the better I looked even to myself. Talk about beer goggles.

Christy and I made it to Grandma's Saloon right when the doors opened at four, and combined with the few I'd sipped at home, I was soon headlong into a blackout. Hours of drunken karaoke followed at the Park Inn: Blondie's "Heart of Glass," Fiona Apple's "Criminal."

Trapped in the seduction of my own mind, I imagined I was channeling Fiona's video where she wanders around a deserted house party in her underwear singing about being the baddest girl around. Countless kamikaze shots followed, along with endless beers. The evening descended into a blur around eight o'clock, with my blackout closing in like the Grim Reaper's cape.

Jed later revealed disturbing tidbits illustrating my state of mind at the tail end of the night. On a bench outside the Park Inn, we had engaged in a deep, philosophical conversation about radio programming trends for nearly an hour before I made the fateful decision to drive.

"You just stood up all of a sudden and said you were going home," he later recalled with a shrug. "Said you wanted to sleep in your bed. I know how that is when you're wasted. You were sort of sedated. Mellow. Kind of like in a trance, but I didn't think you were *that* drunk. You weren't stumbling around or anything."

Even party boy Jed had no clue I was in a blackout—walking, talking, and functioning. People never knew. I then said goodbye and headed off for Superior.

One extremely faint blip of awareness happened just before midnight—I had hit something. Trying to recollect it the next day was like pulling a seaweed-covered fishing line from a murky swamp. I so badly wanted to remember what had happened, but I was operating only on impulse without conscience or inhibition—unable to think, plan, or form intent.

Next thing I knew, it was like day had broken, and I was wandering the aisles of the Spur station where Seth and I had met when I was just eighteen. Not at all distressed, my only focus was on stuffing my face. Stumbling up and down the aisles, I zeroed in on a bag of Nacho Cheese Doritos and a frozen pizza. Attempting to bake pizzas while drunk was pointless, but I did it anyway—always passing out long before they finished cooking.

Just as I tossed my purchases onto the counter, three squad cars circled into the parking lot. Gazing out the window with disinterest, I ignored the officer entering the store—much more interested in getting to my car so I could power down the bag of chips. Their methodical crunching would keep me awake long enough for the pizza to cook. I stood frozen for a moment as I considered adding a can of Pringles to my gas station haul.

Tossing my stuff onto the counter, I fumbled through a crumpled wad of dollar bills left over from the bar as an officer approached me.

"Ma'am? Are you the owner of the silver Ford Probe outside?"

I nodded my head. This much was true. *Sure am.* I was indifferent and unconcerned.

"Were you just involved in an accident?"

Confused by the question, I hesitated while glancing outside at my car idling at the gas pump. The hood was completely buckled in, crunched back so far it touched the bottom of the windshield like a dysfunctional accordion. I chuckled, thinking suddenly of Weird Al and then returned to the present moment. *I must have had an accident?* My blood alcohol report would later return four times over the legal limit for driving.

As my blacked-out mind processed moments using only working memory storage—just like it does when recalling a strange phone number only long enough to dial it—it couldn't download anything. I hadn't formed a new recollection since singing "Criminal" about six hours earlier. It was exactly like I'd beamed from the Park Inn to the Dorito aisle without missing a beat.

Amiably, I nodded in agreement to the officer's question. I wasn't threatened by him. It was obvious, I must have hit something. We needed to figure this out, and maybe I could help.

"Can you step outside please?"

Carefully leading the way, I noticed the cashier peering curiously from behind the very counter I used to run years ago. Three officers waited at the corner near the dumpster I used to fill with discarded cardboard delivery boxes every Saturday.

"Ma'am? Can I see your identification, please?" he stood patiently as I fumbled through my purse, spilling tampons and ephedrine bottles onto the sidewalk, too drunk to care. "We need you to perform a field sobriety test. Have you had anything to drink tonight?"

"A few beers," I admitted. "Maybe three or four at the most."

"All right," he said, scanning my ID. "I need you to stand on one foot and bring the tips of your index fingers to your nose."

I watched his brief demonstration of the test through glassy eyes, but my attempt to follow his lead resembled a seasick bird flapping its arms furiously but going nowhere. The heel-to-toe spectacle was even worse, and the officers stood patiently while I struggled mightily to pretend I was sober. After allowing a couple of attempts, the trio of authorities reached an agreement—I was barely functional, much less capable of operating a motor vehicle.

"Miss Ellefson, we're going to arrest you on suspicion of drunken driving. You're going to jail tonight."

Jail. My first time in lockup—how had it come to this? My life was spinning faster, like a roll of toilet paper seems to after it's halfway gone. The Superior Police Department wasn't *real* incarceration—just a holding cell—but felt close enough to federal prison. After dumping my stuff at the intake desk, I was escorted to a bleak cell. Once the door slammed with a resounding thud, I yelled down the hall to the on-duty guard.

"Is anyone out there? You need to let me out! Listen, I'm pregnant!"

My pathetic pleas went nowhere, and after a while, I gave up and passed out.

The following morning broke with panic and confusion. Struggling to sit up, I gauged my surroundings with a mind sickened by alcohol overdose. Hope. *Hope.* Where was she? My body went limp when I remembered she was with Seth. Suddenly overcome with nausea, I lurched off the bed to hover over the metal toilet. Last night's kamikaze shots soon made a second appearance in the stainless steel bowl.

Later that morning, the guard poked a meal through the slot in the door—a double cheeseburger and tater tots. The few tentative bites I swallowed set off a round of projectile vomiting, the toilet my constant companion for the next few hours.

After pleading guilty for my crime at a five-minute court appearance via teleconference, I signed a signature bond and was free to go. Grateful to be within walking distance of the Alamo, I shuffled home from the courthouse with no car, driver's license, or dignity. Now I faced real *jail time*.

As soon as I reached my apartment, I went straight to bed to agonize through the most excruciating hangover to date. Staring at a wall-sized hanging of the Beastie Boys crammed into a sardine can I'd bought to rebel against the reality of being an adult, I sweated and writhed in my tie-dyed sheets, suffering from alcohol poisoning and shame overload. Once again, Jesus had allowed me to live through another near-death night. I was far from grateful for His mercy.

Soul-searching from my cramped bedroom at the Alamo, I was desperate enough to say a little prayer and begin seeking God for direction. Once the most painful portion of the hangover wore off, I began soliciting friends in the hope they'd assure me I "wasn't that bad."

"I need to do something," I later confessed to Christy after disclosing my harrowing night. "I think I might need to try some AA meetings."

Christy paused. "Do you really think you *need* that? You just messed up. Slow down for a while and be more careful next time."

I wanted to believe her, but deep down I knew she was just telling me what we both wanted to hear.

Later that night, I was gripped by the strong need to make amends to the woman I'd violated. Though I fought the urge and certainly did not wish to comply with it, the prompting of the Holy Spirit I didn't yet recognize would not give up.

I really had no excuses, my victim's name was right there on the police report. Lisa J. Jones. The printed letters felt basic and nonthreatening, but interacting with her seemed more daunting than traversing Mount Everest in my hungover state. Thumbing through the Yellow Pages yielded her phone number and address—less than a mile from mine.

As a huge lump formed in my throat, I picked up the phone gingerly as though handling it that way might soften the blow.

"Hello?"

"Is this Lisa?" My voice quavered as I fought back tears.

"Yes."

"This is Melissa Ellefson. The person who hit you last night." Tearfully, I explained my plan to seek help for my drinking problem.

"Can you forgive me for threatening your life?"

"Of course, Melissa. My ex-husband was an alcoholic, so I certainly understand your struggle. I appreciate you reaching out. I wish you well in your recovery, you're doing the right thing."

Lisa was beyond gracious, her merciful words offering hope and a slim possibility that I just *might* be capable of change. Our brief encounter wasn't an accident—God used my reckless act as a wake-up call that really turned up the heat of conviction, and Lisa was an angel poised to become the catalyst for a long period of sobriety and seed-planting.

My next order of business was much meatier. Recovery meetings had eluded me for a long time, and even though Christy had discouraged them, it was time to take a risk and attempt something I never had.

I headed out the door on foot at the last possible moment, every step of the way wanting to retreat to the safety of my crappy little stucco hideaway.

19

An unremarkable building with the shades drawn was my destination. Never before had I seen people congregating on the sidewalk in front of the Serenity Club, but everyone knew it was an AA group. The building was ironically right across the street from the busy intersection marking the site of my car crash. *What if someone recognizes me?*

Although my dad had done his time in AA meetings, the organization was shrouded in secrecy and shameful to me in 1999. As I approached Belknap Street, an odd memory flared: an after-school special about a girl alcoholic. I'd watched it around age nine, and it had made a lasting impression: *"Meet Mary Connor,"* the narrator droned. *"Junior class vice president.*

Honor student. Cheerleader. And ALCOHOLIC."

The scene showed Mary sitting under a campus tree during lunch hour, discreetly pouring some undoubtedly booze-filled concoction from a thermos. If sweet, sensible Mary was prone to addiction, then no one was immune.

Moving on autopilot as Belknap loomed in the distance, I wanted to escape the impossible task of facing a crowd of despondent teetotalers, but some other power grabbed the door handle before I could escape.

The scene inside challenged the stereotypes I'd entertained in the past —my mind's eye had offered a fantasy world ripe with pale and shaky homeless bums—spun-dry mere hours before entering the hallowed rooms of the famed 12-step program. The hapless characters of my imagination resembled many of the derelicts from the Landing Liquor store of my adolescence; finding anyone halfway normal or high-functioning wasn't on my radar.

Surprisingly, not a single poor, depressed hobo was present at the Serenity Club. Instead, raucous noise and laughter illuminated the tobacco-stained walls. And happy-looking people. The folks gathered around the table appeared at peace, maybe even *joyful?* They chatted, smiled, and sipped coffee, seated in pairs or clusters of three. A trio of women looked over someone's vacation photos, while a couple of men handled coffee duties. Grabbing an empty chair and attempting to blend in was an epic failure. Well-intentioned old-timers wouldn't miss out on fresh meat and soon zeroed in.

A smiling fiftyish guy with an approachable boyish look and a shock of stick-straight black hair reached over the table as I tried desperately to melt into the floor.

"You a newcomer?" I reluctantly accepted his mitt-like paw and shook it as he grinned. "I'm Ernie. Welcome."

"Melissa. Yes. This is my first meeting."

"I thought so. Grab some coffee. And keep coming back."

Keep coming back. One day at a time. Easy does it. First things first. Small wooden signs that looked as though they'd been around for a century peppered the room as simple reminders. A pegboard of colorfully tacky mugs clustered along the wall across from the coffee pot—displaying every kitschy phrase from "It's Five O'Clock Somewhere" to "Sexy Grandma." Likely reserved for the serious regulars, I couldn't imagine I'd ever make it to the mug wall of fame.

Ernie introduced me to Katy that night, a bubbly woman in her forties with a fat tawny braid trailing down her back who would become my first sponsor and a lifelong friend. Through her encouragement, I began rediscovering interests I'd ditched for alcohol. Roller skating, walks by the bay, and gatherings over steaming mugs of coffee at the local diner would soon occupy my days.

Quality time with Hope was something I genuinely enjoyed—imparting my love of Dr. Seuss books, sledding down the big hill in front of our duplex, attempting various crafts, and hitting the roller rink for the first time since I was a kid. Hope loved it so much she decided to have her birthday party there. Meanwhile, I began walking the boardwalk at Canal Park and managed to shed twenty-five pounds over the next several months. The walking and thinking did wonders to calm anxiety and help me to focus on positive forward momentum.

Sobriety also benefited the radio job, until a Friday about a month later when I arrived at work to find both Jed and

Gail seated in the salesroom with an unknown guy. Sporting a smart-looking jacket and crisply ironed dress shirt, he seemed as out of place as I felt frequenting church, which happened very rarely and usually on Easter morning with a raging hangover. Suits didn't darken the crusty upper level of the Pioneer Bank building often, putting everyone on high alert. Depositing my bag on my desk, I gauged them nervously.

"Is something going on?"

"Morning, Melissa," Gail began. "This is my brother Fred; we've got some news for the staff here."

Fred smiled pleasantly and shook my hand. "It's nice to meet you finally. So, I'm told you're something of a selling machine?"

"Ah, it's not all that," I insisted with an awkward wave. "Gail does most of the work."

Fred studied me like I was holding out on him, then quickly shifted from my selling prowess.

"I'm sure you've got a lot of potential, Melissa. Priming the next radio stars has always been an endeavor close to me. I think you've heard our father—the heart behind the station—is pretty sick. The Brill Media group has made an offer to buy the license and we feel it's the best thing for our family."

My radio dreams funneled down the toilet as I ruefully remembered our identity as rebellious renegades bucking the corporate trends.

"Where does this leave me?"

"I'm afraid you no longer have a job here," Fred responded kindly. "The new owners already have a full staff in place, so they couldn't absorb anyone else. We'd be happy to give you a good reference if that will help."

"They're keeping Jed, for now," Gail interjected. "Possibly

just for the transition. We have no idea if he'll remain on staff long-term."

No reason to bother selling anything today. The party was over.

"Thanks for everything, Gail," I said with unexpected emotion as I carried a small banker's box out of the Pioneer building for the last time.

Preservation mode kicked in on the way home as I considered my next move. Even traversing the state entertaining at events for a few hundred bucks in cash wasn't enough income to survive. Once the wedding season dried up, it was slim pickings on the DJ front. Moving back home at twenty-six was off the table. I needed to improvise.

"KDLH-TV is looking for production assistants," my broadcasting professor offered one day, after learning of my predicament.

"I'm not really interested in television," I griped. "I want to be a rock DJ."

"You need a job, don't you?" he smiled. "Perhaps you should expand your horizons."

Later that afternoon, I meandered down Superior Street and impulsively pulled into the KDLH-TV studios. *Why not. I'll check it out.*

Mary Anne, a classy, platinum-haired lady, manned the front desk, and after comparing notes we realized she owned a cabin down the road from my house on Sunny Lane. The shiny front lobby facing the bustling city street featured framed photos of many former news greats my parents had watched from our clunky old Zenith console television set. A gleaming showcase displayed a silver shovel used by news icon Marsh Nelson for the station groundbreaking back in the 50s, and suddenly I envisioned *my* picture among the other broadcasting legends.

Television news was unchartered territory, but writing stories wouldn't be so bad. I scrawled out an application not really caring whether it reflected anything impressive, but later that day the news director called to offer a position in the production department.

The media world was indeed exciting, with everyone racing around chasing spot news and the scanner always screeching a brewing story, the pay meager but enough. Combined with my weekend DJ shows, Hope and I were going to make it. No longer blowing money at the bar every weekend also helped a ton.

The production department offered various technical tasks: floor cameras, audio sound board, graphics, and teleprompter. Yelling "STANDBY" seemed cool, but I wasn't getting my chance on the floor just yet. My main responsibility was reserved for the lowest man (or woman) on the totem pole—running the teleprompter. My writing skills would stay bottled up for now while I resigned myself to the mundane task of operating a little joystick scrolling copy for the glamorous anchors to read.

The months flew by, and each night those framed pictures in the lobby posed a question: *What's YOUR future in television broadcasting?* Sobriety wasn't helping with my habitual procrastination, and I stayed safely sandwiched in my comfort zone, the glitz of worldly fame just out of reach.

The TV crew was in the dark about my criminal record. Hoping for a clean slate, I dutifully appeared in court for my second drunk driving rap in November of 1999, somewhat reassured that my new job could only bring the favor needed to redeem the past.

"I see you were hired at KDLH-TV since your arrest. Good for you," the judge said. "Your sentence is fourteen days on electronic monitoring and six months of probation. I also want you to complete an outpatient treatment program. I'm not recommending jail time because you have a job and a child."

Don't blow it, was his message. Relieved to escape incarceration and blessed by the freedom to work and attend required recovery meetings, not a soul at KDLH-TV knew I sported an electronic ankle bracelet tracking my every move.

Part of the court sentence was some sort of outpatient treatment program, which was distantly exciting and not incongruous with my constant quest for self-improvement. The Recovery Center in Superior had made the list of recommended places, a curious outfit located in a UWS college residence hall—not at all what I envisioned, but the funny little program helped lay some groundwork for an alcohol-free existence. Soon, I was less reliant on Mom's babysitting services—though our codependent enmeshment didn't disappear overnight. She struggled to accept the new me who needed her so much less. My weekend DJ gigs were the bane of her existence, causing intense worry as I traversed the state to earn cash.

My living situation improved too—Hope and I ditched the comfortable but tattered old Alamo and upgraded to a renovated upper duplex apartment in West Duluth. The new living arrangements were beautiful and cozy, located on a secluded and shady tree-lined street. A network of five neighborhood bars clustered just a few blocks away on Grand Avenue, but I wasn't paying attention to them at the moment.

Instead of obsessing about my next drink, I was reinventing myself. My license was still invalid, but Duluth was a much bigger city than Superior and I could easily skirt the local authorities. Hope and I enjoyed the comfy duplex and lived there four years; spending much time at the nearby parks, the small library, and of course, the McDonalds just too convenient to resist. She'd catch the school bus right down the block, with afternoons generally a mad dash to make it from work to meet her. Hope would return to KDLH-TV to round out my workday just like she had in the Z Rock era, and became well-known and loved around the newsroom—even watching newscasts from the engineering post sometimes. A lot of juggling, but I made it all work somehow.

Though I needed Mom less, city council meetings didn't stop on Monday nights, so I trekked up to Caribou Lake with Hope every week. A late night for her, and a lot of driving for me.

Car idling at the corner, I searched anxiously for the tardy school bus. Time I could not spare—I'd peeled out of the station with less than an hour to collect Hope, fly up to my parents' place, and jet back downtown. Making my life work was a full-time job—single parenthood no cakewalk.

Finally, the bus rolled up, and I watched kids file down the steps, plastic backpacks and lunchboxes in tow. Hope hopped off second to last, toting her Barbie gear.

"How was your day?" I asked, as she climbed into her booster seat.

"It was good," she responded, struggling out of her raincoat and reclining against the backseat. "Long day," she murmured, hazel eyes drowsy.

I chuckled as I pulled away from the curb, thinking about Hope's sweet little old soul.

After making the quick drop-off, I returned briskly to the

highway with 25 minutes to make it back to the news center. No leeway—and I still needed to swing by the apartment in West Duluth to grab a file tape for that night's story.

Quickly cresting Thompson Hill and Spirit Mountain, the panoramic and familiar vista of Duluth swelled below as I checked the time again. My heart pounded as I sped—I was still on probation and couldn't afford a ticket—but the expanse of freeway was clear of cops to the Cody Street exit. Railroad tracks that canopied the freeway and a bridge abutment loomed in the distance; I'd passed under it hundreds of times without paying much attention. The cement barrier blocked the view of oncoming traffic—but I moved on autopilot. As I punched radio stations and fluffed my hair in the rearview mirror, I unconsciously moved from the inner left lane of the freeway to the outside lane.

A split second later, a wrong-way driver heading south at a high speed had accessed the northbound lane from the Cody Street exit and barreled right through the space I'd just occupied split seconds before.

Shaking and nauseous, I pulled off to the shoulder, transfixed on the sharp points of my white knuckles as they gripped the steering wheel.

I almost died. I almost died. My mind sputtered. For years, I'd wonder why I had "decided" just a fraction of a second before disaster struck, to change lanes.

The near-death incident on the freeway weighed on my mind as I sat in my outpatient treatment group analyzing everyone around me. A sweet grandmotherly lady and a rough-around-the-edges recovering biker guy led the seven clients seeking recovery, and I will never forget our months spent together. Casey lost his battle with meth a year later. Paul went on to beat heroin addiction and became a successful business owner; I'd later run into him in recovery meetings. Dawn, a single mother in her 40s, relayed awful stories of her neglected children. Brett was around my age and mandated to treatment for his fourth DWI—a real schmoozer.

Vaguely interesting, cocky and slightly flirty, Brett was a possibility in my little black book—that is, until he and Dana, a divorced mother of four, hooked up. Jimmy was an old-school alkie I later spotted drinking from a hotel bar at one of my DJ gigs.

Focusing on everyone else's issues and chestering possible romantic prospects were primary objectives, along with a feeling of special giftedness and a vague comfort in believing that this whole process was a corrective one that would allow me to return to drinking one day. But first, I was laser-focused on people-pleasing my way through the program. A run-of-the-mill curriculum with groups focused on "working the steps," the first three sessions were completed with peers, the next two with a minister before graduating—stuff like writing a goodbye letter to the addictive substance. Steps six through nine were to be done outside of treatment with a sponsor.

My private session with the pastor designated to hear me unload past shame and sexual exploits left a sour taste in my mouth. He seemed just a little too titillated by my past drinking escapades, and I was creeped out by the tight embrace that followed the soul purging. The rush of cleanliness I was promised never came.

The group discussions shared with peers were somewhat helpful though, and unlikely bonds formed over weekly check-ins, step sharing, and familiar addiction fallout.

Mom had agreed to watch Hope during my group sessions—though not entirely ecstatic about it ("Do you really think you need that?"—same thing Christy had said about AA)—and I began to enjoy the routine of dropping her off and heading to my scheduled meetings. Working on myself now was crucial.

Twelve weeks of "treatment" flew by, followed up with six months of aftercare, and I eventually became a trained facilitator. Before long, I was leading groups and offering anecdotes, wisdom, and advice—though I was far from healed myself.

My desire to drink was on "pause;" I'd put it on the shelf to give the program my unwavering attention. But I also kept a few secrets. Deep down I wasn't finished, and when I claimed I was never drinking again, the hollow ring of my words was sure to return void.

The life I'd left behind beckoned from every corner—with alcohol screaming its availability and allure from television commercials, road signs, and street corners—the sight of people chilling out on tavern decks in the summer definitely the most painful. Would I really *never* again taste a perfectly blended margarita in the glow of the setting sun? It just didn't seem fair.

Work complicated things, too. Many who shared the production area with me at KDLH were barely twenty-one and busy sowing their wild oats. At twenty-seven, I was supposed to be terminating that season of life. Drinking remained a nightly occasion for much of the news crew while I refused their parties for a solid six months.

Parked in my production booth one night with my feet propped up on a pillow below the monitor, my mind had grown numb from running the teleprompter. The mindless activity of controlling a small joystick so the news copy would scroll across the camera lens for the anchors to read was extremely unchallenging. Dozing off during commercial breaks was tempting, but screwing up might bring much unwanted notice. Legend had it that the fiery red-headed evening anchor would yell *"WHO'S ON PROMPTER?"* during breaks if the operator was scrolling too fast or slow. I certainly didn't need *that* kind of attention.

Once the broadcast ended, a young guy named Jared who'd just reached legal drinking age breezed through.

"We're going to the bar. Want to come?"

"Oh, yeah, forget it . . . " he responded before I could answer. "You don't drink."

Wait a minute. I *used to* drink. *I could if I wanted to.*

"It's not that I *don't ever* drink," I corrected him, like a little child leaving participles dangling in grammar class. "*I'm just not drinking right now.*"

Jared chuckled at my unnecessary correction. "Whatever . . . we're going out for a few, so join us if you want."

He was in the dark about the electronic jewelry I wore to pay the price for my second drunk driving arrest—simply having decided I never went to the bar for some unfathomable reason.

Strolling to my car minutes later, I watched with envy as my coworkers casually meandered across the parking lot to the adjacent pub, laughing and flicking cigarette ashes into the misty night air. A powerful craving and deep longing twisted my stomach into a tense knot. Despite our age difference, I was unable to squash the overpowering desire to connect in that special way—*over cocktails.* The opportunities for depth and soul-baring just seemed impossible otherwise; I was destined to remain at a surface level, controlling my little prompter joy-stick—but nothing else.

The notion of missing out dominated my thoughts over the next several weeks. Bitter and resentful, I couldn't stop cursing the hand I'd been dealt. Why couldn't I just drink and party like normal people? Combing through the recesses of my mind and years past, I searched for situations where I'd enjoyed alcohol, times when a night on the town provided positive memories. My thoughts lodged on any fleeting euphoria I had sometimes grazed before descending into the abyss, but I found little to work with.

Why had I gotten sober in the first place? The once-powerful reasons were eroding; the harrowing year of 1999 marked by two awful DWI arrests had receded into the backdrop like a Key West sunset—awe-inspiring and unforgettable, but gone in minutes. As the crisis faded into obscurity, discontent grew, and my mind swung erratically between desires. Should I continue to build the sober time clock? Or squander it all for just one more night spent under a bottomless tap?

By February of 2001, a major milestone loomed ahead—eighteen months of sobriety. But I had no idea that relapse was right at the door. Looking back, there must have been abundant WRONG WAY—EXIT—DEAD END signs plotting the course, because my mind had been sliding back into the pit of addiction for months. Constant rationalizing became my eventual downfall—along with the overwhelming delusion that sober time had miraculously morphed my once dysfunctional brain into something capable of moderation. Convinced that my dry run would pay dividends, I honestly believed I'd learned to enjoy a beer or two without unpleasant consequences. Mom even agreed.

"I just want a couple," I whined to her one day. "Not to get wasted. Just on a special occasion or whatever."

"That seems reasonable," Mom agreed.

The weekend after that conversation, another DJ show awaited, this time at Black Woods restaurant in Proctor. I prayed I'd be spared the humiliation of facing acquaintances from high school, perhaps out on the town swilling a few beers and giving me the side-eye while I schlepped DJ equipment like a loser.

My setup was nicely organized—I'd hauled everything inside earlier when the place was dead, then returned hours later, dressed up with an hour to kill.

Go have a beer. I'd already noticed the attractive bar down the hall as I unloaded the equipment. *Just one to kill time.* A switch flipped in my brain, and the idea of sipping a drink turned plausible and rational. My new, responsible self enjoyed a beverage, left a tip, and returned to the DJ booth—no shots, no slurring, no stranger's phone numbers solicited. *I can moderate now.* All that sober time had fortified and insulated me somehow, a healing forbearance period working to morph me into the social drinker I'd always wanted to be. And with that, I threw away a year and a half of sobriety.

The bar was golden, glossy, and attractive, making it effortless to masquerade as a normal patron who'd stopped by for a casual cocktail. The bartender smiled and pushed a napkin my way, oblivious to my history.

"What'll it be? We've got Doc Otis lemonade and Coors Light on special."

"Ummm . . ."

I leaned forward, cupped my elbows, and squinted at the

tap selection. My usual masterful regime was careful study of the selections in a chameleon-like fashion, hoping to convince my server I had no history with alcohol.

"I'll just take any light beer on tap, please. Large, I guess."

A simple, harmless brew, the kind enjoyed after a hard day, a finished project, or a long session of cutting grass.

One beer became two, the second one making the tasty-looking featured hard lemonades seem like an awfully good idea. My body was flooded with feeling, electricity, and buzz. *This is awesome.*

Back at my DJ post, the show was out of focus—more booze my only pitiful wish. After popping in "Land of 1,000 Dances," people piled onto the floor, earning me another drink. No one would question a rum and Coke, coyly stirred with a colorful swizzle stick. People wanted the DJ to have fun, after all. *You have to drive home*, a little voice whispered. I ignored it.

Continued drinking would've been on the menu, but a killer headache intervened before last call. Crestfallen, I packed up my DJ stuff sloppily and stuffed it into the hatchback. The vista of the Zenith city glimmered just below the slope of I-35. Next stop, West Duluth. It was barely a mile to the Cody Street exit, so I drove home only half-drunk. But like a bad penny, the old me was back, and the devil had slipped in unnoticed.

The following weekend my uncle remarried. A couple of years earlier, his twenty-five-year marriage had abruptly ended, but his good looks and raucous personality ensured he wouldn't stay single very long. He hired me as DJ for the reception, and I enthusiastically agreed—looking forward to a big drunk fest.

The wedding reception was a blowout spent blasting my favorite songs at full volume and getting blisteringly ripped on free rum. Wasn't everyone else wasted, too? The guests were busy socializing and didn't seem to notice my condition—although my uncle asked me to turn down the earsplitting music several times. After closing down the banquet hall, I stumbled out to my car and drove home, abandoning the DJ gear since I wasn't functional enough to tear everything down. The following morning brought an agonizing hangover and walk of shame back to the reception hall for my equipment. Just a week into my social drinking experiment and I was back on the highway to hell.

20

I never dreamed I'd find love in a tiny redneck town like Pine City. By March of 2001, I'd been back with booze for a couple of weeks and was drinking excessively all weekend during DJ gigs. One Friday night, I prepared to head ninety miles south to host a community college winter dance.

My road trip required several glass bottles of what had once been Tropicana orange juice, now filled with peach mango wine coolers. *This won't get me drunk enough to be over the legal limit, I'll just get a little head start on everyone else.* My supply remained untouched until I neared the venue, and I'd calculated everything to ensure the amount of alcohol in my system would be within legal limits. *Wine coolers.* Hardly even qualified as booze.

Pine City was home to only about three thousand people, but the community college enrolled twice as many from neighboring towns. Single college men joining the event would've been a nice bonus, though I didn't have high hopes about running into anyone interesting.

The gig struggled to get going, and an hour passed before anyone wandered into the banquet room. A fresh playlist could take my place for a while, so I headed off to find a drink. The secluded setting was so perfectly sheltered I had no problem morphing into something else, and once again I began the process of pretending to be a responsible drinker.

A cozy little bar awaited at the end of a long, knotty pine hall. Just the perfect place to suck down a couple of drinks privately.

"Rum and Coke, please," I requested with a winning smile. "I've spent a lot of years bartending too, so mix me a good one."

Mixology smarts could create a meeting of the minds, and outrageous gratuity might offer stronger drinks and faster service. The barkeep seemed unimpressed, the rest of the scene was dull—with my comrades parked down row sipping Pabst Blue Ribbon silently with their snowmobile helmets. We huddled close, eyes locked with the TV above the bar, but no real connection existed.

The potent cocktails slipped down faster than beer, steadily disintegrating my anxiety. Making a mental note to use rum as medication more often, I drained my glass briskly before requesting one more for the trek back to the dancehall.

"Extra strong," I smiled, wetting my lips for the mediocre server becoming better looking with every drink.

Unaffected, he flicked his eyes to the back row of liquor.

"You want top shelf then? Double shot is $5.50."

"Not even a DJ discount?" I giggled coyly, aware that my schmoozing was going nowhere.

"Rail drinks are three bucks. Doubles $5.50. You won't find cheaper," he added resolutely.

Deflated, I threw a twenty-dollar bill toward him in hopes of repairing our allegiance for later.

"Just keep the rest."

Things had picked up in the banquet room, and as the rum settled into my blood, I prepared for the crowd. The flannel-sporting group was hungry for redneck drinking music or bro-country, and I was happy to oblige for a while.

Once I grew tired of the Southern-fried rock selections, I transitioned to my usual regime: *Melissa's Personal Playlist.* Customary as my buzz ramped up, a profane pop song could easily slip through unnoticed. Wondering where all those hot college boys might be, I stood and bopped my head to the beat of an explicit rap tune.

Suddenly I locked eyes with a guy across the room, smiling and singing every word to the raunchy number. Not what most women would call *gorgeous*—still, his magnetism drew me like a tractor-beam. Tall and lanky with wiry reddish hair, very long eyelashes, and a prominent nose, he somehow oozed charisma. A powerful craving swept through me.

Moving toward the bar, I paused at his table.

"So, you like this song?"

He nodded, his eyes flirty. "I do . . . but I think it's pretty strange to most of these rednecks."

"Tell me about it. I'm really over the Skynyrd requests. You'd think they could expand their horizons a little! 'Gimme

Back My Bullets.' That's one I can tolerate, but that's about it. They're all so overplayed."

Our conversation flowed easily and naturally. "I'm Rick," the guy offered. "I'm here visiting my brother Reid for his graduation from Pine Technical College." Leaning over like we shared a secret, this saucy guy was already up in my personal space. Just the way I liked it.

"Taxidermy major," he whispered, as though no one else would understand. "My bro is going to stuff varmints for a living!"

My effortless laugh was not forced for once, manifesting a carefree, mysterious girl, ripe with independence—a special phony veil I sometimes pulled off with strangers.

"Ah. Visiting the metropolis of Pine City," I responded lightly. "I don't live here, either. Where you from?"

Rick released a small groan. "South Dakota. Far west though, over by the Wyoming border. Is that as bad as saying you live in Fargo?"

I wouldn't have cared less if he was from the foothills of West Virginia or the seediest ghetto around.

"Who knows? I happen to love *Fargo*, even if it made a mockery of our accents. Duluth, my hometown, ain't much better, my friend. I'm from the Great White North, *don cha know!*"

Shrieking with silly laughter, sounding foolish wasn't a concern.

Rick erupted into a chuckle, nodding earnestly.

"I'm sure you get your fair share of crap. *Fargo* is classic, though! Totally on my top ten list of favorite movies. But you think the north is bad? At least you guys are *smart*. Imagine being from South Dakota! Farmers, corn, and tractors. Everyone assumes you're pursuing a career in farming . . . or maybe an auctioneer if you're especially gifted."

Smart. He thinks I'm smart. I filed this sweet little nugget away as we paused to take pulls from our beers.

"Reid's been going to school here for the last couple of years. I finally made it up north. First time in Minnesota."

My stomach plummeted. He didn't even live *here*, surely squashing any possibility of seeing him again. We'd only met ten minutes ago, but that hadn't stopped an instant attachment from forming.

"I better go check my lineup of songs," I finally managed.

My presence at the DJ post was pretty useless now, I'd already checked out for the night. As I adjusted par cans and party lights, my eyes settled on Rick, and I was delighted to find him staring right back. Soon, he motioned me over.

"Sit with us for a minute?" He pulled out a chair and pointed, as eager as a puppy begging to run around the block one more time.

The redneck funfest wasn't the killer party I'd hoped to make it. High time for an extended break.

Once another round of beer arrived, Rick turned with a little smile. Captivating with prisms from the mirror ball dancing on his face, he seemed poised to reveal a thrilling secret.

"Remember when I said I was from South Dakota? I am, but I'm moving."

Biding his time with a coy smile, my interest was off the charts.

"Really? Where?"

Words hanging suspended, my new friend made me squirm

for the answer to the million-dollar question. Finally, he finished his beer with a satisfied look.

"Rhinelander, Wisconsin. Why? Have you heard of it?"

"Of course! It's about three and a half hours away from me! *Plenty close to conduct a long-distance relationship.* My aunt lives in Green Bay. Ah, I know all about Sconnie. I lived in Superior for years," I rambled on. "Why the move?"

"Kind of a funny story, I started college for physics. You know how that is when you think you've got a solid major—and then all the math slams you in the face?"

I nodded in wholehearted agreement. "Math is my nemesis. Truly. My dad keeps telling me I'll use it someday, but I honestly believe it's a conspiracy. He says I might use it to figure price per unit at the store or something like that, but I doubt it."

With a laugh, it suddenly dawned on me that I was enjoying an authentic conversation without one shred of phoniness.

"Very little math needed in broadcast meteorology!" Rick concluded triumphantly. "I switched majors to that, and even though I've never been on television before, one of my professors convinced me I should be a weatherman. I'm taking a job in Rhinelander as a weekend meteorologist."

I gasped. "You're kidding! I switched to mass communications because of math, too! My life's dream was to be an astronaut, but I finally had to face my numerical limitations. I work at a television station . . . actually, in the production department right now, but I'm getting into reporting."

A little white lie I threw out on the spot. Being on TV was exciting, right? Perhaps Rick could overlook my still shrinking 150 pound body if I was an award-winning news reporter. Our commonalities made the chance meeting even more serendipitous. Although I was glad to have lost some weight in recent months, surely Rick (and most men for that matter), would prefer a thinner version of me.

"I'm in the running for a reporting position. It's pretty much in the bag."

Rick was equally shocked by our coincidences.

"Wow! It's almost as if we were *supposed* to meet tonight!"

21

I desperately tried to convince myself the situation had been ordained by God and wasn't an outcome I had concocted—the remainder of the night spent glued to Rick and abandoning the guests. Creating a party atmosphere was insignificant now; my payment check had been delivered. Time stood still as the beers flew, and how I'd get myself home wasn't on my radar. *I'm not that drunk.*

As the clock struck midnight, Rick approached the DJ table. "Would you care to dance?"

My heart flipped. "Yes. Hang on."

The moment I'd visualized for years was before me—a precious slice of destiny where I would sway to a gorgeous love song

MELISSA HURAY

with a mysterious stranger. "I'll Be" by Edwin McCain was the perfect soundtrack for this moment, and as Rick led me onto the dance floor, I was convinced the night had been written in God's book. As we moved across the floor, Rick held me like a priceless sweetheart he'd recovered after a painful absence, his breath warm on my cheek. Too soon, the song faded away, and bright lights jolted on. The most depressing time of the night was upon us: bar close.

Rick watched me begin the distasteful task of tearing down the equipment.

"You need a hand?"

I couldn't get over his perfection. *Quality.*

"You're even offering to help. I could get used to this." I flirted.

As we loaded everything into my car under the black March sky, hitting the highway seemed very unappealing.

Right on cue, Rick said, "You're not driving back tonight, are you?"

"Well, that was the plan," I shrugged as though I was the biggest free bird around. "Do I have other options?"

With a smile, he gestured to his brother, now making his way through the parking lot with some little blonde chick he'd been chasing all night.

"We're headed to Reid's for an after-party. Why don't you join us?"

My eyes gleamed, and in a heartbeat I decided to leave with someone I'd known for a couple of hours.

"I'll take you up on that. It's possible I've had one too many beers to make the trek up I-35."

Equipment loaded in record time, I followed Rick and Reid into the night as my body pumped with adrenaline.

Enthralled with the newness of each other, Rick and I talked for hours, but as the light of day colored the horizon—his mind shifted elsewhere. Stumbling up the stairs of Reid's duplex we collapsed onto his donated bed, laced together with drunken rapture.

Rick was convinced I would be fully willing to sleep with him, but I refused to ruin the potential of the evening by making that compromise. He was okay with waiting only after I broke into a drunken crying jag. Hours later, I woke up in his arms with a raging, head-splitting hangover, but I still felt dreamy.

"I have to get going," I said regretfully.

Rick jotted down his phone number after a lingering kiss goodbye.

"Call me later. Don't forget."

Riding high all the way to Duluth on a cloud of incredible euphoria—I was giddy, lovesick, and already convinced I'd found Mr. Right.

Obsession soon replaced my feelings of delight as the alcohol worked its way out of my system. *He probably doesn't really want me to call.* Now painfully hung over, gloomy, and riddled with doubt, I was certain Rick would be another barroom failure I'd never see again.

After collecting Hope from my parents' house, a mother-daughter day had been planned, but I was shamefully fixated on Rick. Unable to do anything about my state of mind, we went to the park and out to eat while I tried to reboot my thoughts.

Later that evening, Seth's mother called.

"Would Hope like to come to grandma's tonight?" she asked. "Jordan is here, and I thought we could do something fun." Jordan was Seth's brother's son, who lived in the Twin

Cities with his mother. Divorced parenthood provided tons of freedom to drink. Once Hope was squared away in Superior, I savored the building excitement.

The phone rang. "Hey beautiful," a voice drawled.

"Rick! I thought you wouldn't be calling until you got to Rhinelander!"

"Rumor has it I'm still in Minnesota," he chuckled. "Reid talked me into staying another night. Seems I get to extend my little northern vacation."

My panic disappeared as meeting again became a possibility.

"You haven't left yet? What do you have planned for tonight?" *Tone it down.*

Rick paused, and I heard the din of a party in the background.

"We've got a few people getting together. You wanna swing down?"

Swing down? Pine City was ninety miles away. My frantic need to see him made apathy very difficult, but I was trying.

"That might be an idea. My plans for tonight fell through at the last minute."

"It works out then. The more the merrier, right? I don't even know half the people over here," Rick laughed.

After we hung up, I wasted no time gulping a bottle of hard lemonade, then poured a few more into a discarded fountain soda cup for the road.

Ninety minutes later I arrived at Reid's door, where I spent the night opening my soul to Rick. More booze, more transparency. As the party dwindled, I decided to lay my cards on the table.

"Rick, I need to let you know—I have a seven-year-old daughter."

He smiled. "That's cool. I love kids."

"You do?"

I'd really like to find a full-time father figure for her.

"We always had lots of little ones around while I was growing up. Her dad still around?"

"Yeah. Seth. He's a good guy." I clamped my mouth shut in an effort to gauge my words carefully.

"What happened with the two of you?"

While inspecting Reid's CD cabinet, I contemplated how to spin the real answer to shield my psychotic mission of trapping my former husband into a commitment he didn't want to make.

"We never should have married," I finally managed. "The pregnancy was unexpected and hard. We love Hope so much . . . just couldn't handle the stress of marrying so young, I guess."

"It sounds like you're a good mom," Rick smiled. "Me, I've had bad luck with women. I'm what they call *damaged goods*."

Though I found his response very disturbing, Rick's carefree laughter showed the title did not bother him in the least.

"That can't be true!" I argued. "You're a great guy. You even helped me load up the equipment. Most people just turn a blind eye to their pathetic female DJ."

Rick's expression was troubled now, and he didn't seem to hear my heaping praise. "I've never been even *close* to marriage. Isn't that weird? Never even had a serious relationship, and I'm practically crowding thirty. Reid is the same."

Another unsettling red flag I chose to ignore. Rick was a lone wolf, and I was needy.

Heading home the next morning unearthed a well of emptiness before I was scarcely ten miles out of town. Rick was bound for South Dakota where he'd spend the week packing. Though he promised to contact me once he was settled at his new home in Wisconsin, my deep insecurity suggested that was a long shot.

Ten days of doubt and despondency passed until finally I heard Rick's voice once again.

"Well, I made it to Rhinelander. When you coming to see my new place?"

Squealing with glee, I made immediate plans for a weekend road trip.

The first rendezvous was flawless. A real date awaited: Rick brought me bowling with work friends from the news station and heaped on adoring compliments in spite of my pitiful skills. After a disappointing pair of gutter balls, I managed to knock down three pins.

"Woo hoo!" I yelled, slapping Rick's hand. "I just needed to get into my groove!"

Back at the table, I slammed the rest of my beer and topped off the glass. Taps were awesome—someone was forever replacing the empty pitchers, and it was next to impossible for anyone to estimate my consumption. The bowling game provided yet another distraction, and before long shot girls approached the table. Given my solid buzz, even the little hotties couldn't spark my insecurity. Smiling with confidence, I plucked a Jag shooter from the tray while a tall willowy reporter with straight flaxen hair nodded in my direction. Her gaze was somewhat cool.

"So, Melissa. Rick tells us you do some reporting in Duluth?"

Normally I would have been intimidated by such a beauty, but the Jag and beer provided heaps of chemical confidence. Rick was here with *me*, wasn't he?

"That's right. Actually, I started out in the production department, but after a while, the news director wanted me on air! He'd heard about me I guess . . . he was like, 'YOU. I want *you* on air.' He just sought me out! You know how that goes."

As she chewed on my little nuggets of half-truth, I stepped outside my body: a smooth, sexy stranger. Ivy had no clue the story I'd just relayed was only partially true. My actual rate of pay was six dollars an hour, I was not on the air yet, and the news director barely knew my name.

Magical thinking ruled when I was drunk, however, making anything that fell from my mouth poised to burst forth like a promise straight from heaven. Rick appeared and slung his arm across my shoulders.

"Mel is pretty amazing."

Beaming and flooded with warmth, I gobbled up every word that fell from his lips.

The rest of the weekend was spent lounging at Rick's apartment listening to music, drinking unlimited beers, and flipping through old photo albums.

"See this one?" Rick pointed to a snapshot of a busty blonde. "See her boobs? *Fake.*"

I chuckled bitterly, although he didn't notice.

"You've got quite a showcase of chicks here," I managed, struggling mightily to act flippant.

Inside, I was dying with envy. No way could I compete with such gorgeous women, the glamorous reporters and shot girls of the world; not when I was sober, anyway. Studying the images of Rick's perfect, model-like exploits from the past made me feel horribly inferior and wild with jealousy.

Soon it became clear that Rick wasn't interested in knowing me on a deeper level. The glory days were his focus—drunken trips with college buddies, escapades with strippers, brushes with fame that came through his mediocre TV gig—never anything relevant or real. As long as I remained a captive audience, I was a welcomed pal and drinking buddy—nothing more.

Rick's refrigerator held an impressive supply of various micro-brews though, so drinking temporarily muted the disturbing feelings rising within. *It's never going to work out. You're not his type.*

Mornings after with Rick were panic-filled. My eyes fluttered open and I focused on the ceiling and Rick's rhythmic breathing beside me. I had to pee. Thank God I hadn't wet the bed. My mind rambled with disjointed thoughts as I quietly crept to the bathroom to relieve myself. Then, I stepped onto the scale of course, because it was there. I'd climb onto any available one if the conditions were right, then paste an assumption about myself and my worth to the number that appeared. 150 flat. Fake dehydration weight.

My face was pale and pasty in the mirror. Clutching the sides of the porcelain sink, fear flooded me as I realized I remembered very little about the previous night. We'd left the apartment around ten to hit the downtown Rhinelander bars, but everything afterwards was a completely blank slate. *Was I cool with Rick? Had I embarrassed myself? What had I done?* Somehow I knew we'd danced, and I'd carelessly left my purse at an empty table while we were out on the floor. The handbag was in the corner of the bedroom now, offering some reassurance through my ability to keep track of it. The sight of it sitting there couldn't plug the other empty holes, though, and panic grew as we got ready and headed out for food.

"I'm starving!" Rick exclaimed once we were seated at a nearby diner looking over sticky menus. "I feel like I haven't eaten in weeks."

I was quiet and depressed. The one thing sustaining me was the promise of more drinking waiting just a few hours away. Alcohol would pacify my feelings and extinguish the scorching shame bubbling within. Rick sipped his water and studied me, finally realizing I was not okay.

"Is something wrong?"

I shrugged and gazed out the window with the urge to cry building at a furious pace. I couldn't lose it in front of Rick; he'd think I was crazy. I swallowed the lump in my throat and tried to sound nonchalant.

"It's nothing. I was just wondering if you think I drink more than your other friends."

Rick was bewildered. "Why would you ask that? I think you're fine. You're just having a good time."

I relaxed and ate my buffalo chicken sandwich. Everything was okay. I didn't have a problem. My blackouts were of no concern.

Rick and I continued meeting up just about every weekend for the next few months. In early April, he planned another visit to Pine City—a much shorter drive than the long haul to Rhinelander. As an afterthought, he invited me to his brother's place, the brother I was beginning to resent. My plan had been for Rick to come to *my* house that weekend. Where he spent his time was becoming a power struggle.

Yet again, the gathering at Reid's was clogged with strangers, superficial talk, and mindless activities like darts and drinking games. Although Rick greeted me warmly at the door with a kiss when I arrived, he quickly disappeared. Later, in the wee hours of the morning, I was ready for bed, but he wasn't interested in joining me.

"No, I want to stay up a while. The party's still going. You go ahead."

"Come on," I practically begged. "Please? I haven't even talked to you all night."

"Good Lord, Mel, I hardly ever see my brother. Can't you understand that?"

I turned and stumbled up the stairs. *You hardly ever see me.* Now I was begging for scraps.

Morning dawned with a typical hangover and an empty and ravenous feeling from rejecting food for the past two days. Infatuation was definitely the best diet around. I crawled off Reid's bed, trying to gather my wits. Rick was gone, if he'd ever been there at all. Descending the stairs carefully, I located a few stragglers from last night's gang crowded around the TV and absorbed in a golf tournament. I cleared my throat nervously.

"I need to get going . . . "

Watching Rick carefully and waiting for a reaction, I stood in silence until he reluctantly rose from the couch and followed me outside. Feeling the heavy distance between us, tears pricked my eyes as I accepted his lackluster attempt at goodbye.

"Thanks for coming down," he fumbled, seeming to stare a hole through the sidewalk. "And sorry about the whole thing last night. Reid's leaving town and going back to South Dakota in a couple of months—I've told you that. I'm just trying to spend as much time with him as I can."

Feeling foolish and selfish for coming between Rick and his brother, I struggled to explain away how I'd acted, hoping to convince Rick I wasn't an unstable stalker.

"I understand. Really, I get it." Hoping to muster a carefree smile, I reached over and patted his shoulder. "I was just getting upset over nothing. Sorry, I do that sometimes."

Even as I parroted the empty words, the powerful need to capture him that night took over, and "What do you have going on later?" tumbled out of my mouth.

Rick stuffed his hands into his pockets and continued getting to know the ground on a deep level.

"I don't know. We're gonna watch the golf tourney . . . go golfing later, but that's about all."

Golf, golf, and more golf.

His thin attempt to be vague wasn't lost on me; it was exactly how I operated with guys I wanted to blow off. Another party was brewing that night for sure, so I just stood silently. Waiting. He obviously *didn't want me* back, but my dysfunctional obsession had reached such an uncontrollable level that existing without him was unfathomable. The wounds of abandonment were always right below the surface when I felt Mr. Right Now slipping away.

"Do you mind if I come back later tonight?"

The look on Rick's face was worth a thousand words.

"Uh, sure, I guess . . . "

It was better than nothing.

22

I pumped gas at the Little Store and wallowed in my frantic need to flood myself with Rick. After much mental ping pong, I couldn't resist another trip to Pine City—even though tomorrow was a special day. History screamed my terrible follow-through for any important event, most notably anything religious or church-related. Hope was spending the night with my parents; my fibs about DJ shows were so expected now that they went unchallenged. I wasn't really working, I was merging back onto the freeway heading south with a bad feeling brewing inside. Somehow I knew I was about to ruin Easter Sunday in more ways than one.

I made it to Reid's apartment an hour and a half later, but

the infamous brothers were gone.

"Have you guys seen Rick?" I asked the group of strangers sitting around drinking beer. Reid's apartment was basically the community crashing place with various party people letting themselves in anytime they wanted.

"They're up in Hinckley, I guess. They should be back soon," someone offered, referring to a town about twenty miles north. Feeling rejected, I sipped a beer and wondered how long I should hang out before I started looking pathetic. The phone rang, and someone handed it over.

"We're up at Tamara's," Rick said. "Remember her from the dance? She's dating my brother now. You can come over if you want."

Though his invitation was simply a charity offering, I wasted no time putting my dumb arse back into my car and heading north.

Twenty minutes later I hit Hinckley, and easily found Tamara's trailer slightly off the main drag. I hated the girl right away—her high, shrill laugh and abrasive personality screamed we had zero in common, including the dart game the trio was absorbed in when I arrived.

Tammy did plenty of things to reinforce why she sucked, starting with snarky comments about my appearance.

"Everyone up here in Minnesota is a tow head," Rick observed.

Tammy glanced at me with a smirk. "But you're not a *natural* blonde, right? I mean, you have black roots."

"Uh, yeah, it's called 'Minnesota Ash,' maybe you've heard of it?" I shot back.

"She has no people skills, no tact," I hissed to Rick when Tammy was out of earshot.

Left to my own devices most of the night, Rick forgot I

existed while his brother and Tammy put on some serious PDA. After a few hours of drinking and loud Snoop Dogg ("Gin and Juice") drowning out my discontent, the lovebirds escaped upstairs. Rick was completely hammered, but it was my moment.

"Rick, there's something I need to ask you."

I perched on the edge of the couch and stared deep into his eyes. Steeling myself with a deep breath, I let loose.

"Here it goes. Do you consider me your girlfriend?"

Posing this question made me extremely vulnerable, but I *had* to know.

Rick sighed deeply, his intoxicated eyes mere slits.

"No, Mel, I don't. You're not my girlfriend. You're just . . . not."

He retreated into the bathroom as I blinked back tears, fully convinced the world was ending.

I was stuck. I was drunk. In no shape to drive, my only option was to crash at Tammy's unless I wanted to chance a third DWI. Why had I wasted all this time on Rick when our "relationship" was clearly a complete joke?

"I'm going to bed," Rick mumbled when he reappeared. With building hysteria, I followed like a well-trained puppy.

"Can't we just talk about this? I don't *have* to be your girlfriend, but if I'm not, then *what are we?*"

I was ready to bargain for scraps without shame and prepared to stay up until dawn fleshing out the barriers in our "relationship," but Rick was done talking. Shaking his head, he collapsed onto the bed as I curled up beside him and continued rambling.

"I'm sorry if I've been pushing you for a commitment. I can

back off. Just tell me what you want."

His only response was deep, heavy breathing. Rick was out cold, leaving me to cry myself to sleep in the strange house.

Day broke, and I awakened with overpowering dread, alcohol withdrawal, and panic. My heart raced as I lay in the early light, swallowing repeatedly. I was terrified about having a full-blown attack in front of Rick, so I scrambled off the bed to search for my shoes.

He stirred, watched me for a minute, then closed his eyes.

Easter Sunday morning arrived, but instead of praising the risen Lord, I was fighting the compulsion to shake Rick awake to demand an explanation with every ounce of remaining strength. Slipping out the front door, I ran smack into Tamara, dressed in church attire and watering her flowers. Just hours before, she'd been drinking and playing darts, convincing me she was just a lush like the rest of us. Her bright and fresh appearance was shocking. Looking up from the flower bed, she smiled like we were old buddies.

Maybe she wasn't so bad?

"Where's Rick?"

"In the house," I choked, turning and running to my car. As soon as I peeled away, my tears came flooding. Once the horror of Hinckley had receded in the rearview mirror, I pulled into a convenience store for a 32 ounce bottle of Mountain Dew and two packs of Excedrin tablets to ease my debilitating headache.

Still a mess as I reached Duluth, I dragged myself into K-Mart for a pathetic premade five-dollar Easter basket wrapped in cellophane and filled with fun-sized candy and small stuffed animals that looked like they came from the claw machine at the tavern. The plan had been to arrive at my parents' by ten and then head out with everyone for church and Easter brunch, but the entire idea seemed impossible now.

Slowly turning into Mom and Dad's driveway, I tried to appear normal. The headache had subsided just slightly, but my hollow eyes still reflected over an hour of full-body sobbing. After hugging my daughter, I handed her the miserable Easter gift while trying to hide my tearstained face.

"Mom, what's wrong?" she asked right away.

"Nothing, honey," I insisted, through a phony smile that spoke volumes. "I got some bad news and need to talk to Grandma."

After escaping to Mom's bedroom, I word vomited what had happened in a tirade of irrational emotion and then collapsed on the bed crying. Though she tried to shift my thinking to a more pragmatic place, the devil had my mind in a death grip.

"You stay here then," she finally conceded, aware that reasoning with me was a losing battle. "We'll take Hope with us."

My daughter went out with my parents to celebrate Easter, and I spent the day dozing on Mom's bed and weeping. The significance of the holiday was lost, even though it had always been mostly cultural for my parents. The intensity of my hangover blew everything out of proportion as I huddled in bed, crying and blowing my nose constantly, assembling a landmine of snot rags. Why did I always have the most tremendous and devastating alcohol binges just before Christmas and Easter?

Hope and I left later when my withdrawal and overpowering hopelessness had eased slightly.

"Okay if we have something easy to cook tonight?" I asked as we were driving home. "Maybe pizza?"

"Sure," Hope agreed.

We stopped off at a convenience store near our apartment and grabbed a frozen pizza and some chocolate milk, and as I paid the cashier I sensed a slim shred of responsibility emerging. *I am making dinner.* Yes, it was just pizza, but it was *something.* I decided I wasn't going to die after all.

The rest of the week was spent recovering from Rick, but each day the pain faded a little. Friday night provided an opportunity to hit the bars and I resumed my old routine of getting dressed up, trying not to act desperate, and implementing enough controls to prevent a crippling blackout, which never worked.

The night was uneventful, and I stumbled home at bar close with my only known substitute for male attention: donuts, chips, and microwavable crap from the convenience store. The phone rang while I was burning my fingers trying to extract a Hot Pocket from its cardboard sleeve.

"Mel, it's me," Rick said. "Will you give me another chance?"

The pain of the previous weekend vanished as I accepted his apology as a sign from the God I didn't know or pursue. Rick was short on reasons and explanations—but I just chalked it all up to drunken misguidedness.

Two months later, turning a blind eye to his continuous callousness was becoming too much even for a needy woman like me. With only sporadic trips to Duluth, his weekends were consumed by golf excursions and visits to see college buddies in Sioux Falls, Madison, Chicago, and Milwaukee.

Then came the last straw—the email detailing Rick's extensive social calendar for the coming summer. None of his plans included me, and it was almost like he expected a big atta-boy about all the fun he had planned.

Another illuminating moment of clarity where I tapped into the real me, the woman I knew I could be. I had not taught Rick how to treat me, or demanded the respect I deserved. As a result, I was left sucking up his sorry scraps.

Hammering out a matter-of-fact response in anger, I'd reached my breaking point. *This isn't working for me. If you can't commit to a relationship, I am going to move on.* Days later, I received Rick's return message indicating there was no forward path for the two of us. I had the truth, and it felt strangely liberating.

23

What now? Where should I direct my aimless, restless, searching self? At least something positive grew from yet another deadbeat showing his true colors: my buried reporting dream came to life. While pondering the lie I'd spouted about *already* being a news journalist, I huddled in the tiny teleprompter booth upstairs in the engineering department. My post offered a bird's-eye view of the news anchors and reporters preparing to go on set, and suddenly joining them didn't seem beyond the realm of possibility.

"Jared, do you think I could get on-air?" I asked my comrade on the sound board.

"Why would you want to? Then you'd have to actually *talk* to those d-bags. I would much rather be up here."

Ignoring his comments, I knew I had no chance unless I could somehow put together a resume tape. Later that night, I fished some discarded scripts from the recycling bin and brought them home to read to the rent-to-own camcorder I'd been pouring money into for months but would never actually *own*.

A few days later, I charged into the news director's office.

"Ray? I've been practicing. Reading the news. Do you have time to take a look?"

"I'm always open to fresh faces," he smiled. "You could also tag along on some shoots with other photographers and reporters in the newsroom if you'd like to put a real resume together," he added.

"*Really?* That would be awesome!"

A stocky, dark-haired guy wearing a blue hoodie and carpenter jeans hovered just outside Ray's doorway filing edit tapes and overheard my conversation. I had seen him around and somehow knew his name was Dennis, but we'd never spoken.

"You want to be a reporter, huh?"

Beaming and grateful for the opening, I joined him in alphabetizing the stacks of eight-millimeter show recordings.

"I really want to try shooting some stuff. Get a feel for it all—you guys make it look so easy. I know it's probably harder than it looks, but think I could be good at it," I added with an embarrassed chuckle. "Can I tag along sometime with you?"

"Not a problem. Anytime. Let me warn you though, once you find out how TV *really* happens, it wrecks everything—you just never see it the same again."

"I get how that might be," I agreed. "I remember watching the Miss America pageant with my mom one time—this contestant was walking down the stairs for the evening gown competition and tripped on the hem of her dress. I yelled at the top of my voice, '*OH DEAR GOD SHE FELL!*' My parents laughed about that for years, I was so shocked, it was like it damaged me for life."

Dennis howled with laughter. "Oh yeah. That's live TV for ya! You should've seen the time that Nancy Amos from Channel 12 was interviewing the mayor and she got a nosebleed on-air and didn't know it. Man, it was so painful to watch."

As Dennis turned to pack his equipment bag for the day, I stood struck by his easygoing nature, and realized I'd just made my first contact outside the safety of the production department.

"I gotta run," he said when he'd finished. "Let me know when you want to go out. I'm always around."

Winking mysteriously, he trotted off with the dayside reporter to shoot a story on the wastewater treatment plant.

Brainstorming news stories for hours produced some great ideas and tentative scrawled-out scripts. I was ready to track Dennis down the following morning.

He seemed delighted to see me. "Hey! You been working on your big break?"

Nodding, I waved the stack of scripts. "Here's my blood, sweat, and tears. Could we shoot today? I want to get a resume tape to Ray."

"Sure," he agreed.

After the truck was loaded, we ventured out to various locations and messed around with different mock stand-ups and live shots. Back at the station, Dennis regarded me with admiration.

"You sure you've never done this before?"

"Are you kidding? I thought I sucked."

"No way," he laughed. "You've got as good a chance as anyone."

Bonds quickly formed as opportunities to interact with the team popped up. The new contacts were great, but I still was most comfortable with my old reliable friends in the production department.

"Curt's leaving," Dennis mentioned one Friday afternoon.

"Seriously?"

Curt had reliably worked his beats on the city council and school board for a solid five years and seemed to be a fixture at KDLH.

Dennis nodded. "He's leaving for Tampa Bay next month."

Maybe this was my chance.

With the fruits of my labor edited and dubbed to a tape, I delivered it to Ray—praying I would be the next new face at KDLH-TV.

24

Ray didn't pick me, and I was infuriated. Devastated was a more appropriate word, considering my entire future hope rode on his decision.

Joshua Crane was his selection, a relative novice who'd slipped up and said *areola* borealis (as in nipple) on the air, rather than aurora. Ray passed me up for the coveted open spot to hire some unknown guy with only public access experience.

Seething behind my floor camera that Saturday night, I shot daggers at Joshua's stupid bobbing head. Though I was discouraged, I begrudgingly got to know him and continued mastering the newsroom.

Fraternizing with the talent helped. After hours, members

of the news, sales, engineering, and production departments were on equal ground—mingling at the local tavern across from the station's upper garage where it didn't matter if you were on-air or not. One Friday evening, after the late show ended, the newsroom door swung open and Dennis burst in with a few others trailing behind.

"Mel! Great, you're still here. Want to come over to the Garden with us? We're celebrating Andy's new gig."

Andy was a part-time photographer who had just landed a new position in Green Bay. I didn't waste any time following the crew across the parking lot to their favorite hangout.

The Garden Tavern was a stylish and trendy bar, far removed from the dumps I preferred near my house. The largest tap beer in the house put me at ease as I chatted with a few production friends. The anchors and reporters who had also joined the party crowded in a tight circle at the bar, but our two groups remained somewhat divided. I was grateful that Dennis stuck right by my side; he was like a bridge from production to talent, and offered a little street cred.

The party scene dwindled down around ten, and someone suggested moving to another bar. My car—and how I'd get it home—weren't pressing concerns as I hitched a ride with Dennis to a popular college hangout across the bridge in Superior.

Norm's Place was right up my alley—frat boy energy, loud classic rock blaring from the jukebox, and cheap drinks. Folding in with the gregarious crowd of twenty-somethings was effort-less. Dennis ordered a couple of beers and squeezed in next to me at the bar.

"You still think you want to get into news?"

"I really do. Any chance someone else will leave soon? You

got the inside scoop there, brother?" I punched him lightly on the arm, I was starting to loosen up and feel the alcohol.

Dennis shrugged with a hint of embarrassment and aware-ness of our bodies jammed together in a public place outside of work. "You never know. The turnover in that place is phenom-enal. I bet you'll get your chance."

Me, on TV. The idea was unreal.

Dennis made sure my beer never ran dry, and soon I was thrilled to learn my new friend was also a fan of Jägermeister, making us kindred spirits in a hurry. A couple of shooters were in order.

After downing his shot with a grin and a wince, he gestured across the room.

"You want to play the jukebox? My favorites are 'Love in an Elevator' and 'Fat Bottomed Girls.' I'm not a dancer, so that's about all that's left to do here." He shrugged with a grin.

Now he was speaking my language. Tunes and Jag, what could be better?

"I love Queen!"

We jostled through bodies and across the crowded floor to the little alcove where the jukebox was tucked. Dennis slipped his arm around my shoulder as I leaned forward to scan the selections. I didn't mind.

Panic flooded through my body as I came to in a strange place. Dark blue mini blinds, closet door ajar, hooded sweatshirts hanging. A simple desk below the window, Mötley Crüe poster pasted opposite the bed—much like a teenager's bedroom. I fixed my eyes on Nikki Sixx, mouth gaping open in a snarl, arms posed over his spiky black head as though he held the key to unlock my predicament. *Where am I? And where did I get these clothes?*

I pushed back the bed covers to reveal a large red T-shirt and black sweatpants. Struggling into a sitting position, I raked a hand through my hair. A familiar after-bar taste coated my mouth.

I spotted my shoes tucked beneath the desk chair with last night's dress folded neatly on top of them, suddenly filled with a sickening urge to flee. As I prepared to bolt from the bed, the door inched open, and Dennis stepped in.

"My roommates are still sleeping," he whispered, settling in about two inches from my face.

I smiled awkwardly and studied the sweatpants again—so intently I could see the weave of the fabric—speechless and confused. I scrambled for my last full memory: the jukebox. Everything following it was as vacant as a Monday morning church.

Dennis was now staring into my eyes with unbearable intensity.

"You comfy?" he laughed, playfully tugging a pant leg. "All you kept talking about last night was getting your dress off." My face flamed as he continued. "So, I found these sweats, which probably could hold two of you. You were so cute parading around the house in them. Loved your silly dances, too," he added with a twinkle in his eye as I shrank back in horror. "Don't worry, I was a total gentleman. I slept on the couch."

Now that the night was pieced together, I jumped out of bed, turned my back to Dennis, whipped off the evil borrowed clothes, and pulled my dress on with a mad tug. How did I get so drunk? How did I end up at Dennis's house? We barely knew each other. What had started so harmlessly as a casual beer with friends after work now thrust me into an extremely uncomfortable position. My mind ached to put the pieces together as I finished locating my belongings and moved expectantly to the door.

"I hate to make you bring me all the way back to my car, but I really need to get going."

Dennis offered a pleasant wave of dismissal. "No worries. I'm heading out of town today, so I have to hit the road, too."

He grabbed his keys as I followed outside, sensing somehow the conversation was just getting started. It was excruciating, this after-drinking-getting-to-know-you regime—a process I wanted to smother. Dennis hiked himself into the truck cab and turned to face me.

"I had a *great* time last night. You're so much fun, Mel. I've noticed you in production..." he paused to collect himself before going on. "I've wanted to ask you out many times." He looked into my eyes, endearingly, earnestly.

We had a mighty big problem on our hands. Dennis was clearly hoping our little encounter would be the start of something exclusive, but I couldn't wait to wipe all traces of it from both of our minds. Blindsided and unprepared, I struggled with small talk for the fifteen-minute drive to my car.

"See you around," was my breezy, no-strings-attached goodbye.

I hoped it was convincing.

25

The Dennis debacle was neatly filed away. I'd made amends
for my recklessness: the blackout, the *not remembering*—just
chalked it up to a going away party that got a tad too crazy.
Having escaped my coworkers before I got really wasted was
a blessing. Dennis wouldn't say anything, and really didn't
know me yet.

Back at the station, another reporter moved on and hundreds of resume tapes flooded in. Poring over them in an
empty conference room, I stacked my perceived limitations
and inferiorities against each candidate, each one seeming so
much more skilled, polished, and gorgeous than the last. Ray
posted the job opening, and after viewing the treasure trove of

all-star applicants, I begrudgingly applied for an internship to build some skills.

Ray happily welcomed my free labor in the newsroom, with work starting the third week of May 2001. The first real news story I was charged with writing featured a Duluth woman who made it from contestant's row to meet Bob Barker on *The Price is Right*. Likely it was a scrap no one else wanted, but I accepted the assignment greedily.

"Start the story off with a nat/sot," Annette, the anchor that night, instructed.

What the hell is a nat/sot? Afraid of looking stupid, I tracked Dennis down in the break room.

"Nat/sot stands for natural sound," he explained. That means you start with a quick pop of the sound on the tape, like the crowd cheering or something."

Racing back to the newsroom, my copy wrote itself: the finished lead punchy and triumphant: SHOWCASE SHOWDOWN FOR A DULUTH WOMAN WHO WON BIG ON *THE PRICE IS RIGHT*.

I proudly handed my script to Annette. "What do you think?"

Through glasses clinging to the bridge of her nose, Annette scanned it quickly. "Not bad."

Beaming, I hurried back to my borrowed desk.

Tuesday morning, I was late for the editorial meeting, slipping in exactly two minutes before I'd make a scene. Jostling my legal pad and important-looking fake leather folder, I tried to look organized and eager, distantly hoping I didn't smell like liquor. I'd downed nearly a twelve-pack the night before but managed to avoid the bars and hard stuff.

Ray nodded as I slid into place at the end of the table, trying not to breathe on anyone. The taste of stale alcohol was a persistent reminder of the night before *(all I had was beer!)* and though I'd brushed my teeth three times, last night's booze was very apparent by the alcohol fumes I was expelling. Scooting further into the corner, I panted shallowly, hand curved over my mouth as I crouched over my notebook in an attempt to look studious and engaged.

"Tess is going live from the Walk to End Violence, and Eric will be covering the shipping story about the Port Authority's new management," Annette announced, poised at the assignment board with dry-erase marker in clutch.

Ray paused and frowned. "We have a slight problem, though. Paul is sick today, so I need someone to go interview this guy who won an entrepreneurial award."

My pulse kicked into high gear as Ray caught my eye. "Mel, could you handle writing up a package on it? You could shoot a stand-up, too."

"Absolutely."

"Okay, I'll put you and Dennis together then." Annette wrote our names on the board in thick, deliberate block letters. MEL/DENNIS. INVENTOR PACKAGE.

I had won. No one knew I was sitting through that meeting in alcohol withdrawal. They saw me as a worthy journalist, a contributor, an important part of the team.

That night, I appeared on TV for the very first time.

My second scoop involved problem waste: renters who abandoned old furniture, mattresses, and garbage outside their properties. Racing around like a detective, I banged purposefully on doors and interviewed neighbors. I felt *so proud* saying, "Hi, I'm Melissa Ellefson from Channel 3 news. Can we ask you a few questions about your neighbor's garbage?"

I loved reporting, and although I was only an intern, I didn't tell anyone, and neither did Dennis.

Seeing myself on TV was even more captivating; there was no greater thrill beyond my very own face on the television screen. My daily stories sometimes ran on all three newscasts, and the recognition that followed provided the temporary validation I'd craved for years.

After exactly one month of interning, Ray summoned me to his office.

"You're catching on fast," he beamed. "Could you handle doing a live shot for the marathon this weekend?"

The marathon? Grandma's Marathon was Duluth's biggest annual event with thousands of runners converging on the city. Duluthians waited all year long for the big weekend, and tons of people would be watching the news coverage.

"Oh yes, that would be awesome!"

"Great. We'll need a package on the volunteers, then at six, you'll go live from the finish line. The race will be over, but the crowds will still be out."

Race day dawned *very* early. I'd vowed to avoid alcohol the night before and followed through with an early bedtime, up easily at dawn to ensure I could down a half pot of coffee.

Just before five, I met up with David, a newbie weekend photographer, and we drove to the starting line in Two Harbors. Spectators lined the course in the dreary predawn and the excitement was palpable. I'd scored a discarded fleece jacket some former employee had left behind from the coat closet—it featured the KDLH logo, and I wore it proudly with the patch facing out so everyone could see *I was on the news.*

David loaded me down with a tripod that seemed to weigh one hundred pounds, but I didn't care; it just made me more conspicuous. We meandered up and down the course for hours interviewing the volunteers who were handing out water and orange slices to the runners. Around noon, we arrived at the twenty-three-mile mark on London Road, the last major leg of the course.

"How's this for your stand-up?" David asked, scanning the location.

Nodding eagerly and fueled by the crowd, I jumped into action.

"Here at the grueling twenty-three-mile mark, many racers are desperately in need of some motivation. Luckily, the volunteers who donate their time year after year help them push through to the bitter end."

Six takes later I was satisfied.

A few more comments from spectators and we headed back to the station, where I hammered out a script to go with the video. David retreated to an edit bay while I shifted to obsession mode. In three hours, I'd be live on television for the first time, and I was terrified.

"Don't worry, you'll be fine," David assured me.

But nooo . . . Certain my big debut would be a huge disaster without a little chemical help, I needed a drink. *I can't do this sober.*

"I need to run home for a bit," I told David. "I forgot something. I'll be back by five."

Four Mike's Hard Lemonades disappeared down my throat, and my car seemed sucked to the Galley by some supernatural force on my return trip to the station. I gulped a beer in the recesses of the dimly lit lounge and spent a few minutes bragging about my upcoming television appearance. After tossing some change on the bar, I made it to Canal Park half-drunk.

The time before the live shot was hazy, but I was functional, overly cautious, and remembered everything later. Did David suspect anything? To be safe, I kept my distance a few feet away while I smoked.

Another reporter from a competing station stopped by while gathering interviews. Surely, he thought I was a joke intern—chubby, lacking journalistic sense, and certainly missing *the look*. He paused to chat with David for a minute before regarding me with disdain.

"I wouldn't be out here smoking in public. People are going to start recognizing you now," he said reproachfully.

Though I knew he wasn't offering a compliment, I still liked the thought of recognition.

I continued puffing away on the cigarette in defiance, then stubbed it out shortly before airtime. The evening air was stuffy and hot as I stood turned into the path of the setting sun. *No one can smell Mike's Hard Lemonade.* David insisted I face the west for lighting, but I was squinting way too much. Minutes ticked away like hours as I fanned myself with the scripts. I licked my teeth and swallowed.

David's hand was lifted overhead, prepared to cue me.

"Fifteen seconds." Bored, and not the least bit stressed, he dragged from a Marlboro while glancing around at all the pretty girls dressed up to hit the party tents. My heart raced with panic, and my head and chest tightened.

"Stand by." David's hand was still poised. I felt faint.

His finger swept down below the camera lens, but I stood rigidly as petrified rock. I swallowed, but no words came. David gestured frantically and mouthed, *"YOU'RE LIVE!"*

"Uh . . . uh . . . " I stammered. Every second felt like fifty years. Finally, I managed to croak out my lead line:

"We're here at the finish line of Grandma's Marathon, where thousands of runners completed the course earlier today. The race wouldn't happen without the efforts of dedicated volunteers. Here are some of their stories." My package rolled in my earpiece.

"We're clear!" David called.

I hurled the mic to the ground. "That was terrible!"

"It wasn't that bad for your first live shot," David smiled, patting my shoulder.

Ray is never going to hire me now. I just blew it.

We returned to the station, and I passed quickly through the upstairs engineering department. I was coming down from the buzz, getting a headache, and anxious to escape.

On Monday morning, Ray summoned me to his office. *Oh Lord, I'm in trouble. He knows.*

"Mel, I've talked to the general manager about my plans," he began after I was settled in the chair facing his desk. "I've seen you around the newsroom the past couple of months. You've worked hard. I want to give you a shot as a reporter."

Did he sleep through last Saturday's newscast?

"Wow! Oh, that's so great! You won't be sorry!"

My starting salary as a broadcast news professional was the grand sum of sixteen thousand dollars annually. It was an extremely liberating time where possibilities and the power to transform my life blazed into view. Never again was I drunk on the air, though hangovers and alcohol withdrawal punctuated many newscasts. So blessed to have been afforded the opportunity to perform my dream job, I vowed I'd never screw it up.

26

Mind reeling, I scrambled for coverage lies. Fumbling for the phone, I dialed the station and squeaked with a high and screechy "I just woke up" tone, "Hello, Annette? I'm having trouble with my car. Could I talk to Dennis?"

The well of self-worth would vanish if I lost the TV job. Working like a dog and being prompt helped to mute my indiscretions—never once did I reject a request for overtime or a plea to cover someone's shift. Being publicly visible and gaining validation from the world was necessary for survival, each comment of praise becoming a network of unreliable pixie sticks—soon unable to bear the weight of my growing need to be seen.

Dennis picked up the phone. "What's up?"

"Something's wrong with my car. I don't get it. I turn the key and nothing happens. Can you come and get me?"

Dennis knew my alcohol-related secrets by now, but I could trust him to cover. No doubt he wasn't fooled by my story but promised he was on his way.

Wrinkled khakis and a T-shirt would have to suffice—no time to shower. Whipping my hair into a ponytail, I paced the apartment wildly, sweeping beer cans from the kitchen table and frantically stuffing them into the garbage.

Was anything missing? Getting raped or murdered by a stranger I dragged home never concerned me—I only feared they'd take off with my stuff after I passed out.

Dennis honked outside. I clattered down the stairs, head dizzy and muddled, wondering if I reeked of last night's booze. I needed food, ASAP.

After climbing into the truck, my exhaustion was too great to do anything but slump against the window. Dennis looked over with concern as I willed myself not to throw up.

"I was out drinking last night. No surprise, right?"

My eyes welled with tears as we pulled onto the freeway toward downtown.

"I figured. What happened?"

Silent as I sobbed openly, Dennis had seen this song and dance countless times: the promises to quit, the brief respite when I seemed so much more balanced, and then the inevitable plunge back into the sewer.

"I don't know! I promise I'm going to stop, I really *mean* it, but thinking I'm missing out sucks me back in. Last night, Hope was with Seth, and I just couldn't stand the thought of what might be going on down at the bar without me."

Wiping my eyes fiercely, I struggled to shift gears from the impromptu therapy session with Dennis. Some grease would certainly help.

"Can you swing through McDonald's?"

He obeyed and circled the news truck through the drive-thru so I could get my remedy: two egg McMuffins, two hash browns, and a colossal orange drink.

"Mel, I am so worried about you. I want to help, but I don't know how," Dennis finally said, looking very troubled.

"Forget it. I'm a hopeless case."

I attacked my second egg McMuffin, feeling slightly better while lost in the rhythm of chewing and feeding myself. No matter the current level of devastation, nothing could quiet my appetite. My weight had dropped a bit while dating Rick but quickly inched back up to 160. Everyone knows the camera adds fifteen pounds. Surely viewers thought I was much too hefty to command a news desk.

Dennis covered me like a fishnet back at the station and helped make everything look kosher. We already had a series shoot set up that day, affording me the luxury of dozing in the truck between stops, drinking water, and nursing my hangover. Around noon, the previous night's poisoning wore off, and I was miserable. "*Hurtin' fer certain,*" Dad would've called it.

Trying to pinpoint the trigger was a waste of time. Nothing noteworthy had happened the day before—the shooting was smooth, things clicked along—I was on top of my game. Low stress, even—my main story was written and edited much earlier than usual.

Annette had breezed by on her way from the "glam," the brightly lit room where we primped for the show. We lacked fancy assistants and hairdressers, but still enjoyed our own special area with a sofa, bathroom, studio lighting, and plenty of room for prep.

"Mel, we want you to do a set piece at the desk tonight," Annette said in passing.

"Sounds good," I agreed, not yet processing her words. A "set piece" meant *live* conversation with the anchors from the desk, *without* a prompter.

Threading my mic up the front of my blazer an hour later, I gulped air to quiet my thudding heart while fixing my eyes on Jared, my old buddy from days past in the production department. Dying to return to that carefree time now, the sight of him in his baggy jeans and flip-flops was calming somehow, and I was grateful to see him hovering behind the camera, flashing a cocky wink and stage-whispering, *"Don't screw it up."*

The news opening thundered through the room. Annette shuffled her scripts, checked her teeth, and smoothed her hair while I sat frozen. Messing up and making her look stupid would be disastrous. Sitting mutely while she read the top stories into her camera, I waited for the toss.

"The mining industry got a huge shot in the arm from a government subsidy," Annette read. "Melissa Ellefson joins us now with details."

Watching the two of us at the desk through the disabled prompter screen, I smiled at my reflection as I had so many times before and slipped out of myself.

"That's right, Annette. The industry has struggled in recent years, but new hope is on the horizon. I spent the day on the Iron Range talking to legislators about what this means for the region."

My package rolled. Jared yelled, "Clear!"

Deeply triumphant at the flawless execution, I released the remainder of my pent-up anxiety in a long, slow, exhalation. Annette was pleased, too, and flashed an *atta-girl* wink as I crept off the set.

Victorious, the deal was sealed: *I am going to get drunk.* And the bender that kicked off with euphoria and anticipation ended with oversleeping for work, an excruciating hangover, and the need for Dennis to come to the rescue.

The drinking debacles just repeated themselves—starting with a solid day of news, praises for my writing and storytelling, and the feeling of conquest after proving my worth to the world. Once I'd contributed so richly to the flow of ideas that birthed television news, it was *my time.* Friday nights I was off the clock at six, with my prerecorded package running again later on. A brief stop by my apartment to slam three beers made up for lost time before heading off to the Galley.

My life was divided into neat thirds like a Tupperware serving plate designed to prevent the Jell-O from running into the peas: news professional, devoted mom, blackout bar fly. The useless barriers I tried to enforce seemed to provide inoculation from the evils of regular binge drinking.

The scene at the Galley was hit or miss—some nights only offering low action, vagrants sipping cheap taps, and the droning fans from the fryer—but what made the atmosphere so magnetic was its potential to flip on a dime. This Friday night was shaping up all right, I'd run into an old boyfriend and allowed him to shadow me like a lost puppy for an hour but was soon sidetracked by a group of guys shooting pool in the corner. A long, blond specimen bent over his stick, the neon above capping him with an angelic halo. After sinking his shot, he moved toward me, raking a hand through his streaky tresses.

"You look like a rock star," I slurred, as he took the stool next to me. "Sebastian Bach."

"You're that news chick, aren't you?" he grinned, with a flash of recognition. "I guess that makes *you* the celebrity."

I'd been *recognized*.

"Yep," I confirmed, with a sheepish shrug. "That's me."

"You look better in person," he drawled, moving in closer.

What a pick-up line. I was hiding my weight well and covering it with fake sex appeal. Tanning, teeth whitening strips, a French manicure, and dark lighting did the trick.

I drained the rest of my bottle. "Let's get out of here. You want to head over to Soup Town?"

With such an invitation, what guy could refuse?

"Let's roll."

A harmless beginning, but another wrecked state of mind and body awaited in just a few hours. Alcohol served as my rocket fuel for a while, but I couldn't effectively drink the next morning away.

My new friend and I must have hit the Superior bars, but the next day I couldn't remember much. Dawn broke, and Sebastian Bach was gone; last night's companion was just another fly-by-night, flavor-of-the-hour I'd never see again.

27

Since age fourteen, filling the hole my father's failures left behind and finding someone to hold captive had been my relentless quest. Daddy issues be damned, the habitual pattern of scouring the taverns for an exception to the traditional barfly persisted. The futile mission to cross paths with my soul mate at the neighborhood watering hole never waned. Each time the excitement built: the preparation, the initial adrenaline rush, the anticipation—but the same old outcome loomed. A drunken interaction, names forgotten, only snippets of the night before saved for the morning. Then the regret, guilt, and obsession would begin again.

The week began with a strong commitment to sobriety, but

the looming weekend brought intense cravings for one more spin on the merry-go-round. *You won't black out. You're going to have a good time, not look for a guy. You'll remember.*

Empty pledges and endless bargains to the God who was nothing more than a magic genie in the sky blew away like puffs of wind. Marathon blackout drinking binges always won—horrendous ordeals requiring days of recovery afterward. My panic attacks were full-blown Sunday through Tuesday; recovering from a bender was now a three-day minimum.

The Galley was a solid constant once I had recuperated—the crusty old watering hole a portal of brief escape void of long-term satisfaction, its no-frills offering a smelly room, beer, and whiskey-swilling lonely people. Just like the old supper club joint from childhood, my favorite place to hide out was like a significant other I didn't want to be seen with. Reeking of grease from the fryers cranking out an endless stream of deep-fried delights, it was a familiar disappointment, like the piles of pull tabs crowding every corner like stubborn snow drifts refusing to melt. The Galley's crusty walls offered a welcome escape from reality where I was at peace with what I'd become.

When my favorite barroom grew stale, four other nearby establishments offered a slightly different flavor of bar fly. My nightly circuit often included visits to the Rustic, Champs, and sometimes Mr. D's. Nothing new under the sun, same old players, same results every night, yet my search for a diamond within the walls of gloom continued.

Waking up was virtually impossible and felt like something I didn't deserve. Wednesday and Thursday nights kick-started the coming weekend with copious amounts of alcohol but were a shade less outrageous because work loomed in the morning.

Still, powering through blinding hangovers was exhausting, and by Friday night I was ready to throw caution to the wind.

The daily grind nearly killed me—my only saving grace the newscast's end and the seclusion of my apartment. Once safe from watchful eyes, my throat opened like a storm drain and fortified my soul with cheap beer and another night at the gates of hell.

Beer was my seemingly harmless fodder, but it kick-started the craving for hard liquor, attention, and risk-taking. The bar where everybody knew my name was an expert soul-sucker—its price tag forever climbing.

By the summer of 2001, the weeks rolled by like a merry-go-round of dizzying seasickness I couldn't wait to ride again. My life pivoted uselessly around a foundation of drinking binges and Galley visits. Shame and worthlessness grew through the knowing I should be bonding with Hope instead.

The Galley welcomed me and my excuses anytime; my fellow comrades also had important destinations *they* never reached. Grand stories and empty promises flooded the bar as life screamed by, kids grew older, and precious moments were blown. Comatose and oblivious, we sat anchored on our respective bar stools, waiting for something to happen.

My mediocre drinking trough offered a faux sense of belonging. The imbibers gathered nearby also didn't want to be lectured about unbalanced lives, so we commiserated well. We all had big plans, things to do, and people to see—but when closing time rolled around once again, we still occupied the same old bar stools, engaged in conversations I wouldn't remember.

Forever jam-packed with a plentiful supply of compliments to feed my sick ego, the Galley gang was a peaceful dealer of self-delusion. A carousel of possibilities: sometimes the painful scene featured only career drunks and lonely widows, but one night I hit the jackpot when an old boyfriend sauntered in.

Cameron and I had met a year earlier, but things never progressed beyond the bar stool. Oh sure, we'd talked vaguely of doing normal, *alcohol-free* activities—meeting for a jog, taking a martial arts class—but nothing materialized. Dry events made me very antsy.

My old flame was seated directly across the bar, head bent over his wallet as he counted out bills. Moving through the crowd until I was hovering behind him, I leaned over and placed my chin on his shoulder.

"Want to get out of here?"

With a surprised jump, Cameron half-smiled while I beamed with satisfaction at the impression I had made and summoned the bartender. Time to pour on the charm.

"I need to tell you something. I am sorry for the way I treated you. The way I stood you up."

Appearing unimpressed, he drained his beer. "More than once."

"You're absolutely right. I'm asking you to give me another chance. Please. I'm serious."

Noisy as a crowded amusement park, the bar didn't seem the proper place for a heartfelt conversation, but somehow my drunk mindset insisted I was fully capable of conveying sincerity. Cameron was quiet, staring off at a TV.

"One last chance."

My head swelled with triumph. "Let's do a shot. Hey, bartender. We need a couple Jag bombs down here."

The curtain closed and the blackout began. Whatever

happened after ten that night was memory unsaved.

Imprisoned in bed the next day, I was still drunk and now saddled with an excruciating, nauseating headache. My head surged and throbbed with any slight movement. Cameron was nowhere to be found.

How did I get home? I crawled out of bed and immediately collapsed to the floor, unable to hold my weight and twisted in a heap of pain. My ankle was sprained, a regular happening when I was stumbling around blacked out. Hobbling about the apartment searching for clues, I checked the door and was mildly relieved to find it deadbolted. *No one was here last night.* Cameron must have ditched me at the bar.

A big mess awaited in the kitchen from a run-in with the microwave and some macaroni and cheese, and an unfamiliar bag of corn chips was scattered across the top of the stove. Muddy tracks (mine) paraded a crazy path through the kitchen. Using my supreme sleuthing abilities, I deduced that I must have used the swampy trail in the woods leading from the gas station as a shortcut.

A dim recollection surfaced at the sight of the footprints. I was lying in the miry swamp, staring drunkenly up at the stars for what seemed like hours. No other memory was available, just the heavens peeking through the branches arching over my head. Unable to get up, I relented to the mud for unknown hours where no concept of time existed. Somehow, I made it from the nearby bog to my apartment.

A few years ago, we were up north in Superior visiting some family. I ran into an old Keyport coworker. "Did you hear about Jenny?" she asked. Jenny was a fellow bartender who apparently had died tragically and unexpectedly a short time before—she had left

*the bar on a subzero night, fallen into a culvert near a river where
her leg became trapped, and drowned.*

Instead of being terrified of a possible drowning in the
quagmire, I was wallowing in self-pity over Cameron. The
unexpected encounter, so glorious and satisfying in the moment,
was now a distant memory. How did all the talk of rekindling
our old flame vanish so suddenly?

I grabbed my cell phone impulsively and dialed his number
while packing the kitchen trash to the brim with discarded beer
and hard lemonade bottles. A pathological urge to transfer the
evidence to the outdoor garbage can overwhelmed me and my
heart pounded, momentarily drowning out the headache. I
feverishly hoped I'd be shuttled to voicemail, but he answered
on the third ring.

"Cam? It's Mel."

"Hey," he said slowly, with unmistakable hesitation. "I was
just getting ready to leave the house for a softball game."

"Oh, I see. I won't bother you then. I just thought I'd call
and say hi, because I wasn't sure if you had my number anymore," I gushed.

"I think I lost it. But I have it now. I better get going."

Dead silence.

Idiot! Maybe he had no recollection of our meeting, either.

"I'll let you go then. Have a good time at your game."

What a jerk-off! Didn't he want to make plans? What had I
done to ruin the new beginning?

I hobbled upstairs on my sprained ankle after garbage duty,
head screaming and throbbing from the exertion my wasted
body couldn't bear.

Bloodshot eyes and pasty skin greeted me from the mirror.

The stench of the bar permeated my hair and last night's clothes, and the exquisite pain of a massive headache flooded my brain until I was convinced it would explode. Lowering to crouch on the edge of the bathtub, I began to pray as sobs wracked me.

A flood of depression and remorse gushed in, drowning me in a cascade of shame. *Please God, please help me.*

28

Sticking with Dennis helped to normalize my drinking. He'd never rat me out. My best buddy and I cranked out some serious news products and offered any competing news team a run for the money. Canvassing the state for a range of stories stretching from forest fires to serial sex offenders, I shed my mask and let it all hang out. Dennis knew the real me, the authentic Melissa, and he liked what he saw. He was falling in love with the version of self I tried to hide.

We shared many beers, and Dennis always made sure that my blacked-out self made it home in one piece. Right around Christmas of 2001, I celebrated six months of news reporting.

"I love the work you're doing," Ray said.

My boss's praise proved that drinking hadn't affected my dream job. No one knew I started my career buzzed on hard lemonades, and I was confident the frequent bar excursions wouldn't bleed into my professional life.

Christmas was approaching, and Mom invited Hope over to help decorate the Caribou Lake cabin house. Forever prattling about recreating a "Currier and Ives" holiday scene, Mom envisioned vintage wooden sleds and caroling to the few neighbors on Sunny Lane, something she'd been talking about since I was a kid. Another free evening was taking shape, and beer would make things happen. Dennis had droned on all day about my Christmas present.

"What it is?" I demanded.

He just smiled and shrugged—he maybe even blushed a little.

Adult beverages waited at the end of the workday—I'd already knocked back a few and was running low on provisions. I wasn't worried; the liquor store would remain open for hours and the Galley was a safety net until well after midnight. I was still deep in the priming phase at my apartment, loving the thought of endless possibilities. A drinking buddy would sure come in handy.

The phone rang. Dennis seemed to read my thoughts like a brother.

"Are you going to be around for a while? I have your gift. Can I swing over?"

"That works if you can get here soon," I said, cracking open my third beer. "I'm heading to the bar in a bit. What's so important that you can't just give it to me at the station?"

"You'll see," Dennis said mysteriously. "It's not a work thing. I need to bring it over to your house."

Probably some kind of goofy thing. Dennis arrived at my door fifteen minutes later with some beer (he never mooched from others) and a package the size of a cereal box.

"Thank the Lord you didn't come here empty-handed," I said, distracted by the shiny pink wrapping paper but more interested in the beer. My can was half empty as we trudged up the stairs and settled in the kitchen. Dennis's offering sat like a pink elephant in the middle of the table.

Finally, he pushed the gift toward me. "Open it!"

"A DJ headset!" I exclaimed, tearing off the paper. "Cool! I've been wanting one of these!"

I eased the flaps on the box loose to take a look at the new gadget, only to find wadded tissue inside surrounding something smaller.

My apprehension increased.

Oh Lord, I hoped it was earrings, or even a bracelet.

Popping the jewelry box open revealed a diamond ring in a gold band etched with hearts.

"Wow" was all I could manage. I slipped it on as Dennis watched every move.

"What does this mean?" I finally asked, with mounting apprehension.

"What do you want it to mean?" he responded, eyes shining.

I shrugged slowly and cracked another beer.

The dark and gloomy Galley was the ideal place to deny reality while flashing my new jewelry. Others, too, were curious about its symbolism. Instead of trying to explain, I downed three shots of tequila and two Jag bombs.

Driving to work in the stark and sober light of Saturday morning with a monstrous hangover, the ring was an invasive species hitching an unwelcomed ride on my finger. Knowing something was terribly wrong, I slipped it off and zipped it into my wallet.

Dennis zeroed in on my empty hand right away.

"Where's the ring?"

"I just don't feel like answering everyone's questions," I responded timidly. "They'll want to know who it's from, and I'm just not up for a big coming-out party."

Dennis was crushed, and I spent the rest of the day trying to schmooze my way back into his good graces.

The days leading up to Christmas Eve weren't supposed to be spent poisoning myself with cheap wine, but somehow I ended up downstairs in my landlord's apartment swilling White Zinfandel.

Gerard was hosting a little party that included a few families—and Beck, a big Navy dude around my age. As Hope played with the other kids, I happily offered a sympathetic ear for Beck's sad life story—his former wife had ditched him for another guy while they were living in Virginia with two small kids.

I could certainly relate to his tales of a broken love and as the White Zin flowed, eagerly dove into a long exposition about the abrupt ending to my own marriage.

"He said he never really loved me in the first place, probably," I concluded, for shock value more than anything.

"He's a fool," Beck said with resignation. "You're a good woman, I can tell."

This was pleasant news, but was being tagged a *good woman* enough? Was Beck just waiting for a nice, desperate subject? He was an easy target—and growing flirtier as the night wore on.

Laid back, affable, pleasant, nonthreatening—much like Mitch, my first boyfriend. But not challenging.

"It's getting late, I better get Hope to bed," I finally managed.

Escaping upstairs, I tucked Hope in but had no plans of sleeping myself. After she drifted off, I continued drinking in my bedroom, blowing smoke out the window screen, and talking on the phone until the wee hours of the morning.

The next day I was hungover, guilty, and full of self-hatred. My hangover set the day's tone and turned the joy of a Christmas gathering with old friends into dread and despondency. Hope and I were headed to my old friend Amy's house for a little holiday get-together, but today would be a struggle.

With trembling hands and a queasy stomach, I wondered how I'd make it through the day. More beer. Drinking in the morning didn't happen often, but I needed it badly now, and a warm, flat beer chugged in the shower calmed the shakes. After three more, I was stable. Shower sipping under the hot water made it seem as though it never happened.

The booze didn't run dry for the rest of the day, and I did a passable job blending in. No one had a clue I'd started drinking right away that morning, and I kept up my deception by extracting bottles from the garage fridge when others were occupied.

Later on the gathering was winding down, but I was in no mood to stop drinking, so I summoned Dennis on the way home.

"What's up?" I chirped. "Want to come over and watch Hope for a bit so I can meet with a couple of DJ clients?"

My stories were getting more and more ludicrous.

"Sure," he responded flatly.

I wasn't fooling him, but he still arrived dutifully at my door fifteen minutes later so I could close down the bar.

How I hated myself the next day. Sick and hungover on Christmas Eve, exhausted, clingy, fragile, and dreading the holidays. My mind scrambled with mad rationalizations to ease the regret I felt after driving home half-drunk with Hope. I would push through the holidays, only for her.

Dennis made a special trip to my parents' house for dinner where I picked at my food, hardly talking. After we ate, we moved to the living room to watch a holiday show, and I nursed a beer, so sick I couldn't even stomach it.

"Santa is coming here?" Hope asked. "Will he know we're at Grandma's?"

"Yes, he knows, honey," I assured her. "Grandma called the North Pole."

"We should probably get to bed so Santa can come," I insisted a short while later, practically shoving Dennis out the door.

"Is everything okay?" he asked with concern. "Did I do something?"

I couldn't believe he was blaming himself for my ridiculous behavior.

"Dennis, no. It's all me. Listen, I'm sorry for what I said about meeting DJ clients. You know that was a load of nonsense."

With a wave of dismissal, I gave my best enabler a stiff hug before sending him on his way. Dennis had a heart of gold and was truly fearful for me, but my treatment of him was poor and heartless. I was too unhealed to offer anyone anything. He deserved so much better, and I knew it was high time to return the ring.

I caught him in the KDLH-TV parking lot shortly after New Year's Day, tentative and uneasy after ignoring his calls for the past week.

"Mel, hi," he greeted me. "It's been a while."

"Dennis, I can't do this." I swallowed hard and held out the ring box.

"What? Why? What's going on?"

He slammed the truck hatch and leaned against it, looking stunned, like someone had just slapped him with a dead fish.

"I have to give it back. It's just not right. You support my drinking; you enable it. I've *got* to quit, and as long as we're together, it's never going to happen."

Dennis threw up his arms angrily. "What are you talking about? You know how much you go back and forth! I get nauseous just watching you! I'm not going to be riding you all the time to quit . . . you've got to do it for yourself!"

I stared at the pavement, transfixed on tiny hairline cracks I wished would expand before my eyes and suck me down into the concrete. "I know you're mad. I just have to do this."

Choking back tears, I held out the ring box again, and he reluctantly took it.

"You haven't even given it a chance!" Dennis yelled. "How can you *do* this?"

"I just have to! Please understand."

Before he could say anything more, I turned and left the garage. I was a jerk, but keeping the ring was not an option.

Now that Dennis was gone, sobriety became my focus once again. I managed a squeaky-clean New Year's Eve—a major feat—but it required full apartment quarantine after Hope had been delivered to my parents' house. The evening was spent gorging on Jeno's pizza rolls and crying—convinced everyone else was out having the time of their lives.

Nose to the grindstone, I avoided party people and focused

on Hope and my work, the new lifestyle holding on for a month. But by February, I'd fallen off the wagon again. Unable to pinpoint the problem, I eventually decided I'd made a grave mistake by dumping Dennis. I yearned for another ring.

Right before Easter, I called him out of the blue.

"I've been an idiot. Give me another chance?"

Hours later, we were inside a mall jewelry store where Dennis wasted no time opening a charge account.

"You can have anything you want in the whole place. Anything under $2,000, that is," he said, grinning.

Caught up in the glitter of the moment, I perused the gleaming cases until I had the perfect diamond.

"Do you think we should go for it?" I asked, admiring the rock on my outstretched hand.

Of course, the saleswoman thought so. "When's the big day?" she nearly demanded.

"Uh, I'm not sure," I stammered, blindsided.

Looking to Dennis for reinforcement, inside a voice screamed, *YES! A WEDDING! That's what's supposed to be the end result of all this ring shopping!*

The saleswoman quickly changed course after sensing my reluctance.

"I don't mean to rush you! You've only just begun," she beamed, flashing a huge fake smile. "I have a friend who has been engaged for *three years*. Can you believe that? When she shows her diamond off, she says it's an 'I love you' ring!"

Finding this tale much more palatable than the end game of marriage-for-the-rest-of-my-life, my panic over the major purchase and commitment it represented subsided. The new jewelry looked great under the blinding department store lights, and we left with it tucked into a tiny black box.

"Put it on!" Dennis laughed, almost drunk with excitement, as we strolled the mall. Tense and uneasy, I plucked it from its fancy satin bed and slipped it onto my ring finger.

Days later, I noticed a huge dark spot right next to the surface of the stone. How had I missed that in the store?! The diamond *was* enormous, but I couldn't escape the stupid carbon flaw.

"It has a black mark," I stuck my hand right in Dennis's face. Squinting, he claimed he couldn't see anything.

"It's *not* going back," he said firmly.

Beyond jubilant during the second engagement, Dennis talked wedding plans while I continued to inspect the very noticeable black dot that screamed everything wrong with the situation. Overcome by a deep feeling of dread, I agonized over the latest impulsive reaction I knew was another colossal mistake. The engagement charade continued for a record three weeks until things became unbearable again.

Trapped and panicked, I called my brother for advice. He was blunt, diplomatic, and straight to the point.

"Go to work tomorrow and return it. Mean what you say, be direct and clear, and don't go back on your words."

I followed Dave's instructions to the letter.

"You've got to be joking," Dennis choked in disbelief after I'd dropped a second ugly bombshell.

"No, I made a mistake. I know this is a horrible thing to do, and I'm sorry. Please don't hate me. It's still under the return policy."

Dennis's face was beet red with fury. "Eff the return policy!" he yelled. "I don't care about that. There's something seriously wrong with you!" He threw the ring box into his truck and peeled out of the parking lot.

The next day he had cooled down and was begging me to reconsider.

"Come on, Mel. You haven't given us a chance since day one."

While it was excruciating listening to his earnest pleas, I stood firm.

Heavy binge drinking continued with the Galley always the first stop on my trapline. The vacant and purposeless clientele welcomed me as their local television star, and I never lost sight of the slim chance that I may meet my next husband within its grease-stained walls.

29

Everyone recognized me that Friday—the bar was a hotbed of activity, and I felt staring eyes as I sipped free rum and cokes and laughed without insecurity. Time flew as the red carpet rolled out in the form of complimentary adult beverages—rum, margaritas on the rocks, overflow from a pitcher of daiquiris the bartender whipped up for a table of ladies celebrating a bachelorette party. I sipped it all as my prerecorded news cut-ins ran on the televisions. Watching people glance from the TV to me was thrilling. I was even more interesting than the bride-to-be, sauntering around in a long white veil stapled with condoms in all the colors of the rainbow.

"I saw your story tonight," my friend Bob remarked as I

scored the only empty stool next to him.

"What is the deal with that smoking ban, anyway? Will it ever go away?"

I shrugged and helped myself to a cigarette from his pack.

"It won't pass. So, smoke up, right?" Laughing like a hyena, I slapped Bob's arm. No one expected me to be a goody-goody at the Galley, least of all my barroom buddy. It was a secret club that allowed me to cut loose and forget about being a community representative.

The night played out in an unremarkable fashion. The bride and her crew moved down the street, and hope of excitement was fading as the clock struck midnight. So far, I'd been content to play the jukebox and drink with Bob. He had a crush on me, but he was old enough to be my dad and too shy to pull any fast ones.

While engaged in a very deep and meaningful conversation about the history of the Beatles, two guys in softball jerseys sauntered in.

"George Harrison is totally underrated," Bob babbled. Distracted by the boys, the British Invasion drifted out of focus.

"Give me some quarters," I commanded.

Bob scrounged around on the bar and instructed me to play "While My Guitar Gently Weeps."

"George Harrison wrote that, you know."

As the guys hovered over the jukebox, I sidled up alongside them jingling the coins in my hand, eyes moving over the stockier one with the softball jersey. The gold cross he wore purposely hanging from the collar of his jersey was captivating, seeming to indicate he had values beyond the usual Galley crowd.

"You play for J-Z's? Do you know Dave Kessler?"

J-Z's was the bar his jersey advertised. Dave Kessler was a bogus name I created in order to make my move. It sounded like a local weatherman, but I couldn't remember for sure.

The guy leaned closer, smiling slyly. "Sorry, I didn't catch that." A flash of recognition, and then, "You're on the news, aren't you?"

I bobbed my head and smirked. So simple. Work was the furthest thing from my mind and we'd already established my status, so I changed the subject.

"Where are you going next?"

Another state awaited just minutes away, a fantasy-land oasis where the nightlife continued until two-thirty in the morning. Superior, Wisconsin. Almost always successful in recruiting guys willing to tote me across the bridge, I figured these two would be my next victims.

Turning to ask his friend something, the guy with the gold cross placed his empty beer on top of the jukebox and moved back toward me with a smile.

"I'm Jack. And this is Gavin," he said, gesturing to his friend. The other guy was not nearly as cute as the cross-wearer and appeared very drunk. "Sounds like we're heading over to Superior. You want to join us?"

Yes, yes of course I did. The rest of the night was spent with my new friends, dancing and partying until bar close.

Sprawled out on top of my comforter in black platform shoes, waking up the next morning was a surreal jumble of confusion. I didn't realize right away that I wasn't alone until I rolled over into a big surprise.

Jack was stretched out in that damned softball uniform. I clutched my head, grateful that extreme drunkenness had kept me in my clothes. He stirred, and a smile crept across his face.

"Good morning," I said brightly, reaching to open the window blinds. "I better take you home. I have to go get my daughter." I started moving around the room, tidying up.

Jack climbed off the bed and caught me around the waist.

"I'm so glad I met you."

His hug seemed to show true affection, but perhaps he was simply still drunk.

We moved into the kitchen where I chatted aimlessly, my usual defense mechanism when a giant black hole had eaten my memory. I remembered meeting Jack at the Galley and driving to Superior, but that was the end of it.

As I pondered my final recollection, I was hit with a brief dancing flashback and recalled the cross necklace. His jewelry was branded into my memory—the gold Christian symbol I'd zeroed in on early in the night, convinced it was a holy force drawing us together. But it fell off when we were dancing, and the night ended with a desperate floor search.

We never did find the pendant, and I dimly remembered scouring the floor on my hands and knees, swearing I wasn't going anywhere until it was recovered. I was convinced its disappearance was a very bad omen, and even with only limited scraps of recollection, something still screamed I *had* to see Jack again.

"Sorry about your cross," I said, as we were heading out to my car. Jack looked puzzled.

"Cross?"

"Your cross? Remember it fell off?"

"Oh yeah, I forgot about that," Jack muttered. "No big deal, my grandma gave it to me . . . I saw her yesterday, so I wore it. For her."

"I know how that is," I rambled. "My grandma hates tattoos . . . Her name was June. Junie. That's my middle name. Anyway, I got my first tat when I was nineteen, and I always tried to pull my sock up over it—well, Gram saw it one day, and I told her it was a stick-on when she asked. It's on my ankle."

Jack said nothing and stared straight ahead like a vacant zombie.

"So, where am I taking you?" I asked with forced brightness. Long ago, I'd mastered the art of general questions; much better than saying flat-out, "Hey, where do you live again? I know you probably told me several times last night, but I was too ripped to remember."

I had grown terrified of losing my mind, of pickling my brain and inducing dementia or Parkinson's or some other old-person disease of which I was distantly aware. My blackouts were completely out of control, and alcohol was affecting my short-term memory, too. After a three-day binge, disjointed thoughts clogged my mind, and problem-solving was out the window for days.

Jack gestured to the next exit. "You can get off the freeway right here. That will take us right to my place."

Hmmm . . . he sounds like a homeowner.

We pulled up to his Lincoln Park house a few minutes later, and although it wasn't located in the greatest neighborhood (can we say level 3 sex offenders?), it wasn't *that* horrible. My eyes tried desperately to capture any positive points, however flimsy they may have been. A normal, stable person would've acknowledged a dumpy, unkempt bungalow and a yard strewn with beer cans and bottles in a ghetto neighborhood—a picture desperately waving several red flags that alcohol, codependency, and fear of abandonment had trained me to ignore—but I somehow pruned the bad parts away.

Reality indicated my new friend was irresponsible, selfish, and most likely an addict, but my alcohol-saturated brain filtered all of that out, instead fixating on the rusty old swing set and deciding Jack must surely love and care for his kids.

After rummaging around for a scrap of paper, we exchanged phone numbers.

"I want to hear from you," he said hypnotically, leaning into my open window, right into my soul.

I headed off to fetch Hope in a daze, with Jack consuming every thought. It was only day two, and I was already hopelessly hooked.

Quiet Sundays filled me with dread; I really viewed the Lord's day as the worst of the week—hating the long wait to my next drink. Shifting to daughter mode, we went to a movie and then spent a laid-back evening at home putting a puzzle together. After Hope was asleep, a number I didn't recognize flashed on the caller I.D.

"Hello?" I answered suspiciously. A buzz of background noise bled through.

"Mel! How's it going?"

"Jack? I didn't think I'd hear from you tonight. What's up? Whose phone is this?"

"Eh, it's my buddy's. My cell service was cut off, payment check for the bill bounced. That's what the bank people said, anyway. I got a NSF fee, but eff it. Bunch of crooks." He paused. "I'm over at Champ's playing darts. We're almost done . . . should I stop by?"

Oh boy. After an awkward pause, I attempted to decline

the offer I badly wanted to accept. "I don't think so . . . Hope is sleeping, and she hasn't met you yet. I don't think it would be a good idea if she woke up and found you here."

Jack's tone was so easy and convincing. "Come on. I just want to *see* you. Please? I haven't been able to get you off my mind all day," he added.

I quickly weighed the cost of Hope's disapproval against the flood of bliss from Jack's beer-fueled platitudes. "I guess it would be okay for a little while . . . but you can't spend the night."

He was silent as bar noise rattled through.

"How am I supposed to get home then?"

"Don't you have a car? Don't you drive?"

"That's a long story . . . "

The epic tale undoubtedly involved a bad record and drunk driving incidents. I'd finally cleared up my rap sheet, earned a valid license, and had evaded law enforcement for the past four years—I'd even finagled a decent used car for the first time in a decade. Was Jack just another directionless, gold-digging lowlife?

"Just come on over. I'll call you a cab later on."

As soon as we hung up, I opened the fridge and popped a beer. I'd planned an alcohol-free evening, but now I needed to get on Jack's level, and fast. No doubt, he was hammered. Within twenty minutes, I'd polished off five beers in my efforts to catch up.

Grabbing a sixth, I moved outside onto the deck until I saw headlights creeping up the driveway.

Jack stumbled a little in the glow of headlights and drizzle as he meandered up the sidewalk. Since it was raining, we headed inside and parked ourselves at the kitchen table. Soon, we'd finished off the rest of my beer stash as well as a bottle of old

Christmas wine. With all the booze long gone, we stumbled into the bedroom and passed out. My good intentions of sending Jack home had vanished.

I'll just tell Hope he's an old friend.

My eyes cracked open around seven the next morning with my dear little daughter standing over the bed, staring at the two of us incredulously.

"Who's *he*?!" she demanded.

"Hope, this is Jack," I smiled broadly so she'd think the whole situation was totally normal. "He's an old friend of mine. He came over for a visit since he was right in the neighborhood. Isn't that great? He didn't have a ride home though," I shrugged, gauging her furious expression. "So, I let him stay."

"An old friend, huh?" Her eyes narrowed, and she took off in a huff.

Jack scrambled off the bed. "Crap, Mel, I'm late for work. Can you give me a ride? I need to stop at home, too. My uniform is there."

"I have to work, too," I managed, moving into damage control mode. "Everyone is going to be late at this point. But at least Hope has a fun day planned!" Beaming, I turned to gauge her reaction while trying to ignore the scowl of disdain scrawled across her face.

The three of us piled into the car, and I dropped Hope at the Boys and Girls Club for the weekly field trip day that served as babysitter on a budget. She was still ticked off and stage-whispered, "He better not be around when I get home," as she climbed out of the car.

Next stop—Jack's house. Eyeing him with confusion, I watched as he slouched way down in the front seat.

"Oh damn," he muttered.

A short, stocky woman with purple-tipped hair and several facial piercings glared icily from the drooping porch.

Killing the engine, I faced Jack. "Who is that?"

Rolling his eyes like he'd just been majorly inconvenienced, he reached for the door handle while offering a little pat on my hand. "Don't freak out, Melissa. I know what you're thinking—but hear me out. It's my ex, Lacey. She still has a house key, due to me being stupid," he muttered, gazing up at the house. "Hang on. I'll be right back."

I watched as he ambled up the cratered sidewalk, not believing my eyes. Just last night he'd disclosed his pending court date for his third drunk driving offense. Not only that, he'd fathered kids all over the state—three children by a trio of women.

Despite this information about Jack's true character, I waited and seethed in my car for the next fifteen minutes as he and the woman on the steps argued. *Is it really his house? Or is it "theirs"?*

Jack returned just as I was about to leave and climbed timidly into the car. I pulled out onto the street, waiting for a damned good explanation.

"I know what you must be feeling," he began feebly. "But you don't understand Lacey. She's a psycho. She thinks she can come over anytime she feels like it and do her laundry."

I stared straight ahead. "Do you live with her?"

"No! No, I told you . . . she and the kids moved out months ago. I see them every other weekend. The kids, I mean. Honestly."

I merged back onto the freeway. "Where are we going again?"

Jack pointed toward the nearest fast-food entrance. "Right here."

"You work at Taco Bell?" I asked in a tiny voice.

"Yeah, I *told* you that last night," he answered emphatically. "A bunch of times."

Before getting out, he once again locked me into some sort of Vulcan mind probe with his deadly eyes. "Mel, please believe me," he implored, as the once flat tone shifted to one of heartfelt passion. "I *don't* have a girlfriend. I'm telling you the truth. I want to get serious with *you*."

Greedily sucking up the exact words I longed to hear, I decided to overlook the multiple DWIs, the unplanned kids, and the Taco Bell career. This guy was a winner.

"What are you doing Saturday?" I asked. Despite all I'd just learned about Jack and his lack of ambition and integrity, I was still desperate to arrange our next get-together.

30

Saturday night promised to be an upscale and lavish party. A fat payday was coming—I'd collect eight hundred dollars to provide DJ services at a wedding dance near the Canadian border in the popular skiing getaway of Lutsen, Minnesota. Jack was tagging along, and I figured the long drive would provide lots of quality time together.

After delivering Hope to Seth's house for the night, I returned home to load up the sound system. The July sun was sweltering, and I was drenched with sweat once the car was packed. With a few minutes left to fix my hair and reapply makeup, I chugged my fifth beer in front of the bathroom mirror. That was enough.

Minutes later I was at Jack's door, feeling shy and yearning for a few more drinks. Even several beers hadn't blunted my nerves; I needed to be smashed to interact with people now. Drinking didn't take the feeling away until I totally blacked out.

The entire neighborhood seemed to be watching as I navigated Jack's cracked sidewalk, overgrown grass and broken toys cluttering the path. The missing front porch step required a gigantic stride to clear the gap, and empty beer cans littered the doorway. His lack of handyman skills was blatantly obvious. I ducked my head into the small entryway.

"Jack?"

"I'm in here," he called.

Carefully stepping over cases of empty returnable bottles and discarded clothes cluttering the front entryway, I located Jack slouched on a futon oblivious to the piles of litter. Empty pizza boxes, dirty dishes, and discarded toys covered every inch of carpet space. I couldn't believe my eyes. This was only 2002, but now I'd say his house was right out of a *Hoarders* episode.

"Have a seat. I'll get you something," he mumbled.

Jack hauled himself up from the futon and disappeared into the kitchen, where he ducked his head into an old rusty refrigerator. The nearby sink overflowed with dishes and the garbage can intended for outdoor use was stuffed to the hilt with empty boxes and bottles, resembling the one belonging to Oscar the Grouch on Sesame Street. I stared at the ceiling, afraid my eyes would explode if I continued to ponder Jack's living conditions.

"You want a beer? Or a shot? I've got some Fireball here."

I checked my watch. My rule about cutting myself off until we made it to Lutsen went out the window. One more for the road couldn't hurt.

"Yeah, I'll take a beer," I agreed.

Jack passed me a bottle, then popped his longneck and flicked the cap into the corner. I gingerly took a seat on the edge of the futon and joined him in staring vacantly at the muted television set broadcasting a PBS outdoor fishing program. Before we hit the road, I had to pee. I looked around with apprehension.

"Can I use your bathroom?"

"Go ahead, it's in the basement," Jack responded vacantly, his eyes not leaving the television screen. "I think there's still some toilet paper down there."

Roger that. With a smile, I headed downstairs thinking, *Yep, this is all totally normal. He's just living a bachelor's lifestyle. GUYS. Can't live with 'em, can't live without 'em.*

The basement was frightening and should've been condemned. Every piece of garbage, junk, and refuse that Jack and every other preexisting tenant didn't have enough ambition to haul to the local dump was thrown in a heap. Old mattresses, clothes, garbage, and boxes stained with water and mold were piled in mountains that reached the rafters.

I located the vile toilet, standing alone against the wall and looking worse than the filthiest truck stop john imaginable. Against my better judgment, I crouched over it and scored the last three squares of toilet tissue clinging to the roll.

Back upstairs, we finished our beers and took off for Lutsen. With my buzz reignited, I chattered all the way up the North Shore, educating Jack about the failure of my marriage and a blow-by-blow account of the last ten years. My mouth never rested when I was half in the bag with a captive audience.

Eventually, we landed on the subject of his most recent DWI arrest.

"You sure seem to like doing things in threes," I commented.

Jack stared blankly. Why hadn't I noticed his dimness? Could it be that every encounter we'd had so far involved mass quantities of alcohol?

"Three kids? Three DWIs? Don't you think you should stop having kids and DWIs?" I prompted.

The conversation was ludicrous, but I continued mining for scraps.

Jack shrugged. "Yeah, I guess. Haven't really thought of it much."

"Well, what have you *learned*? Anything at all?" I prodded.

Jack pondered my question. "I learned not to drink and drive?"

"Uh-huh. Are you seeing a pattern at all?"

Jack shrugged once more, and I left him alone.

Soon we arrived in the quaint skiing village and found the reception lodge. Jack was really helpful with getting everything hauled inside and set up. *What a good guy.*

"I'm going to hire you eventually, but right now you're an intern," I joked. "For tonight I'll just pay you in beer. Is that all right?"

Jack was flat broke, so I'd be buying his drinks anyway. Requiring labor made me feel less desperate.

My DJ post was located up in a knotty pine balcony above the dance floor, offering a bird's-eye view of the entire crowd. What a unique and exquisite location—my table faced the staircase, so anyone heading up to request a song was in full view. Far away from guests, I was perfectly suited for excessive drinking.

The swanky little alpine bar was the perfect place to get a little more tuned up before the actual reception. Crowded with people who'd overflowed from the wedding ceremony, no one knew I was the DJ—I appeared to be any other guest. Gauging the snooty and elite crowd made it clear I needed more beer fast.

Jack was totally out of place. We slid into a nearby booth where I decided it was high time to start asking questions about his parents.

"How's your relationship with your mother?"

Jack gazed through me. "My mother? Uh, okay . . . regular, I guess."

"Uh-huh . . . what do you mean by *regular*?" I continued, staring into his face.

My little inquisition wasn't working—it was impossible for Jack to string together a complete sentence.

Jack cocked his head. "You know what I mean. How most people's relationships are with their mothers."

Uh huh. Jack, you and I are not like most people.

"How about your dad? What's he like?"

Jack squirmed. "Things are okay. My dad's been told he's a little, well . . . I guess you could say he's a little ... slow. A little off."

Nodding hypnotically, I wondered if Jack was also lacking something upstairs.

The bride and groom would be arriving soon, so I ordered two beers to bring up to the DJ post and shuffled Jack to the knotty pine perch. He parked himself behind me in a chair and didn't move unless I told him to.

The dance started well enough—I can remember peering over the railing, high above the crowd, to watch women swirling in short cocktail dresses as they flanked the bride's voluminous ball gown. The sounds of big band and swing tunes filled the hall with energy, and the crowd devoured the peppy horn and jazz solos.

But as the sticky evening descended into total darkness, my functionality dissolved. The great divide from the bride and groom was a blessing—though I could only guess how I'd acted and what I'd said while performing my emcee duties.

With dreadful anticipation I expected a complaint from the married couple, angry comments scrawled on the wedding feedback form, or even worse—a call to the DJ company I represented to complain about my reckless performance.

Past experience indicated that once I grew tired of the bride and groom's requests, I'd spend the night spinning music from Melissa's Favorite Playlist—which never failed to include Metallica, Guns N Roses, and songs with explicit lyrics. The wishes of those who had hired me were made abundantly clear, but none of that mattered when I was eight beers deep.

I knew all too well what blacked out Melissa was capable of. At a reception months back, the bride and groom complained about the loud music and song selections that didn't include many of their requests. I had shouted into the mic, "Okay, fine, if you don't like what I'm doing, I'll just play Barry Manilow for the rest of the night."

The couple was *not* amused by my comedy routine and did call my boss to complain. I would never have known what took place—had they not reported it to my manager. Jack's dimness made him a cloudy witness unable to grasp the gravity of the situation, but history revealed my pattern at drunk DJ shows.

When the party died down, I abandoned the equipment in the stale and muggy loft and dragged Jack outside to camp before the waters of Lake Superior. The night's second act seemed to stretch for hours—I held Jack captive for a deep conversation about our future while we drank leftover beer from my trunk. I don't remember passing out, but soon a blood-red sun crept over the horizon and biting flies were everywhere.

And *oh*, my *head*. Was I drinking bleach the night before? Jack and I had crashed not far from the lodge and the grand windows overlooking the lake, making me wonder how many had seen the DJ passed out on the lakeshore. Dozing until nine was not nearly enough—but we had to get the equipment out of the party location before I was accosted by a worker.

Praying I'd escape the lodge employees, I dragged Jack into the stifling hot upstairs loft. Cursing myself as I fumbled through the work I should've handled the night before, I managed to get everything loaded up with some help from my roadie. I was horribly sick, fighting the urge to throw up, and sweating like a pig.

Reclining the front seat as soon as we hit scenic highway 61 for the drive back to Duluth, Jack slept all the way without a care in the world while I panicked and obsessed. My latest beau was a road to nowhere, but my desire to mold him into husband material was as all-consuming as ever.

Still feeling like trash as we neared the Twin Ports, my head rang with liquor assault and a wasted, wiped-out feeling—the price paid for days of heavy alcohol abuse. Sunday morning meant the party was over for now—always a horrible revelation. Dragging through the rest of the day with my mind firmly focused on Jack, I knew our little funfest had to end, but still, just one renegade thought recycled through my mind: *When will I see him again?*

Two full days were required to recover from the wedding dance, and unbelievably, I didn't receive a complaint from the pristine bride and groom who'd requested only big band music. On Tuesday, Jack called to invite me to his weekly softball game.

I wanted to go—badly—but I couldn't *be* with him if drinking was not part of the plan, so I decided to ship Hope off to Mom's house. I'd never done that on a Tuesday night, but I figured it was necessary *just this once*.

I dropped by Mom's office that afternoon, attempting to look frazzled and stressed.

"Could you watch Hope tonight? I just got called into work."

My mother was silent and exhausted by my constant requests for her babysitting services.

"Melissa, this is getting a little old. I really don't believe you have to *work*. What are you really doing? Huh?"

"Please, Mom," I whined. "Why would I lie? Do you think I *want* to go to work? *Really!* Why don't you believe me? Go ahead and call my boss if you want!"

I weaseled until she gave in.

The softball game was boring, but once it ended, the bar beckoned as a welcome reward. Now I could get my drink on. I examined the other girls who'd followed their boyfriends from the team and made endless comparisons. They clustered in their own little group while I hung with Jack.

"Those chicks are talking about me, I know it," I whispered, as Jack collected drink orders from his buddies. "They keep looking over here."

Jack shrugged. "Screw them. I used to date that one redhead—Missy. They all think I'm a player."

He threw down a wad of bills and signaled for the waitress. "You want something?"

I looked up, dazed and wondering, *Are you a player?*

"Ah, sure. Just get me a beer. I'll be right back."

I headed for the bathroom, passing by the table of mean girls without making eye contact—then made a detour for the bar as soon as they were out of sight.

"Two shots of Jägermeister."

Licorice cough medicine, just what the doctor ordered. Liquid courage to counteract the cattiness.

Jäger usually made me snaky, and sometime around bar close I instigated a fight with Jack: a big power play called "pick your friends or pick me." He made his choice and walked off with his bros.

Turning toward home, I stumbled through the trail in the woods, but not before a pit stop at the Holiday station for nightly provisions. While I polished off a bag of powdered doughnuts, I deposited a drunk and nasty message on Jack's voicemail. Then I set my alarm. I had to be up for work by eight.

Morning broke with a demonic hangover and suffocating desire to rush over to Jack's house in the 'hood. Like a vampire thirsty for blood, I feared a trip to the nuthouse if I couldn't get a suitable explanation. The best option was to corner him like a wounded dog when he couldn't escape. I probably wasn't sober as I fired up my engine and drove like a maniac to his trashy tenement.

"Jack?" Marching into the cluttered living room, I fully expected to find him shacked up with some tramp on his old futon. Looking like death warmed over, he appeared in the kitchen doorway and regarded me with dull, bloodshot eyes.

"Hey."

Moving to a chair, he plopped down with his shoes. Apparently, he had somewhere to go. My utter desperation could no longer be contained.

"What's going on?" I railed. "You told me you wanted to get *serious*. Serious! Doesn't that mean—oh I don't know—'be in a relationship'? Then last night you totally snaked out. Where is this going?"

My screaming and intensity carried no effect. Jack finished tying his shoes, seeming to process my words while doing so, then regarded me with blank, vacant eyes.

"Get serious? I said that?"

My head pulsed with a rush of nausea as I witnessed my trembling, pathetic attempt to demand someone's love. I snapped to attention.

"You know what? Screw this."

Bolting for the door, I reached my car without looking back.

Jack made it to the doorway.

"Call me," he offered, as I squealed away.

The crying commenced: furious, bitter tears over a low-life I'd known less than two weeks. The booze was talking. Hangovers magnified anything remotely unpleasant about ten thousand times. What goes up must come down, and what is chemically depressed will later be overly stimulated. My central nervous system was struggling to recalibrate after being flooded with hours of depressing alcohol.

A few days later, I was as good as new and regaining my wits. Jack was history by the close of July 2002. Though he continued to leave drunken messages, I never lowered myself to his level again.

31

Jack's influence was gone, but my drinking continued to rapidly worsen in the coming months. Though I truly yearned to change, one more binge forever awaited around the corner.

By the fall, Dad's health was deteriorating—providing yet another excuse for me to spend any free time boozing. The internal bleeding my father had previously battled was once again a serious problem—the veins the doctors had surgically repaired years ago were breaking down. Hard to believe more than ten years had passed since he'd been treated, and the drinking hadn't stopped. The procedure on his esophagus had been a medical Band-Aid that desperately needed true behavioral change to work—just like the imposed AA meetings and addiction treatment everyone else wanted much more than he did. Dad's liver was truly failing, and he radiated the dreary reality that death was not far off. The old routine resumed— with Mom emptying pails of black, blood-tinged vomit while keeping up a shiny exterior to mask any true alarm.

After several transfusions and a few days in intensive care, Dad was always discharged good as new, the pints of healthy blood infusing him with borrowed strength and someone else's motivation. The growing urgency of his liver failure and what had caused it weren't grasped as he bragged about having been admitted to the hospital with the lowest hemoglobin count doctors had ever seen.

"Dan, you have to quit drinking or you will die." The medical team had ceased to sugar-coat the situation years ago, but whatever the present crisis, their pleas landed on deaf ears. Over the years, various therapeutic interventions had followed the hospital stays, but it was too late for that now. Dad needed a new liver, but was unwilling to comply with the rigorous transplant list requirements.

By the time I'd reached my early twenties, I'd accepted that Dad wouldn't make it to old age. Having no real awareness of generational curses, I never considered interceding for his healing and hadn't yet experienced the power of prayer or the breaking of demonic strongholds through deliverance. The very real work of the enemy had infiltrated our family line, and the demonic vice grips that bound my father seemed indestructible. Suggesting he seek *prayer* for all of this would've been viewed as psychobabble stuff that Holy Rollers promoted. My parents were never believers in the power of the Holy Spirit, preferring to save it for Jesus Freaks who spoke in tongues and executed supreme fakery from charismatic revivals. Back then, I hadn't personally encountered this power either, and didn't understand the transformational force. Things may have been different for Dad if I'd taken up my authority in Christ.

Still, his investment in his own healing was needed, along with repentance, and a desire to turn from sin. He apparently wasn't desperate or broken enough to cry out to Jesus. I could've prayed and pled the blood all day long, though I'm not convinced Dad *wanted* to get well. The book of John describes Jesus's encounter with a man who had suffered a long time, waiting day after day beside a pool that was rumored to have miraculous healing powers. Jesus asked him an interesting question, "Would you *like* to get well?"

The guy was nothing but excuses.

"Everyone else gets here first, I can't get into the water, I have no one to help me." Jesus offered a solution: "Get up! Pick up your mat and walk" (John 5:8; NIV).

Notice he wasn't *automatically healed*; he also had to put in some effort—he had to be willing, and he had to believe God *could* heal him. Jesus touched the man beside the pool of Bethesda despite his self-pity, but the man's willingness was still needed.

Dad had his own pet list of rationalizations. "It's my malady, it's a disease, I can't help myself, I'm in pain, I don't gotta do nothing I don't want to."

It's hard to comprehend why someone would choose to remain oblivious to the loads of stinking garbage filling every corner of their lives. Sort of like boiling a frog or being a hoarder. Circumstances grow up around us, slowly and insidiously, and after a while, we are unable to discern the way out. Perhaps

Dad viewed his comfortable old bottle of Silver Fox as a safer alternative to facing the pain of change. I guess I'll never know the true reasons this side of heaven.

Dad frequently binged on vodka, supplemented with beers throughout the day. His final afternoons were spent watching game shows, calling radio DJs to request songs, and talking willingly and happily to telemarketers. Mom dubbed him the Energizer Bunny because he just kept "going and going"—somehow rebounding from each health setback. With his poorly managed diabetes and pack-a-day smoking habit, he was far from a picture of wellness. But his same old dry wit, love of Barbershop music, and relentless and proud pursuit of my changing careers remained constant.

Thanksgiving of 2002 was nothing like the years we enjoyed large holiday gatherings with grandparents and extended family. Dad was barely functional and spent two full days in the bedroom taking nothing by mouth. Hope, Mom, and I shared Thanksgiving dinner in the silent house while Dad slept in an adjoining bedroom.

But he bounced back a couple of days later, well enough to attend a birthday party for Amy's daughter. Huddled in the basement with the guys, he was just like his old self, watching football and laughing.

It was mid-December, and Hope spent her usual Monday night with my parents until after the ten o'clock news. By the time I made it to pick her up it was nearly eleven, and we rushed out the door because school came early the next day.

"I saw your city council story tonight," Dad piped up as we were leaving. He watched my news reports religiously and offered humorous critiques of the rest of the broadcasting crew.

"I loved that jacket you were wearing. What do you call that color, Missa? Is it aqua?"

I smiled, pleased that he was interested in such small details of my life.

"Yeah, I think so. It's from Cimarron—that store that gives us wardrobe. Wait. No, it's called sea foam, I think."

Dad chuckled. "Whoa, Melis, you're quite the little celebrity now; pretty soon you'll be running that anchor desk on the weekdays, and—what's her name? The redhead? She'll be gonzo."

I laughed and shook my head. "Annette. It's Annette, Dad. I don't think she's going anywhere."

"Naw, you could handle it, Miss-liss. Mark my words. You'll be running the whole shebang one of these days."

As I headed for the door, a strange feeling rose up, and I paused on the patio in the mild December night.

"*Bye, Dad!*" I yelled, deeply struck with the feeling that I should turn back. As I hesitated, I heard his deep voice drone.

"Bye nowwww. Don't be a stranger."

"See you later!" I wanted confirmation.

"Good Lord willing, and the creek don't rise."

Comfort was wrapped in those words: *All's well that ends well.*

I turned down the sidewalk and loaded Hope into the car, not knowing these would be Dad's last words to me.

Early the next morning, Mom checked on him before leaving the house. She went to work thinking everything was normal, and tried calling home as she always did while wrapping up the workday. The phone rang endlessly and as her frustration rose, Dad managed to answer.

"Hello."

His voice was hoarse, weak, and barely above a whisper.

"Dan! Why are you still in bed?!" Mom barked.

His weak response revealed his predicament.

"I'm sick," he managed, deep voice straining with the impossible task of releasing the words. "I'm throwing up blood. I need an ambulance."

Mom summoned the paramedics and rushed home. Later, she called to explain the situation, but I wasn't alarmed. I'd been through the ambulance drill countless times. Three days passed in intensive care, but Dad's condition didn't change.

Although my father had been conscious during the hospital transport, he was placed into a medically induced coma shortly after arrival and had remained there.

"Dad hasn't been able to process the drugs he was given when they first admitted him," Mom explained. "His ammonia levels are so high that they've kept him unconscious since then. His liver and other vital organs appear to be shutting down."

Seriously?

I called in to work that morning and met Mom at her office after Hope was settled at school. Mixed feelings pinwheeled through me as we drove downtown to the hospital. Should I be agitated by the inconvenience or alarmed? As we took the elevator to Dad's floor, Mom's profile resembled that of a nervous schoolgirl, not a fifty-three-year-old woman.

After checking in at the reception desk of the intensive care unit, a nurse stepped out to meet us. He introduced himself, then referred to his charts.

"Will you be waiting for a bit? Dan's peaceful right now, and I'd really like to keep him comfortable. He's been so agitated since he arrived, trying to tear out the IVs and get out of bed."

Would Dad pull through? Knowing the answer to this delicate question would enable me to stop feeling obligated to make all these hospital visits.

"Can you just be straight with us? How serious is it?"

The nurse studied me like I was a stubborn carpet stain that wouldn't scrub out.

"Are you asking if Dan is going to die? Dan's liver is *very sick.* But do I think he'll die? No."

Sliding into a booth at the hospital coffee shop a few minutes later, I studied my mother. Her dewy and vulnerable appearance had faded into something ragged and worn. Spending more than three decades with my dad had clearly sucked the life out of her. She blew on her coffee and looked up wearily.

"So, what do you suppose this means?"

The feeling I'd been stuffing down was difficult to pinpoint and then equally hard to suppress. Disappointment. Despair. Being held hostage as doctors haggled over Dad's fate. When would it end?

"I have no clue. And neither does anyone else here."

The rest of the day passed quietly, and on Sunday morning Mom called while I was cooking breakfast for Hope.

"What do you girls have planned for today?" she chirped.

She's going to drag me downtown.

"Not too much. You going to see Dad?"

"I know this is your day off, but I think you should come. It's important."

"If you say so," I responded with reproach.

Hope and I picked Mom up and headed back to the ICU. Wanting to keep the mood light, I fielded various superficial topics and cracked jokes.

"Dad will make it through like always," I insisted. But once I stepped into the elevator, fear took over, and anxiety swallowed my comedy routine. I wanted a drink. Why didn't hospitals have bars?

Hope hovered nearby, appearing more like a twelve-year-old than a second grader. We reached Dad's floor, and Hope and I waited while Mom checked us in. People were clustered in the small waiting room, some huddled together crying and whispering in hushed tones. It was a place for the dying.

Mom returned. "They'll be out in a moment to get us."

Disappointment flooded in with the reality of actually *seeing* him. I'd hoped to avoid it. As I stared at the floor tiles, another nurse pushed the swinging door open and beckoned to us. We stepped inside, and the ICU greeted us with silence more deafening than the dead of night, its presence somehow ear-splitting.

Once we'd moved into an adjacent room behind the nurse's station, I gasped at the shocking sight of my father. A clear tube snaked through his nostril and his hands were puffy and swollen from the tracks of the IV. His raspy, labored breathing was alarming—his useless chest rising and falling abruptly and forcibly.

Studying him in amazement, I'd never seen Dad in such a state of submission, controlling nothing. Each time he'd been hospitalized—no matter how sick and close to death—he was still able to sit up, crack jokes, and look forward to his next beer. But in a coma, his body was completely limp and controlled by machines. Seeing his tongue lolling off to the side of his gaping mouth seemed intrusive. I had to look away.

Hope wept silently beside me, clutching an old snapshot of her grandfather. They'd been playing dress up, and Dad was draped in a pink feather boa with plastic play high heels teetering on the ends of his bare feet.

Mom broke down as she reached out to stroke Dad's hand, tears spilling over her cheeks.

"Oh, poor Dad," she murmured, her voice cracking. "He wasn't a bad man. He was just dealt a bad hand."

I gathered her in a hug as the nurse moved away and returned with a box of Kleenex. Mom dabbed her eyes and composed herself.

"How are his ammonia levels?"

"They've come down some, but no one can really say how much damage has already been done. I wish I had other news for you."

Wait and see. Mom and I turned back to Dad. I grazed his hand expecting it to feel cold—but it still pulsed with life. After studying him for a long time, a deep desire welled up from within my heart. *Please don't ever let me drink again.*

32

Two days passed with no changes in Dad. Still unconscious—possibly brain dead. Mom called the newsroom Wednesday when I couldn't escape.

"Melissa, I have a decision to make. The hospital thinks it's time to take out the tubes and move Dad to a hospice unit. I just want to make him comfortable. He used to say he never wanted a tube up his nose," she added, sounding defeated.

My body tensed with the starkness of her words, the thought of her hand pulling the strings of Dad's impending death.

"What, and then he just starves?"

"No, not like that. They keep him hydrated and comfortable. If he rallies and shows signs of improvement, then the care plan would change."

"What other choice do you have?"

"That's about it. His organs are failing, and we think the tube might make him unable to let go. Dave agrees with letting Dad pass. He's arranging a flight to Duluth."

Alone at my desk, I found numbing in the buzz of newsroom activity and spent the rest of the day distracted with work. My dad was dying, and I probably should've been distressed, but I was more worried about scoring the right sound bites.

The six o'clock newscast ended without incident, and I excused myself for dinner. After choking down a quick sandwich, Mom called again, and I almost regretted answering. Dealing with her open sobbing was unbearable.

"I'm at the hospital right now. Marie from the office came with me. Dad's in the hospice unit. Everyone is so gentle, and it's quiet. Dad seems more at peace now that nothing is attached to him. Oh, and there's a beautiful porcelain angel next to his bed with her arms spread out. You need to see her, Melis. Absolutely breathtaking."

Shut up about the angel.

Voice faltering, she completely broke down. "We'll be here for a while longer," she choked. "Can you come?"

Yeah, I really should. But I'm not going to. The thought of crowding around Dad's deathbed was more than I could handle.

"I can't tonight . . . I have an interview with Congressman Oberstar set up at the station. Tomorrow, though. For sure."

Hanging up the phone guilt-ridden, I stood in the empty kitchen berating myself for being so stupid and weak. I didn't know it was already too late.

Back at the station, I interviewed one of Minnesota's

longest-running legislators mechanically, then finished the night in the edit bay hiding from watchful eyes. Driving home, I purposely went by the hospice wing of the clinic, even though it wasn't on the way. Blank, dimly lit windows reflected back.

Morning broke on December 12, 2002. I fumbled for my phone on the bedside table with anxiety and adrenaline fueling me. Mom had called at 7:07 a.m. I retrieved the voicemail and pressed the phone to my ear.

Hope wandered out of her room and curled up sleepily on the couch as I dialed Mom's number.

"Hey, Mom. What's going on?"

"Dad died in the night," she said simply.

I propped my head up with my hands and turned to my daughter.

"Honey, Grandpa passed away."

"You mean my grandpa is dead?" she squeaked in disbelief. As she sobbed, I wrapped her in my arms, repeating assurances I didn't completely believe but had heard somewhere. He was no longer suffering and was in a better place. It was a blessing.

In my heart, I want to believe Dad is with Jesus, although I didn't quite understand the plan of salvation back then. Dad loved the Lord, and while his alcoholism was certainly not God's will, He did permit Dad to execute his free choice to live and ultimately die as he pleased.

Hope recovered quickly and decided to go to school. I dropped her off an hour later, then called my boss and put on an impressive show of waterworks while revealing the news of my father's passing. *Crocodile tears,* Dad would've scoffed.

Ray tender response was more the cause of my flooding emotion than my father's demise. "Take all the time you need," he urged.

My next stop was Mom's office. A social butterfly even in the face of death, she'd gone straight to work the day after Dad's passing, insisting it was helpful to have people around.

I pulled into the parking lot of Duluth Teacher's Retirement Fund a few minutes later, scanning the first-floor windows and hoping to make the pick-up snappy. Mom's company had moved from the wino hub on First Street up to a nice office complex on Central Entrance six years earlier, and it was much more pleasant to visit her now. Still, I wanted to avoid the uncomfortable interactions with people jonesing to offer their condolences, the cringey scenarios so unbearable without alcohol. Really, I'd only masked the pain of living life by anesthetizing normal human emotion for so many years.

Ron and Marie, Mom's long-time coworkers, peered somberly from the copy room as I attempted a half-wave, gazing back in an apathetic trance. Mom leaned out the door, clutching her sweater against the wind and gesturing aggressively for me to come inside.

Oh, Lord, here we go. As I shot her a bratty look, she threw her hands up and I climbed out of the car. Marie had joined my mother outside on the sidewalk, and cupped my face with her hands when I approached. Every fiber of my being screamed to look away, but she was so distraught that it seemed heartless.

"Oh, kiddo . . . this is a really hard time for you."

Others crowded around and offered brief, awkward hugs and words of consolation. I'd known my mother's coworkers for years, but we'd never exchanged hugs. The rigid and uncomfortable scenario reminded me of AA meeting embraces offered in the name of unity.

"So how are you doing?" my mother's boss asked.

"I'm all right." I managed.

"It probably hasn't hit you yet. It can take a long time to sink in."

Nodding, I repeated the same flimsy sentiments as people trickled by with their words of sympathy.

"Thank you. I really appreciate that. Yes, it's a blessing."

Knee deep in the awkward scene, my cell phone vibrated and I scrambled to retrieve it. It was Amy.

"Melis, how are you doing? I've been a basket case this morning. I just can't believe Big Dan is gone," she sobbed.

As I delivered canned words of sorrow, I was again surprised by my lack of grief. The art of detachment offered a robotic feeling of separation, but compartmentalizing feelings into a lockbox never worked long-term.

After the office reception, it was on to funeral planning.

Connie Cremation sure is fascinating. I couldn't take my eyes off the lady who'd greeted us at the front desk of West Duluth Cremation Services. Her name wasn't really Connie Cremation—I'd spaced it out after ten seconds. The statuesque woman who ushered us inside was fiftyish, and sported a glimmering tongue stud. I was stunned. Still clinging to oral jewelry at fifty?

The tongue piercing clashed with her otherwise '80s look, a peculiar hodge-podge that married a bulky denim stonewashed skirt and macramé coat sweater with a thick herringbone chain. The kinky hair trailing down the middle of her back was a soft shade of burnt orange; short frizzy sides anchored almost painfully by copper barrettes.

A few paces down the hall, we gathered around a large oak table where I examined Connie's hands busying themselves with

Dad's file. Her nails were long and sculpted, the gaudy diamond wedding set occupying the ring finger of her left hand making me slightly jealous. After arranging the paperwork into neat stacks, she folded her hands primly and began talking death certificates.

"How many copies will you need, Mrs. Ellefson?"

"Just one," I answered, hoping to speed the excruciating process along. "Dad didn't have any accounts we need to close."

Connie jotted that down, then turned to us seriously. "Okay. Now I need to ask some *personal* questions about Daniel. Also, I am new at this. Usually, my husband takes care of these arrangements, but he went out on a death call just a little bit ago, so please bear with me."

Her apologetic smile made me feel just a little sorry for her.

"First of all, did Daniel have a pacemaker?"

Mom and I exchanged a look, then shook our heads as Connie Cremation considered this.

"You're *sure* he doesn't have a pacemaker?"

"Yes, I think we're *sure*," I responded peevishly.

Connie shuffled paper again with more conviction this time. "The only reason I *ask* is that if Daniel *did* have a pacemaker, and we began the cremation process, he would blow up. That's all."

That's all? Suddenly on the verge of ridiculous, hysterical laughter, we sat in disbelief as Connie provided a detailed analysis of the cremation process and the number of boxes required for the new version of Dad.

Mom and I exchanged glances while our hostess left the room to retrieve Dad's personal items from the hospital. She returned a minute later with a small manila envelope.

"That was all Dan had for jewelry," she said.

Mom tipped the envelope into her hand, and a ring and

necklace slid out. My throat closed in a tight knot of emotion as I studied the necklace with Dad's medic alert charm and his wedding ring, wrapped unceremoniously with yellow masking tape. My eyes welled up as I remembered how skinny he'd become at the end, existing only on booze. His grooming deteriorated, and he went days without showering, but his long bony fingers were never missing the wedding band.

Mom inspected the engraving inside. "Dan and Sue, circle of love—1966," she read, turning to me with teary eyes.

No one could deny Dad's loyalty.

Connie's husband Ethan joined the funeral planning party a bit later, a stocky little gentleman with jet black hair clad smartly in a navy-blue suit. His strong resemblance to a portly Dracula was amusing. Marching over, he reached out and pumped our hands enthusiastically.

"My condolences. But please don't worry, Mrs. Ellefson. Daniel is in very good hands."

Turning to me, he smiled winningly as though a 160-watt lightbulb had just exploded in his head.

"And I know you," he grinned, as if I had been holding out on him. "You're on the news!" Continuing to smile broadly, he stared while I stood, feeling like a bastard stepchild.

"Yes, that's right. Channel 3 news."

I desperately hoped he would leave it alone, but no such luck.

"Hey! You know what? Mark Evans from Channel 6 and Daryl Parker from Channel 10 work here too!"

The mortuary was the last place I expected to cross paths with someone from the news world, but apparently, funeral director jobs were popular side gigs for television personalities. The last thing I needed was to encounter a couple of station competitors while making plans for Dear Old Dad's cremation.

Half expecting Drac to whip out a job application as he went on discussing the possibilities for Dad's upcoming memorial, I zoned out as he chatted with Mom, daydreaming about singing to those who came to pay their respects.

I used to joke with Dad that when he died, I would belt out Elton John's "Daniel" at his funeral. *Ah horse apples, Melis, I can't stand that song!* Dad had scoffed.

When the tour of the funeral chapel finished, we moved on to the sales area, where urns made of everything from plastic to platinum awaited. Along with the vases for ashes were coffins galore, and I gasped at a $4,000 casket while Dracula and Connie chattered endlessly about the quality of their end-of-life products.

The few tears I'd shed so far had been confined to Mom's examination of the ring Dad would never wear again, but my eyes blurred once more as we moved through the sales room. The urn I'd spotted embossed with musical notes was perfectly fitting for Dad.

Suddenly, a memory flared up from deep within my limbic brain: I was four and riding to the store with him in his prized baby blue 1972 Dodge Dart, the only new car he'd ever owned and purchased the year I was born. On our weekend rides together, we'd roll the windows down, and he'd blast his Barbershop 8-tracks from the cheap factory stereo. I learned every word from "Top of the World" to "Keep Your Sunny Side Up," belting out each song with impressive intensity. *God loves it when you sing,* Dad always used to say.

Ethan and Connie shook our hands solemnly when we finished, and the odd bond we'd developed made me smile. With obvious gifting for their line of work, they'd fostered a strange feeling of peace for my mother and me.

As I looked back one last time, Ethan winked discreetly.

"Your dad is in good hands," he whispered as we walked out. I believed him.

Dave made it to Duluth a few days later, and we met at Mom's house to plan Dad's service. Poring over old pictures, our common goal was to select the best depictions of Dad's life here on Earth. No one wanted his memory diminished to that of a sad alcoholic taken by liver failure. The highlights we chose represented a variety of life experiences: Dad toting a surfboard on the sand of West Palm Beach, standing with his Barbershop quartet, Mom and Dad smiling and jubilant at a UMD prom, Dad bouncing Dave on his lap as a chubby, smiling baby. And my favorite: Dad and me dancing together at a wedding reception. My long braids trailed down my back to the waistband of my pleated skirt, and Dad was clapping with a look of delight: clad in a horrific beige three-piece suit.

"Dave, you know Dad didn't die because the tubes were removed," Mom offered casually, as if referring to the status of her 401(k) plan.

Tubes, tubes, tubes. I cringed as Dave methodically polished off a sloppy joe.

"I know, Mom," he said, rolling his eyes. "Dad's lifestyle eventually caught up with him; it wasn't like it happened overnight."

Completely no nonsense, Dave had a knack for putting things into neat and orderly packages without a lot of outward emotion. I admired the lack of sappiness. Dad had spent nearly forty years as an alcoholic, and time had eventually run out.

33

My television career had launched with a silly little fluff story about a local lady who won big on a well-known game show. A couple of years later, I'd risen to a couple of the most serious news beats: school board and city council. Most reporters dreaded the assignments that required a great deal of preparation, study, and attention to voluminous agendas. But self-worth had blossomed from my years spent tracking long and tedious meetings, and I'd finally secured a spot among the veterans.

The dreary chambers were often filled with the same directionless people shouting from soap boxes about not wanting a strip club or alcoholic wet house in their neighborhood, but diligence sometimes paid off. A catfight could unexpectedly erupt, or a loony hemp-wearing granola grandma might go off on the mayor. Freely offered public speaking opportunities could quickly turn more enticing than spot news, but grinding through the long meetings was necessary to stumble on a possible side show.

Media row faced the council front and center in creaky wooden chairs—with the news folks afforded prime seats in a crowded space where every nook was a precious commodity. Stifling from all angles, the chamber grew extra stuffy once May arrived, every paper meeting agenda doubling as a makeshift fan.

Many Monday nights I'd spent next to the City Hall reporter from the local newspaper. Tall, dark, and inaccessible, I'd accepted long ago that Bryce Hayworth would never look twice at someone like me. The underground message was clear—print media viewed themselves from a perch high above broadcast news crews—the brand of journalism I peddled was too surface-level and sensational. But something had shifted this particular Monday. Bryce smiled and leaned close as if we were old friends and respected colleagues.

"How are things?" Familiar heat rose in my cheeks as his breath tickled my ear.

"They're going okay," I managed.

Sneaking a glance at him later revealed a sunburn tinting his chiseled face, making him look boyish and *real*. Something softer lurked beneath the surface of this dry print journalist. Perhaps he even went on fishing trips and enjoyed picnics in the woods.

Just a few days had passed since Dad's death, and I'd continued working without missing a beat. After the council meeting, I was headed to Mom's to spend the night. Hope was waiting, and I'd drive the two of them to the airport in the morning for a flight to Denver and a weekend with Dave's family. Late Friday I'd join them, but the last exam standing in the way of my bachelor's degree had to be dealt with first.

Thoughts of drinking had left me alone, and I figured that as long as I didn't lose the mental picture of Dad lying helpless in his hospital bed, I would be okay. *John Barleycorn* drifted to mind—the literary work and autobiographical novel written by Jack London about his struggles with alcoholism. He'd been a favorite author of Dad's.

"Long time no see! How's life?" Bryce was especially chatty.

"My Dad passed away not too long ago," I impulsively decided to reveal.

Bryce's eyes clouded, and I suddenly regretted my fat mouth and weak boundaries. "Oh no, I'm sorry to hear that. Was he sick?"

Sick, how? Sick physically, mentally, or both? Revealing the true cause of his demise felt abrupt. *Was he sick?* Yes, he drank himself to death.

"Liver failure," I breathed, enjoying the shock factor.

Bryce's eyes widened.

The council session drifted out of focus as I spent the remainder of the night curiously aware of my new buddy.

"When are you done with work?" Bryce asked suddenly when the meeting ended.

"Ten-thirty," I answered too quickly. "Why?"

"Want to go grab a beer later?"

Uncomfortably aware of the heat in my face, racing pulse, and prickling sensation in my arms and legs, I resisted the urge to fan myself with the agenda.

"That sounds great, but I have to bring my mother to the airport very early in the morning. Maybe another night?"

"What about Wednesday?"

After exchanging phone numbers, I promised to call the following day to finalize plans.

The next morning, Mom, Hope, and I were out the door by six, the interaction with Bryce looping endlessly through my brain. Just before daybreak, I'd leapt off Mom's stiff and unyielding sofa, cheerfully hauling luggage out to the car in the frigid December predawn.

With time for breakfast before boarding call, we gathered in the little airport café after the luggage was checked. Spotting the daily paper on an empty table featuring Bryce's city council article from the night before, I grabbed it excitedly.

"I hope you aren't going to read," Mom frowned. "I thought we'd have a nice breakfast together."

Sliding an orange plastic tray in the cafeteria line, I bypassed breakfast pizza and dried-up looking potato wedges, finally settling on a scoop of slippery eggs that probably came from a powdered mix like the astronauts used in space travel.

"Ah, chill out. I'm not going to look at it now," I answered, my Bryce-fueled euphoria affording a high level of grace and tolerance.

At the cash register, Mom handed over nearly twenty bucks for the three unimpressive trays of breakfast food, then took a seat and forked eggs into her mouth as I continued to glance at the *Duluth News Tribune*. I finally shoved it across the table.

"See that? That's Bryce's article. The guy I'm going out with Wednesday night."

Mom scanned the page. "Oooh, he looks smart. Maybe he'll be a good one."

"Who's Bryce?" Hope asked darkly. "I thought you liked that Rick guy."

"Rick's history," I laughed. "Haven't you been paying attention, girl?"

Even Hope's constant regulation of my love life wasn't going to derail my bliss. Refusing to touch the pricey eggs, I guzzled coffee instead and continued to reread Bryce's article, captivated by his insight.

34

Three days stretched ahead with no responsibilities. I left the airport at seven, the entire day a blank slate to fill however I wished. More sleep sounded good, so a blissful nap called as soon as I got home. Then I lounged around the quiet apartment all day knowing excitement could be generated later. Putzing on the Internet, watching old music videos, and reading passed the time without urgency. A brisk walk in the chilly air redeemed the lazy day, and I returned home satisfied and sweaty as night fell.

What now? A fleeting urge to summon some coworkers crossed my mind, but I quickly nixed it since I was supposed to be on a plane bound for Denver. I checked my phone for messages. Nothing. *I'll go tanning,* I decided, gathering my purse and heading out once again.

Emerging from a baking session under the hot bulbs half an hour later, I climbed into my car and headed toward home. Nothing was left to occupy me, and my brain swiftly changed directions. *I am going to get drunk.* The sustaining image of Dad lying comatose in his hospital bed seemed to have lost its punch.

The neon sign of a cowboy roping a runaway horse into submission blazed into view, and I turned into Rodeo Liquor. Before I knew it, a 12-pack was riding shotgun in the front seat. With renewed energy, I clattered up the stairs to my apartment, the inner battle vanishing as I cracked a beer. *No one will find out.* Being a recluse for the next three days seemed a compelling necessity. My daughter was safely tucked away in Denver, and I wasn't expected for work until Monday. I felt like a ghost who could wreak havoc without leaving tracks behind.

Five beers disappeared as I mechanically scanned internet dating profiles, passing the hours without inner conflict. I was slowly getting primed for another night of beer-fueled excitement.

The supply was running out though, and I wanted to save a few for later on, so I hustled out the door toward the Galley, tossing my now-empty beer can into the weeds before slipping through the side door. The scene inside was more tedious than visiting hours at a nursing home, with nothing to do but pass the next couple of hours chatting with the sixty-year-old bartender. While I shared a long and dreary commentary of the events leading up to my dad's death, she chain-smoked Newports and half-listened.

Teetering on the edge of a blackout, I later retrieved a faint memory of leaving the bar and heading down the street to Champ's, hoping some excitement and fanfare awaited.

Stumbling along the cracked and uneven sidewalk of Grand Avenue, I sensed my rational mind failing and amnesia moving in. My deeply ingrained procedural memory knew where I was going, but my brain wouldn't be coming along for the ride.

What happened at Champ's? The bartender refused my demands for last call, and I was deeply disturbed about it the next day. Had I been flirtatious or downright freaky in my quest to score drinks and attention? Getting cut off at Champ's was serious business, considering career alcoholics were its bread and butter.

As day broke, my thoughts raced to Hope, and I relaxed after realizing she was in Denver. Then came a terrific flood of panic, as I wondered if I'd dragged anyone home from the bar. I crawled out of bed and passed through the kitchen and down the stairs to find the door deadbolted from the inside. Knowing I'd been alone in the apartment relaxed me a little. Outside, the solitary set of footprints visible in the dirty snow eased my conscience.

But an upsetting alarm bell sounded when the memory of the bartender flared. I remembered begging and weaseling as she stood firm: "No. You've had too much to drink. You're done." Had anyone seen this? Had I made a spectacle of myself? My inner demons were on another maddening mission to send me to the asylum.

At least I had no place to be. Cradling my throbbing head in a pillow, I dozed restlessly until three in the afternoon. The headache had subsided then, enabling me to sit up shakily.

Bryce! I hopped out of bed, suddenly activated. *Bryce was waiting.*

My excitement quickly faded as I imagined what I would say. What if Bryce knew how drunk I had been the night before?

That's ridiculous. How could he possibly know? He lives on the other side of town! Besides, what would someone like him be doing in a dive bar?

I punched his number quickly, hoping the sound of his rich baritone voice would ease my anxiety, but it rang three times before going to voice mail. My heart plummeted as I imagined Bryce blowing me off. *He probably reconsidered going out with you because he found out you're a drunken fool.*

After leaving a carefully staged and casual-sounding voice-mail, I hung up feeling dejected. Drunk. Drink. *That's right!* Six beers waited in the fridge. A little chemical help would make me feel better, ease the pesky inner voices, maybe even "make" Bryce call! It was only three in the afternoon, but a brewski couldn't hurt. My hands were unsteady as I popped the cap. After draining the bottle, I jumped into the shower. The phone rang as I was toweling off, making it really seem like the beer helped to move things along.

"Melissa? It's Bryce. How are you?"

"I'm good. I've just been cleaning house all day," I fibbed.

"So dedicated." Bryce chuckled as I flushed, standing there naked and dripping on the bathmat.

"I'm still working. Want to meet up at nine?"

"That sounds great. How about Mr. D's? It's pretty close to my house."

"D's sounds great," Bryce agreed. "I haven't been to that place in ages."

Gleeful again, last night's troubles were long forgotten. More beer awaited soon, but I needed to be patient for now. I planned to bring my A-game tonight. I was *not* going to screw up the chance to impress Bryce.

Distracting myself with projects around the house protected me from my leftover beer until seven, then I was free to happily polish off the rest of my stash. I had limited myself to five—plus one measly swallow of Pucker carefully measured into a shot glass.

That night, Mr. D's would serve its purpose well; a bit of a rowdy sports bar, but still a fun place for a casual drink with an attractive male colleague. As I turned into the parking lot, I watched an old drunk man stumble up the sidewalk and disappear into one of the seedier adjacent taverns. Drinking at Mr. D's definitely brought me up a notch. Sweeping into the bar, I wondered if anyone recognized me from the news. *Surely, they must.*

My date was back by the pool tables, awkwardly sipping a beer in a brown leather jacket and glancing at a hockey game droning on the television as though it offered enough reason to be drinking alone. He looked relieved to see me.

"You made it!"

Wedging ourselves in between a lady in a Polaris windbreaker and a long-bearded man with his eyes closed, I ignored the lack of space and got busy ordering a round with the organized execution of someone with an advanced degree in boozeology.

"How about a shot? You've had a hard day, right?"

Bryce shrugged as I signaled the bartender again.

"I'm not really a shot guy, but why not? Just don't mess me up too bad," he added with a chuckle.

"A couple of Hot 100s too," I winked, flashing a wad of bills. "I call it 'Bad Medicine.' Wait, no. Fireball—or Hot 100 . . . what do you say, Bryce? You want to drink like the big dogs?"

Ultimately, I settled for Hot 100, and the additional alcohol kick. For the next three hours, Bryce and I rattled on about our jobs, lives, and pasts. I matched him beer for beer, shot for shot. Shortly after the chatty revelry, I slipped into oblivion—the place where memories didn't live.

Bryce was struggling to keep up with my endless requests for rounds of alcohol, and the remainder of the night was preserved in snatches.

When did we leave the bar? I didn't know, but dimly remembered being parked in Bryce's car where he finally delivered the kiss I'd been waiting for. What was it like? I only had a faint clip left behind of the moment our lips locked. Retrieving the brief memory later was more like watching it on a screen happening to someone else.

The time after the kiss was blank—I'd slipped into blackout again. My memory then jogged forward to a scene in front of my house—where I'd brazenly begged Bryce to come inside "just for a minute." He'd been resisting, but eventually, I won the battle.

Two hours later, Bryce pried himself from my embrace. We'd been purposelessly rolling around on my bed, though every stitch of clothing remained intact. He must have understood on some intuitive level that going too far would've been a fatal error.

"Mel . . . it's three-thirty in the morning . . . I *really* have to go. I have that important meeting with my publisher in a few hours."

No fight left in me, I watched him leave the room through my drunken haze and then promptly passed out.

35

Sabotage. I always destroyed every opportunity with decent, smart, attractive guys. Bryce was the total package: good-looking, chivalrous, and educated—but I'd blown it anyway. Thursday morning dawned with electrifying shame to compound what little memory remained of our disastrous rendezvous. One thing was crystal clear—I'd behaved exactly how I'd vowed not to. Recalling my date scrambling out the door in the wee hours of the morning was mortifying. Wishing I could wipe all traces of myself from the world, for the third day in a row I rolled over and buried my head in the pillow. Sleeping until three in the afternoon was easily becoming a habit. When Hope wasn't around I had absolutely no self-regulation.

Later that afternoon, I managed to introduce some eggs to my queasy stomach and then wasted the next several hours watching mindless television. I'd soon be jetting off to Denver, but my throbbing head and guilt-ridden mind blunted any excitement. Sad and defeated, the much-anticipated night with Bryce had ended in an epic failure at my own hands.

The hours slowly ticked by as I hovered over the kitchen table with a beer, glancing distastefully at my math notes. I was still plodding through advanced algebra at UWS, the final class needed for graduation requirements. Communications majors didn't require much math, but this course had been a major stumbling block.

Professor Westley had approached me with concern around the mid-point of the semester. "Melissa, I am afraid you're in danger of failing my class. Would it help to meet at my office for some extra guidance?"

I accepted his offer and showed up weekly at Ross Hall, strangely the same place I'd attended treatment a few years back. The rehab had closed the previous year, and now housed faculty offices. Through one-on-one instruction, I was able to finally understand probability and other elusive math concepts.

The professor's special help was hard to recall with a horrible hangover intensified by depression though, so I shoved the notes aside in frustration and tuned the TV to VH1 Classic. Zoning out on old videos from The Doors and Cream for the next couple of hours helped to quiet my spinning mind. Staring a hole through the television, I considered packing my suitcase, but the obsessive thoughts crowding my mind squashed any motivation. *You're a drunk and a lowlife loser. No one is ever going to love you.*

The relentless attacks of the enemy coalesced with my own self-talk until I couldn't tease out the owner of each voice. Very limited memory of the night with Bryce remained, reassurance was nonexistent. Who knows what I had done? Anything was on the table.

My day had begun with a vow to avoid alcohol, but once it was eight o'clock my resolve crumbled and I found myself popping the cap off another beer.

Once I'd emptied the fridge, I ventured down to the West Duluth bar district for several more. Bored and subdued, I glanced around at the clientele, wondering what I had expected to find. *Someday, this place was going to burn. Would my whole life be inside?*

Sliding from the barstool, for the first time in ages I remembered the starry walk home, the Milky Way visible in spite of the dull light pollution spilling down Grand Avenue. Nights like these made me wonder if I *could* control my drinking.

Morning dawned, and the reality of my math final blazed into focus. Last night I'd pushed it off, but the remaining linchpin to my bachelor's degree was inescapable now. Everyone at work thought I had graduated years ago. I carried residual shame about this little white lie and the truth behind it—alcohol was the only roadblock to the elusive degree I'd chased since 1991.

Fighting back panic, I moved shakily to the bathroom for a quick shower, wondering why I was so hung over when I hadn't had nearly as much as usual. I grabbed my school bag with fifteen minutes to race over the bridge into Superior, my entire spotty college career hanging in the balance over this one final test. If I failed, my degree would be down the toilet.

I rolled into the parking lot of UW-Superior shortly after speeding over the Bong Bridge, wedged myself into a staff parking space, and bolted up the stairs of the historic Old Main building with about ten seconds to spare.

Professor Westley delivered a warning look as I charged into the room and slid into an empty desk in the very last row. I really didn't want to disappoint him. Being late, in withdrawal, and dreadfully unprepared nearly pushed me into a full-blown panic attack, and I struggled to manage the familiar flow of adrenaline rushing into my system as the test was circulated. The equations were simply gibberish, and my hands trembled so badly I could barely hold my pencil steady.

Somehow, I managed to complete the final, hand it in, and escape the halls of Old Main, never to return again.

36

Delta Airlines delivered me to Denver International hours later, and though it had been nearly ten years since I'd made it out to Colorado, my mental dread spiral blocked any enjoyment of the four-day getaway. Playing at the park with my brother's sweet children was impaired by obsessive thoughts of Bryce and fears about my college career. The vivid scenes of receiving a failing grade remained as long as booze-induced depression dominated my system.

By Sunday night, I was slowly shaking the web of self-pity shrouding my future. Five days later on Christmas Eve, we were back in Duluth, and Hope and I stayed with Mom for the holiday. Dad had been dead for twelve days.

"I need something to drink."

Rummaging through Mom's refrigerator yielded a treasure: a single beer representing the end of Dad's stash. *This will be my last one.*

The holidays passed uneventfully, and other than the lone beer I stayed away from alcohol and even avoided the revelry right down the street at the West Duluth bars on New Year's Eve.

Halfway through January, I addressed the stack of mail I always avoided and found a yellow envelope from UWS tucked between junk flyers and magazines I thought would make me smarter but never read (like *Popular Science*). That canary-colored letter held my final grades. With a pounding heart, I tore it open to reveal a string of As and a B minus in math, bringing my cumulative GPA up to a respectable 3.0. *I had earned a bachelor's degree.* Professor Westley's comment beside my final grade brought tears to my eyes: *Melissa demonstrated great improvement and a willingness to work hard.*

My gaze fell on a favorite black-and-white photo of Dad and his Barbershop quartet sitting in a stack on the table, and I realized I no longer had to fib about my college education. I was filled with sudden awareness of how proud he would've been.

"You see that?" I said, holding the letter up to his picture. "I did it!"

Dad loved to tease me about the little white lie reflected in my bio on the KDLH website. My profile claimed I held a bachelor's degree, but he knew the real truth.

"What a load of BS," he used to rib me.

Three more weeks passed, and I was riding high on my newfound success and feelings of mastery. I was a college graduate, *and* I was stone-cold-sober—more than sixty days this time. It had been years since I'd been able to manage such a long dry spell.

The first week of February was spent finalizing plans for Dad's upcoming memorial service at my childhood church. My father had left us only two months before, but a quiet peace had settled, and we didn't long for his return.

The memorial service was flawless and beautiful. Dave and I had spent hours assembling poster boards with pictures of Dad from birth to death, and nearly two hundred people gathered to remember him. My mother had been worried about the turnout, but we found out he was quite well-loved. Dave and I delivered perfect, appropriate speeches for the service.

"In my Father's house there are many rooms," I kicked my memorial address off with a Bible passage from the fourteenth chapter of John I didn't completely understand, but it sounded good, and I knew it was commonly used at funerals, and then moved on to a subtle bit about Dad's struggle with the bottle: "Alcohol exchanges the drabs of reality for the spangles of fantasy," I read, paraphrasing Jack London's *John Barleycorn*. Standing at the altar scanning the crowd, I realized I had moved many to tears.

On a high following the speech, I reminisced with family and old friends and the atmosphere in the church basement turned congenial as guests chatted and returned to the "life goes on" mode. Sunlight filtered through the high, narrow basement windows, turning particles in the air to golden fairy dust, and I felt cozy and secure as chatter buzzed around me.

Picking at the plate of food I didn't plan to eat, I disengaged from the table conversation to reflect on the many Sunday mornings I'd spent in a musty classroom in that very basement, along with my dutiful attendance at confirmation classes. It seemed to have yielded little. Despite all the churchy exposure, countless Sundays were still spent staring at the ceiling thinking secretly to myself, *I'm not sure you exist, God.*

I had even disclosed this to my mother one day after becoming unable to bear the shame of my unbelief any longer. She wasn't shocked and assured me everything would make sense someday. Back then, God was more of a lovely fable than the Living Word. So far, no one had shown me how to access His power in my life.

Still, my childhood church had served as a haven in many ways, providing some stability and sense of community. Vacation Bible School was a major highlight every year. "For God so loved the world," is the promise in perhaps the most famous Bible verse. That scripture doesn't have a thing to do with our behavior—it simply says to *believe*. Believe in the One who was sent, and you will have everlasting life. Believing and accepting Jesus also manifests in the fruit of a changed heart and life. I wouldn't internalize this truth for many years, yet John 3:16 was the catalyst and the seed, planted by Pike Lake Presbyterian church.

Through the din of departing guests, I overheard Uncle Mark and his wife planning to make their next stop the Le Grande Supper Club for a quick drink. The woodsy bar and lounge had been a favorite hangout of Dad's—also known as *The Venture,* its former name from the 1960s when Dad was a young boozer.

Melis . . . your uncle left me stranded at the Venture one night after we'd had a few. I had to walk all the way back to Caribou Lake in 20 below . . . no gloves, my hands down the back of my pants to keep warm.

Dad held many memories of the family gathering place that sometimes offered good times and blessed release, but at other points served as a catalyst for many feuds with my mother when he stayed out drinking all night.

The Le Grande and the Chalet had their own elusive power, and the life force they produced certainly didn't intend to ruin lives. The aging supper clubs cemented family and friends together in a way that only alcohol and camaraderie could.

"We're just going to stop for one, for Dan," Mark's wife mentioned casually, as they said their goodbyes to my mother. Uncles, aunts, and cousins who'd traveled from out of town prepared to head back to hotel rooms in groups. Soon, everyone was discussing meeting places and the gathering turned from remembering Dad's life—to prioritizing the still-living. Hotel rooms, poolside tables, and hot tub cocktails awaited. Alcohol helped to bring loved ones back, and the fact that it had claimed my father's life didn't really connect with anyone in a meaningful way.

"We'll have to hit the hotel lounge later," someone said from the departing crowd. Nonchalant, festive, and harmless, the drinking talk eased the awkward stiffness that came at funerals, offering conviviality and lifted moods.

Dave and Jenn appeared, each burdened with armfuls of leftover food from the buffet table. We hauled everything out to Mom's car, discussing plans for the evening in the fading daylight.

"We're going back to Mom's, and then we'll head out to Northland in a while. You're still coming, right? Social hour starts at six-thirty."

The fancy-schmancy gathering hosted by Dave's best friend included me, too. *Social hour.* Digesting the word, I imagined sitting alone at this swanky place with my big brother and all of his successful friends.

"I'll be there."

Dave glanced around. "Where's Hope?"

"Seth's parents offered to take her home. They knew about Mom's house guests and my dinner plans with you guys."

Another open night. As I pondered the casual drinking comments of the others, a powerful urge gripped, me and I wholeheartedly believed that *this time* everything would be different—the goal of social drinking I'd failed to master would magically work now: two or three but *no more*. The sixty days of clean time I'd pulled together seemed insignificant as I drove slowly from the church back out to Highway 53.

Pike Lake Liquor loomed in the distance with a cluster of cars buzzing through the parking lot, everyone gearing up for a lively Saturday night. People trickled outside under the neon signs with an added pep to their step as cases and quarts were harmlessly tucked into trunks. *Why couldn't I be one of them?*

The liquor store looked so friendly and approachable that a six-pack of Mike's Hard Lemonade had joined me in the passenger seat just minutes later. I glanced over at it repeatedly as I drove down the hill to West Duluth—barely resisting the urge to pop open a delicious drink for the road. The neat little six-pack seemed to belong there.

Once I rolled up my driveway, it was *game on*—I plucked a lemonade from the cardboard holder and swilled it before I was in the door. Half an hour later, the rest of the six-pack was gone.

While sipping the syrupy little bottled cocktails, I spent a fair amount of time ensuring I'd blend seamlessly with Dave and his friends as I combed through my closet with a critical eye. I finally selected a long black flowered skirt and drawstring shirt—an ensemble I believed represented the perfect mix of mourning and moxie. At six, I returned to my car and made the ten-mile drive east to the Northland Country Club. I didn't feel drunk, just comfortably numb and ready to face a group of successful strangers.

The stately Victorian mansion was set back in the woods—pristine and wonderfully secluded. The temptation of a hidden bar was a dangerous trigger that never grew old. Reflecting on the night in Pine City when I'd met Rick, I parked my car and walked toward the white-pillared building. Though the whole debacle with the guy from South Dakota had been a recipe for disaster, the anticipation of another night with an unknown ending was still a harbinger of excitement. The sky had clouded as night drew on, and a thin glaze of snowfall made the sidewalk slick.

The ground level of the country club was quiet as a library, with massive mahogany doors leading to a foyer and a small bar in the corner. A maroon carpeted staircase commanded the center aisle up to the second floor, the high loft ceilings creating a cavernous atmosphere.

Feeling like a trailer park girl in a Walmart skirt desperately trying to masquerade as someone high-class, I realized the hard lemonades had lost their punch and I needed more booze, fast.

Moving through the foyer and into the dining area, I spotted a large banquet table beautifully set in the center of the room. Creeping closer, the place card in the middle indicated it was reserved for our party. I was the first to arrive.

Feeling odd and out of place hovering in the empty room, I returned to the less intimidating foyer. A jacketed young guy had emerged and was now jostling bottles behind the small bar.

"Are you open?" I asked as though it didn't matter.

"No, this bar isn't," he answered apologetically. "But there's a lounge upstairs."

I thanked him with a broad smile, tasting the magic words. *Lounge upstairs.* Ascending the grand staircase reminded me of Stephen King's *The Shining,* and I wished I'd end up snowed in that night, hidden away and cared for with a fully stocked bar and servants for assistance.

Little action awaited in the hideaway—but alcohol was available, and that was the point. Two guys huddled at the bar mesmerized by a basketball game; the remaining patrons young men in tuxedos smoking cigars and sipping from brandy snifters.

After forking over five bucks for a beer, I minded my own business. Not much to see other than the guys across the way. The huskier one gabbed on a cell phone and glanced in my direction occasionally. Happily hidden away from Dave and the rest, I could safely drink. I wondered how many beers I could chug before the rest of the guests showed up.

37

Soon I migrated to the opposite side of the bar, flirting with the two guys I'd mentally ripped apart at first. Bart, the huskier of the pair, was kind of dorky, but I didn't resist his offer of free beer.

"I'm waiting for the McNamara party," I mentioned, referring to my brother's close friend and sure to point out I wasn't just a gold digger on a quest to pick up rich guys.

Bart nodded. "I know Pete McNamara."

Signaling the bartender, he requested notification when Pete and the others arrived. I watched, mildly impressed, and may have pursued things further with this awkward rich boy if Pete hadn't appeared in the doorway then, just in time to find me slamming a root beer barrel.

I trailed downstairs, rationalizing the scene by insisting I was just killing a few minutes.

Pete chuckled and offered a knowing look. "Right. I know what Bart's all about. Seems I arrived just in time."

Tripping down the grand staircase would be my last full memory—the rest of the evening faded into a blur and time stood still. Hazy recollections later surfaced of being at the table guzzling 32-ounce glasses of very strong dark beer, somewhat odd for me since my preferred swill was pale light brew I consumed like water. Many of my brother's crew resided in the Colorado Rockies and were connoisseurs of fancy microbrews though, so I imagine I was just going along with the gang. Distantly I knew shots would have been inappropriate, but I was still doing a bang-up job of getting blisteringly wrecked out of my mind on "just" beer, and it didn't take long for Dave to notice my incoherence.

"What is going on with you?" he hissed, jerking me from the table and out into the hallway. "How much have you had to drink tonight?"

Unable to support my weight, I slid down the wall into a heap on the floor. The Jekyll-Hyde was in full effect.

"I hardly had ANYTHING!" I screamed. "It's amazing you even included me in your little thing here," I slurred. "I'm sure you don't even WANT me around! I'm just gonna go home."

"There's no way you're driving!"

Dave's firm comments quickly flipped my moody attitude to one of tear-soaked hostility.

"Well what, then? What do you want me to do?" I sobbed.

We moved to a private area to talk, where I continued to cry and snuffle through my snotty nose. "I know I have a problem, but I just can't stop!"

Dave tried to help, but the haughty country club within earshot of a dozen or so of his friends was definitely *not* the place. I needed to go far away before I soiled our family name even further.

"You need your meetings!" he commanded.

"But I've *tried* that!"

My brother called a cab and shoved me out the door, but I'd be very grateful for it later. I don't remember my lovely chariot arriving, saying goodbye to anyone, or what they may have witnessed.

My next recollection was the driver peering at me in the rearview mirror.

"Mel? It's Tim. Do you remember me?"

Tim was an old alcohol buyer from Landing Liquor, a helpful gap-toothed wino I'd encountered back in high school who supplied me with beer and strawberry schnapps. With his kinky bright orange hair, I always told him he looked like Ted Nugent. Squinting in the glare of the dome light now, I tried to distinguish his face, but it no longer resembled that of a favorite rock star. He'd morphed into the grim reaper.

Damage control began early the next day with the enormous hangover that shepherded in Sunday. My mornings-after were so debilitating now that I could barely function for days after a blow-out night of drinking. The phone on the bedside table rang, and I struggled to open my eyes, squinting at the display. Mom. *Here we go.* Dave had already been in touch, recounting all of my precious behavior. I was suddenly despondent and desperate.

"Was it your Dad's memorial that set you off?" she demanded.

Wiping my eyes with the blanket, I wished I could sleep for a hundred years and tune everything out forever.

"I don't know!" I squeaked through a voice thick with tears. "What do you want me to say? I don't *plan* to do these things, Mother! They just happen! Once I start, I can't stop. I don't understand it."

She sighed, and her tone softened. "Honey, you are thirty years old now, but it's plain to see you still don't like yourself."

Hope would be home soon, so I hung up the phone and summoned another cab for the good old walk of shame back to the Northland Country Club to collect my car. Home again an hour later, I suffered on the couch like the living dead, staring hopelessly at the television and dozing until Seth's parents arrived.

"Mom, want to go see a movie?" Hope asked as soon as she walked in. I shouldn't have needed every remaining shred of motivation to honor my daughter's simple request and felt pathetic sitting next to her in the dark theater, painfully sick. Halfway through the show, she seemed to sense my despair and reached over sweetly to grasp my hand. With tears glistening in my eyes, I felt God brushing me through my beloved daughter. I needed to live for *her*—not the approval of others, a guy, or my beloved beer bottles. For the rest of the movie, I tried to focus on the precious gift of Hope—but memories of the night before continued to rot my brain like fruit left out in the sun.

Later, when she was tucked into bed, I called Dave and Jenn.

"I'm sorry about my behavior last night," I wheedled.

Dave was not quick to say my actions were cool with him, and we talked seriously for quite a while.

"What are you going to do about it? You need to put yourself into treatment or see a psychologist. Seriously, Melissa, please consider it."

The conversation with Jenn was a little different and much more bearable. She'd pretty much dismissed my antics.

"Big deal. Everyone does stupid things when they drink. My friend Angie gets mean. I have to watch her. Maybe your Dad's thing just got to you."

Her response was much easier to swallow than the shrink or rehab my brother advocated.

Once again, the voice I wanted to believe was louder than the one that spoke the truth.

38

My Dad certainly had faults, but I never intended to degrade his memory the way I had the night of the memorial. Getting drunk in front of Dave was excruciating. Though he knew pieces of my addictive history, he'd distanced himself from the progression through college and an eventual move out West. Now, the starkness of the battle was right in his face. The horrible and humiliating experience of my straight-laced brother seeing me completely wrecked out of my mind was enough to keep me sober for over a month.

After a while, Dave was back in Colorado and the pressure subsided. I stumbled upon an amazing opportunity with a local Marine recruiter who introduced me to a program for news media to attend a week-long military conference in San Diego, California. Instantly mobilized by the prospect of a trip to a warm destination, I completed the required paperwork and flew out with Dennis two weeks later.

Any feeble attempts at sobriety vanished as the state of Minnesota faded into the backdrop. Excessive drinking moved into focus, the distance providing the perfect scapegoat for a week of insanity and getting totally ripped every night. Dennis had no objections—knowing my sobriety efforts never lasted long made it more likely I'd make some more bad choices that included him.

With the stage set perfectly for a week of drunken antics, we shot stories, traveled to locations, and cranked out endless news packages from sunrise to sunset. Once night fell, our reward came at the hotel lounge that served jumbo margaritas and Mexican appetizers. Self-control wasn't on my radar; every night was spent closing the bar down and then somehow stumbling back to my hotel room to pass out.

The week in San Diego was ending before I knew it, the final night spent gathering with people from the conference. The great band playing in the trendy hotel bar helped blot out the reality of the party's end. Dennis had been subdued the whole week, keeping his distance and allowing me a leash to hang myself. Noting his careful evaluation of me in social situations, he would've been furious if I showed even the slightest interest in anyone of the opposite sex.

Lucky for him, no one had caught my eye the entire week. Of course attractive men were everywhere—just not the type who'd be interested in a slightly chunky, eccentric girl forever masquerading and painfully uncomfortable with herself. The easy-going nautical types crawling Half Moon Bay were way out of my league. No matter. That final night I'd be double-fisting it and bonding with booze. I wasted no time summoning the bartender with my orders.

"Two margaritas and two large beer taps," I requested, winking. Watching him walk away, I decided he was the best thing I'd seen all week. *Probably married.*

Dennis looked bothered. Ignoring him, I swilled beer and practiced my refined talent of drinking even the Marines under the table.

"Let's dance!" I yelled, trying to drag Dennis onto the floor as the band broke into a jazzy rendition of "Brick House." *"I love this song!"* I drained my glass and tugged on his arm. "Come on, please? Let's have *fun!*"

Dennis would not budge. Never before had I seen him bust a move, and tonight wasn't going to be his big debut. Finally, I settled for yanking him to the edge of the floor to serve as a captive audience for my "Brick House" moves.

Back at the bar, my schmooziness increased with the stunning bartender, who was very attentive to my drinking needs. I showed my appreciation by showering him with handsome tips.

"What's your name?" I asked when Dennis was occupied with another conversation.

"Kenny."

His grin revealed dazzlingly white teeth. I was spellbound.

"Well, there Kenny, you are a mighty good bartender," I gushed, tipping my glass.

He laughed and refilled my beer.

Ditching Dennis so I could talk to Kenny *alone* had been impossible because so far he'd been stuck to me like flypaper, but eventually he retreated to the bathroom. Leaning as far across the bar as possible, I whispered drunkenly to my new hot prospect.

"Do you have a wife or a girlfriend?"

Pretty blunt, but there wasn't time to pussyfoot around the subject.

"No, I don't. Are you single?"

Thrilling. *"Yes, I am."*

"I figured the guy you're with was your boyfriend," Kenny answered with a surprised look.

"Nope, he's not. Everyone assumes that, but he's my *coworker*. He's a good friend. That's all. Do you want to stop by after work?"

He caught my eye from the mirror above the bar and smiled again.

"Sure. What room you in?"

Dennis returned as I was giving Kenny directions, and took his seat silently. His look of annoyance soon escalated into fury. "Did you just ask the bartender out?" he finally exploded.

"Yeah. What about it?"

Trashed beyond recognition, my memory all but failed. Around closing time and pretty close to the point of passing out, I desperately tried to hold it together for Kenny by presenting myself as flirtatiously tipsy rather than falling down drunk.

"I just have to clean up, and then I'll be over in about half an hour," he promised, shuffling me out. I somehow stumbled back to my room.

Kenny made good on his word and arrived at my door armed with a bottle of wine, but I was dead to the world. My roommate found the whole situation hysterical as she recounted it the next morning. I'd just spent thirty minutes under a blisteringly hot shower but remained barely coherent.

"We tried to wake you up for like fifteen minutes," she explained, filling in the night with the gaping unknown ending. Finally, I looked at the bartender—what was his name? Kenny? I was like—well is she *dead?*"

Funny, right? While my roommate enjoyed a good laugh, I pretended to chuckle along in hopes of conveying an accidental night of excess. But inside, I was truly horrified by my brush with death.

The mind-blowing hangover worsened as I imagined Kenny trying to rouse me from my dead, drunken sleep. The stressful day of travel awaiting would be marked by withdrawal, shame, and depression, but at least I'd never see the roommate or the bartender again. Longing to crawl back into bed and die, instead I needed to paste on a phony smile, make it through one final gathering, and head to the airport.

Everyone met up the final morning of the conference for a huge breakfast organized by the military officials who'd been our escorts all week. A tasty buffet, lots of normal, happy people—and me.

Riding to the event with Dennis, I flipped down the visor mirror only to discover an alarming scarlet rash on my face, chest, and neck. Hives from the withdrawal.

Dennis was still aggravated but had softened because I was a trainwreck—covered with red splotches, in withdrawal, and fighting back tears. As we lined up for the food, I knew I was going to be sick.

"Excuse me," I managed, before bolting out of the room.

I stumbled into the bathroom and locked myself into a stall, barely in time to empty the contents of my stomach (which was mostly bitter-tasting bile), then reemerged only to collapse into a wing chair in the little attached powder room. My fragile state made pulling it all together unfathomable.

After dabbing my mouth, I huddled a few minutes more in excruciating withdrawal sickness praying no one would find me. No such luck. Seconds later, the door swung open, and a cute blonde woman came in, greeted me with a nod, and retreated into a bathroom stall. After finishing, she washed her hands and stood fixing her hair at the sink.

"Pretty hungover, huh?"

Was it that obvious? I simply nodded, there was nothing to say.

"We took it easy last night. I've been so busy with the activities all week, I haven't even had *time* to drink! The pace of this trip has been outrageous, don't you think? I need to go home so I can relax!"

I lacked the strength to respond, but begged to know the answer to the question that had tortured me for almost fifteen years: *How can someone forget to drink?*

"Hope you feel better," she offered with a sympathetic grin.

Casting a wan smile in return, I rejoiced once she was gone and returned to feebly collecting myself. I was pouring sweat and felt like I might pass out, so I wet some paper towels with cold water and blotted my face and neck while silently screaming, *WHY CAN'T I JUST BE LIKE HER?!* She looked cute, popular, and fun. She didn't get falling-down-drunk every night.

Please God, help me get through this, I begged in my usual plea of desperation. Somehow, I gathered my wits enough to make it back into the conference room.

After the breakfast gathering that marked the end of the trip came the draining hassle of airports, luggage, and connecting flights. Jammed next to Dennis on the plane, the only escape was sleep that wouldn't come. Needing the sugar to survive, I mowed through a large bag of fun-sized Snickers bars. When I was hungover, my brain craved sugar like a drug-addicted lunatic.

As I agonized over my latest tragic fall from grace, I methodically polished off the bag of candy and folded each empty wrapper into makeshift origami in an effort to avoid Dennis's pitying glances. He wanted to have a deep heart-to-heart—but I was in no mood. I spent the remainder of the flight analyzing the week in San Diego, wondering if anything could be salvaged. I'd put together ten high-quality stories, a few even picked up by national networks. The affiliates across the country didn't know I was powering through a massive hangover as I stood executing a flawless stand-up near soldiers qualifying for marksmanship status. But a closer look revealed my pasty skin and bloodshot eyes. I witnessed amazing things on the trip—like the Crucible—the toughest test of strength, will, and endurance a Marine recruit would ever endure. I even got to see the small beachside bungalow that had been the site of Tom Cruise and Kelly McGillis's rendezvous in *Top Gun*.

The trip had been the thrill of a lifetime, but a solid week of sickness and hangovers blotted out the bright spots. As thoughts drifted back to Kenny, deep regret flooded in as I realized I had failed again. Could I reach him somehow? I couldn't even remember his last name. *How could the party be over already?* A little consolation was tucked within the fact that my indiscretions had been carried out many miles away. Dennis would keep quiet.

I arrived home near midnight, so depleted that I could barely schlep my suitcase to the top of the stairs. Hope had spent the week with Mom, and I'd pick her up first thing in the morning. My daughter's consolation for a week without me was a bagful of cheesy souvenirs: tacky magnets and an airport T-shirt screen printed with: SOMEBODY WHO LOVES ME WENT TO SAN DIEGO AND ALL I GOT WAS THIS LOUSY T-SHIRT. Looking at my sorry offerings flooded me with the most worthless feeling imaginable.

39

A quiet week at home with Hope followed the mind-numbing trip, but soon the memory of the harrowing plane ride spent in alcohol withdrawal faded. The nonstop glowing reviews of the boot camp stories I'd shot helped to ease my inner turbulence. No one cared about my boozefest. I pasted my ego back together and tucked my near overdose away.

Liquor cravings were muted until Friday night, Hope was invited to a birthday sleepover party, and an intense urge to drink took her place. Without resistance, I threw on some shoes, grabbed my keys, and headed off to Rodeo Liquor. The guy manning the store was sipping a tall boy of malt liquor from behind the counter. Somehow it was reassuring to know I wasn't the only who once thought sipping beer at work was acceptable, though I was terrified of doing it now. We chatted for a few minutes, and he offered me a can of whatever I wanted while I shopped.

After I'd finished off the free beer and collected a 12-pack, I trudged back to my apartment and cranked up some Aerosmith tunes. Not knowing what the night would hold was tantalizing, and the hard rock and secret beers primed the night for action. Alcohol *made* things happen. Magical things. The film of a movie reel was already cranking in my head.

Minutes later, the phone rang. It was Leah, a producer from KDLH.

"There's a party over at Kent's from Channel 9 tonight. He invited the whole crew from the station. You want to go?"

This was fantastic news, and a school of bipolar butterflies erupted in my stomach at the sound of her words. "Sweet! Why don't you come over here first? We can have a couple before we go."

Leah agreed, and as I waited for her, a tiny voice suggested that getting drunk in the presence of the competition might not be the greatest idea. My compadres? Ah, it would be harmless. We were all off duty, having a few cocktails, right? No big deal.

Another beer quieted my concerns, and Leah soon arrived with her blonde hair done up in a French twist. Amused, I wondered if I was underdressed in my jeans and black drape sweater. After lounging in the living room laughing over a few old photo albums for a while, I soon became antsy to add some excitement to the party.

"I want to show you a bar down in my neck of the woods. We could have a quick one, then cab it over to the party. You up for that?"

Leah shrugged. "Why not?"

We returned to Rodeo Liquor, picked up another 12-pack, then parked and headed into the Galley. The decision to leave my car in the lot and retrieve it in the morning felt like a very responsible one. My old Galley pals slumped on their worn stools with smudgy tap glasses in front of them, calling out greetings. I was friendly but wouldn't be staying tonight. I had better things to do. See ya later, lowlifes.

After downing a couple of quick taps, we hailed a cab over to Kent's. The news party was in full swing when we walked in, and I was in my absolute prime for a while.

Right away, I stumbled into my good Caribou Lake buddy Amy and her husband Pat. We'd connected back in February at Dad's memorial service, but it was even better to drink together. She was the last person I expected to see at a gathering of newscasters, and my drunk self couldn't get over the good fortune of running into one of my favorite people.

"What are you doing here?" I yelled with delight. I didn't know it right then, but I would later realize that Jesus was the reason our paths had crossed.

Amy and Kent's girlfriend worked together, I later learned. Only because of Amy's presence, I escaped being thrown to the wolves and left passed out at yet another frat house.

There is precious little that I recall about the night. The parts I do remember were spent with Amy and Pat. My behavior was frat-party appropriate at first—gushing over people, helping myself to trays of shots, and having off-color conversations with various reporters, weather guys, and photographers. The kitchen doorway was my post for quite a while.

I would not have another memory for the next five hours.

Amy was my supervisor—my trusted childhood friend, the babysitter who made sure I didn't defame myself beyond recognition or worse—get dragged into a bedroom by some drunk and aging former frat boy.

She couldn't protect me from everything I wanted to do, however. The next day I learned I had given the DJ a *lap dance,* (clothed, but still)—and those harmless station competitors had front-row seats for all of it.

Amy shook me awake around three in the morning, her familiar voice sounding just a little like it was addressing a small child who had fallen asleep at the circus.

"The party's over. Come on, Melis. Pat and I will take you home."

I stumbled outside to their van (incredible that I could walk at all) while mumbling about bailing on Leah, then passed out again until we reached the Galley.

Amy insisted on driving my car the few blocks to my house, though I told her she didn't need to. After she and Pat made sure I was safely inside, I stumbled upstairs and did what I do best—attempted to bake a Tombstone pizza.

But of course I couldn't stay awake for the twenty minutes of cooking time. The next morning, the oven was still cranked to 400 degrees, the air was filled with a thick haze of gray smoke that filled the entire apartment, and the pizza (which had been baking for the past eight hours) was a hard little black briquette.

40

The pizza and the potential of burning the house down were the least of my worries. I was so beside myself over what I had done I considered checking into a psychiatric ward. The shame I felt was indescribable. After working so hard to secure the reporting position at KDLH, I always tried to present myself as a serious news professional. Now the people I wanted so desperately to impress had seen me at my absolute worst.

The morning after dawned as a day of death, quite possibly the worst of my life. The entire week following Kent's big bash marked the roughest and most depressive post-drinking binge assault. Terror, panic, and helplessness were eating me alive.

I received a small taste of the impression I'd made on people in the coming days via my colleagues and their wide-eyed stares. They'd seen me in a full-on blackout, and there was no erasing what they'd witnessed.

To this point they'd been blind to my destructive descent, but Kent's party showcased my complete loss of control. The people I wanted to impress saw the very same things my mother did when she found me passed out in my own vomit at fifteen.

Normal partiers didn't understand how excruciating this event had been for me, how *terrifically degrading*. The gravity of the situation was impossible for anyone to grasp—I'd just experienced an *alcohol relapse*—the inevitable return to active use I always eventually caved to. It hadn't been just a little slip-up or "went overboard" sort of thing. No. I had once again said *yes* to the gravitational pull of my deadly addiction—and making that choice carried a very high price tag. Nothing I'd tried so far had been able to permanently save me from *the return*, and each time I drank again I risked death, rape, or grievous harm. Normal drinkers couldn't begin to understand the magnitude of my personal consequences.

Compounding my horrific shame, I also learned I'd been propositioning Amy's husband! *My long-time best friend!* While blacked out, I was completely unpredictable and not the slightest bit trustworthy. Unaware, out of my mind—I'd sidled up to Pat when Amy was out of earshot and said something indecent, something sexual. Stunning. Even more mind-boggling was the fact that *she* didn't hate me. Pat declined my offer, of course. He was a man of honor, just trying to steer clear of a drunk old friend.

The morning after the party, I crawled out of bed *only* because Hope was waiting. After throwing on a baseball hat, I regarded myself in the mirror with disgust. Looking *rough*.

My daughter was happy to see me and climbed into the car excitedly while jabbering about the party. The piñata, the cake, the late-night giggling, the girl talk. Suddenly, she stopped in mid-sentence, and her nose began to twitch. She sniffed the air, eyebrows furrowed.

"What? What? Why are you doing that?"

She met my eyes with a steely gaze. "I smell something peculiar. Something that smells an awful lot like *beer*."

Frozen and flooded with shame, I could do nothing but lie. "I don't know why you would say that. All I can smell is bacon. Was Faith's mom cooking bacon?"

Hope dropped the subject but clearly knew the truth. It was awful to realize she didn't trust me. I remembered Dad and his NFL vodka mug all those years ago. History was repeating itself.

Back home, I called Amy to do damage control. "I am so sorry. I guess I'm not over my dad's death. Sorry you had to babysit me."

"Ha, Melissa, don't worry. You were trashed. Who cares."

A forgiving friend who loved me unconditionally, she had already moved on. Her grace made me even more weepy, ashamed and guilty.

"Remember that video camera Kent's girlfriend had?" Amy said suddenly. "They taped you sleeping. Poor Melis."

She laughed, but not in a cruel way.

"Oh, Lord," I squeaked.

"Don't worry about it," Amy chuckled. "She was getting everyone in their drunken stupors."

"Amy? Don't say anything to your mom, okay? You know she'll talk to mine and I won't hear the end of it."

She paused. "Dang it, I'm sorry. I already told my mom

about running into you. But I'll call her back and tell her to keep quiet."

I hardly felt better.

Lying on the couch for most of the day while Hope played quietly in her room, I was wracked with guilt over my inability to offer attention, but physically I couldn't. The crushing depression of my latest relapse had me bound tightly in the web cast by my old amigo *John Barleycorn*, the fair-weather friend who always hit the highway once morning dawned. I was left with the bill for his services, and the debt was hell to pay. With the price tag climbing ever higher and the relapses intensifying, I was rapidly going from out of control to comatose.

The darkest hours of my descent into full-blown addiction looped endlessly in my mind. The night with Bryce, my dad's memorial, the lost week in San Diego, and now a drunken party with my colleagues topped off by a video camera. Each incident was a new rock bottom. How low would I go?

Mom called later in the afternoon, stirring me from a restless doze. She knew everything about my party performance. Apparently, Amy hadn't been able to get to *her* mother in time to deliver the warning.

"I heard about your little episode last night," Mom railed. "You were completely wasted, hitting on Pat and everything." She clucked her tongue in disgust. "*What* got into you, Melissa?"

I sat and absorbed her verbal tirade for a few minutes, knowing I deserved its explicit truth.

"I'm a mess," I finally admitted. "I'm trying. I really am."

"You will get this," she relented, softening and sounding heartbroken. You will overcome this, I know it. Each one of these horrible episodes is bringing you closer to quitting for good."

Somehow I made it through the day. For normal people suffering through a hangover, relief usually followed after a good night's sleep. Not for me. Monday nearly rivaled Sunday for worst-day status. I had to go to work and *face people*, and this reality filled me with unspeakable dread.

The Channel 9 guy who'd thrown the party also covered city council meetings with me. There was no way around it: I would have to face both Kent *and* Bryce. Sobbing uncontrollably in the shower that Monday morning, I dreaded the coming day and felt so hopeless I would've done anything to escape. I have no idea what kept me hanging on.

Overflowing with shame, I had to endure the disgusted and pitying looks of my coworkers. Somehow I powered through the council meeting and the noticeable smirk from Kent when I arrived. He'd been chatting with Bryce, and knowing glances were exchanged as I took my seat. *She gets crazier with every sip!* I was way beyond that now. I'd gone from party girl to psychopath.

My drinking was out of control, but work wasn't suffering one bit. I was promoted from General Assignment Reporter to Weekend Anchor, making me feel even more invincible.

41

Kent's party carried a powerful impact and enabled me to gather a full two months of sobriety. Figuring some drugs would help my recovery efforts, I visited a free clinic and convinced the low-paid resident to prescribe an antidepressant. It helped that I was weepy and distraught the morning of the appointment.

"Let's start you on some Lexapro," he said, after a five minute chat. "It can't hurt, might take the edge off a little at least."

Nodding, I accepted the prescription listlessly, mistaking my alcohol withdrawal for a deep depression needing pharmacological assistance.

By the end of May 2003, cravings for alcohol dominated every thought once again. The Lexapro made me flat, work was boring, and I was sick of covering the school board. Following the same old beat had become a buzz kill, and half of my interview targets never responded, requiring endless calls and borderline begging just to score a lousy sound bite.

Outside the fanfare of anchoring weekend shows, my usual focus was painfully dull stories about the school district's budget deficit. The business operations manager was a frequent subject—and one of the few who didn't mind my endless requests for on-camera interviews. Chris Paulson was a dry numbers guy in his early 40s whom I didn't consider much beyond our short conversations. Patient and dutiful as he spoke, I would nod and pretend to be enthralled by his finance junk.

I made it to work the last day of May to find Annette finalizing the day's assignments. My name was next to PAULSON QUITS.

"Chris Paulson?" I asked. "From the school district?"

Annette nodded. "He's leaving for a job down in the Twin Cities. I'll have you interview him about the new position, and we can pull some file footage and talk about his career."

Simple. Dennis and I headed over to the school administration offices. We'd finally settled into a comfortable routine without pressure for a romantic relationship.

"So, what's this all about?" Dennis asked. I dragged the tripod down the hall like an unwilling toddler as I explained the details of Chris's new position.

"Too bad," I concluded. "He was such a reliable interview."

Soon I was prepping the lavalier mic for Chris and making small talk as Dennis set up the camera. We quickly collected the necessary sound bites, then Dennis packed up while I continued chatting like I had all the time in the world.

"I'll be right there," I promised as he headed to the truck.

"Now that you're leaving, you need to give me all the dirt on the district." I flashed Chris a grin while tucking pens and budget printouts I'd never look at again into my bag.

"Sure. But you have to go out for a beer with me if you want the scoop."

"Ummm . . . " I stared in disbelief, then returned numbly to the chair facing his desk. "I assumed you were married?"

"I was," he answered after a long pause. "You could say it's been over for the past five years. Divorce was finalized a month ago. I married my friend, you know what I mean? No spark. We never had children."

My mind raced as I processed the unexpected turn of events. This business professional guy was asking *me* out? After doing a double-take, I realized I'd overlooked his decent appearance. Serious, dark brown eyes, short hair streaked with a little gray. Lean and youthful looking. *Are you sure? You want to go out with me? Relax. He isn't proposing. He's asking you out for a* beer, *not a lifetime commitment.*

"That'd be cool," I finally managed. The fact that I had quit drinking was an artifact of rapidly declining importance.

Dennis reappeared in the doorway looking slightly exasperated. "You coming?"

"Oh yeah," I mumbled, having forgotten all about my side-kick. Pausing on the way out, I offered Chris a lame handshake that couldn't conceal the building excitement. *We had a secret.*

"Good luck on your new position. You leaving next month?"

Chris nodded. "Yep. But I'll see you before I go, right?"

Flustered now, I muttered, "Yep. Yes. Uh, keep in touch."

Dear Dennis clearly suspected something suspicious had

transpired while he was out of earshot.

"What did he mean he'll see you later?" He asked as soon as we were alone.

With a heavy sigh, I hoped to show his prying was very unwelcomed. "I have no idea, Dennis."

Chris called the newsroom Wednesday. "Mr. D's tonight sound good to you?"

"That's great," I agreed, acutely aware of my coworkers' presence. This business professional just seemed so elite.

Almost on autopilot, I'd been sober more than a month, but that wasn't important now. Something inside suggested that Chris's status and stability would rub off like luck from a Buddha's belly and change my relationship with alcohol.

Prepping for our date involved a 6-pack of Mike's Hard Lemonade, drained in less than an hour. After arguing with my closet, I finally settled on black denim capris, a flowy rayon shirt, and classy wedge shoes. *Casual, yet sleek.*

Six easy blocks separated me from Mr. D's—late afternoon and not a cop in sight. I parked and climbed out of the car, teetering on my wedges. *Oh Lord, what am I doing?* Yes, I had six cocktails under my belt, but painful anxiety still brewed. Ducking into the safe haven of the dark bar smothered it. Soon I was swallowed in cool smokiness, secure and guarded within the anonymous depths.

Chris had saved me a stool, relaxed and unassuming now that he'd ditched his usual tailored suit for a blue polo shirt and jeans. Dragging on a cigarette and enjoying a tap beer, he was a comforting sight like a well-worn blanket—suddenly Joe Average—not Mr. Business Professional.

"Hey."

I parted my lips slightly, dimly reassured that they shimmered with gloss and probably looked inviting. Perhaps the sight of them would distract my date from the size of my butt in the too-tight capris.

With a delighted grin, Chris turned and blew smoke out in the opposite direction. "Melissa! You made it. Can I get the lady a drink?"

Arranging myself on the bar stool beside him, I crossed my legs, hoping it made them look longer and leaner as I pondered the tap selection.

"Let's see," I said deliberately, roaming back and forth over the spouts as if I never drank and couldn't decide what sounded good. I never wanted people, especially *men,* to think I was a lush—though they always found out eventually. Finally, I pointed to his glass and smiled.

"I'll just have what you're having."

Chris gestured to the bartender and ordered a large, frosted tap beer. Smiling, I watched the barkeep pour off the foam.

"Perfect."

The next two hours were spent drinking, talking, and schmoozing—coincidentally locked into the same exact stools Bryce and I had occupied not long ago. Things were going smashingly so far, but my drinking ramped up as the night spiraled on—the alcohol just flowed faster down my throat as bar time evaporated.

What if I don't get enough to drink? The dusty light of the setting sun broke the darkness occasionally when someone entered or exited the bar. As the clock struck eleven, the encroaching blackout swallowed me like a net.

Piecing together events later revealed Chris and I had

wandered across the street to Champ's, but I have no clue what we did, whom I may have seen, or worse—who had seen *me*.

I jolted awake the next morning, sick and disoriented. My heart leapt like a trapped animal as I flew to the window. *My car was gone. God help me* . . . I paced about the kitchen, clutching my head, aching to remember while my brain reeled and swam and struggled to make memories. Only bits and pieces scampered to mind. Chris? Mr. D's . . . beer, shots, I was smoking, giggling, whispering in his ear . . .

With a lurching stomach and eyes filled with tears, I clapped my hand over my mouth as the enormity of the situation came crashing in. Although I hadn't touched a drink for over a month, one night was all it took for the madness to return. The latest failure felt soul-crushing—everything, the mental stability, self-esteem, confidence, I'd worked so hard to build was destroyed.

I spotted a scrap of paper leaning against the napkin holder on the kitchen table. *Melissa: Call me when you get up and I'll bring you to your car. Chris.*

I dialed his office and croaked, "Chris?"

"Morning, sweetie," he cooed. "You ready to go?"

Fifteen minutes later, he was at my door in his business attire. I'd thrown on jogging pants and a baseball hat—barely able to face him.

"Oh, dear God, I am so embarrassed," I squeaked. Mortified was a more appropriate choice of words.

Chris pulled me toward him in a familiar bear hug. "No big deal, kiddo. We all overdo it sometimes, right?"

He hadn't figured me out yet—still locked into the honeymoon stage where babysitting a drunk girl was cute. That would get old real fast.

Once we were back on the road, I sat in humiliated silence as we meandered down Grand Avenue.

"Where is my car?" I whispered.

"We left it at Champ's. You were kind of bad off, Mel. At the end of the night, you collapsed in the doorway—throwing up all over. I basically carried you to my car and went back inside the bar because you'd left your keys and purse. All spread out . . . everything. Cell phone. People were going through your stuff but I think I got there in time. Make sure you check and see if anything is missing."

How helpful. Codependent. I couldn't take any more information. Clutching my head, I moaned, "You have no idea how stupid I feel."

Chris just smiled like I was his little project. "You're in luck, honey. I have good news. I like giving people second chances."

After we'd collected my car, Chris headed back to work, and I returned home and collapsed into bed. Hope was at her dad's, and I wasn't expected for her until after work. Because I didn't start my shift until two, I was allowed some time to deaden my horrendous hangover.

Rolling out of bed at the last possible minute, I still felt wretched and dreamed of calling in sick but instead forced myself to shower and made a feeble attempt to look presentable. I arrived at work fifteen minutes later and settled in at my desk while Annette rattled off the day's assignments. My stomach turned as she talked and sweat beaded on my upper lip.

"Hang on a sec, Annette," I managed. I bolted to the bathroom just in time to puke up whatever was left in my stomach. The hurling trend continued in the form of bitter stomach bile every fifteen minutes for the next two hours.

"You don't look good," Annette observed. Then half-joking she asked, "Are you pregnant?"

"Ah, no," I chuckled, trying to make light of the situation. "I ate a burrito for lunch. It was kind of old, left over. That's what did it, I'm sure."

Annette wrinkled her nose as I leapt up from my desk for another round of dry heaves. Eventually, I couldn't make it between bathroom runs and retreated to the worn-out couch in the glam, where I covered myself with someone's coat and tried to sleep.

Annette peeked in half an hour later.

"Are you okay? Should I call someone in for tonight?"

Shaking my head, I struggled into a sitting position and wondered if the room reeked of alcohol.

"No, I'm better now," I insisted with an unconvincing smile.

The thought of having a replacement for my evening anchor spot was unthinkable. Annette bought a bag of Wheat Thins from the vending machine and deposited it on my desk. After nibbling the crackers and downing a few Diet Cokes, I came back to life enough to manage the newscast at six.

Chris and I met up again for cocktails, and I got nearly as trashed as I had on our first date but skipped the antidepressants. Convinced the *pills* were the cause of my deathly reaction to alcohol, I figured I had found a way to avoid a repeat embarrassing performance.

Chris took a quick liking to me and moved fast. As he prepared to start his new job in the Twin Cities, he rambled a lot about taking things to the "next level." Marriage, "down the road" even! But after he left town at the end of June, I squirmed away. He was another stable and employed guy I eventually decided was a total turn-off.

The pathetic cycle of brief sober stints followed by inca-
pacitating blackouts was one I could not break. My tolerance
was increasing at an alarming rate, and I could easily put away
nearly a case of beer along with intermittent shots.

The morning after another blowout at the Galley, I peered
nervously into the refrigerator to find only one can remaining
in yesterday's case of beer. It was possible that someone else had
helped me empty it.

As the wasted nights spiraled on, finding a way to say
goodbye to booze for good never left me. At night I cried softly
and begged God for help. *I have faith that you can help me.*

My battle to stay straight permanently was a losing one
without the Lord Jesus Christ as my rock, and suddenly the
seeds planted long ago began whispering this truth. I knew on
a deep level that my worldly attempts to change *myself* through
willpower, the ideas of man, and white-knuckling could only
take me so far. Though each one helped me cope temporarily, I
was still massively unhealed at the core and hanging by a thread.
The answer to my problem would not be found in any world
system. I needed something supernatural.

42

It was a gorgeous, hot, sunny day—so muggy that my head pulsed mercilessly with the hangover I was trying to ignore. I drew a glass of water from the tap and sucked it down while pretending it was the Living Water of Jesus, a healing stream capable of purifying all the poison and toxins bubbling within. I had heard of that somewhere.

Arriving at work in the sheepish way I always had after a night of drinking, I sat paranoid and disconnected, wishing I could turn into myself and disappear. Who had I talked to the night before? Would someone ask questions I wouldn't be able to answer? Settling in at my desk, I scanned the assignment board and the newsroom. Was anyone mad at me? Did they know about my secret battle?

The Galley beckoned two days later after I'd slammed a few beers at home. The place was dead, but several stools down an older couple hovered over cheap taps. Since there was no one else to talk to, I sidled over.

"What's up with you guys?"

"Just hanging." The guy wore cut-off jean shorts and a T-shirt that read, "I DID THE DUVAL CRAWL." His female friend peeked out from a fringe of stringy brown hair and probably weighed all of eighty pounds. Her half-open eyes indicated she'd probably been bellied up to the bar awhile.

"This is Carl," she mumbled, pointing to the guy. They giggled and began kissing passionately. I looked away.

"So, is this your girlfriend?" I asked Carl, trying to keep the conversation going.

He ordered another beer and laughed. "Naw, I just met this nice young lady." He kissed her cheek, and she lit a cigarette. Checking the clock, I noticed it was almost one in the morning.

"What are you guys doing later?" I needed some company. "Do you want to hit the bars in Superior?"

The woman shrugged. "Sure. You driving us? Carl and I ain't in no shape."

With two DWIs already under my belt, I once again drove drunk across the Bong Bridge to capture another precious hour of bar time. Pulling into the parking lot of the Keyport, I bragged to Carl and his lady friend about my history with the bar.

"I just about built this place. I worked here four years and managed the karaoke business. Have you ever sang here? It's the best sound system and song selection in town."

But a lifeless lounge greeted us. A dead bar to match my

decaying soul. None of my old customers were on hand, the bartender was an unknown college kid, and the karaoke was already shut down for the night. Carl and his lady continued taking their relationship to the next level while I sat dejectedly sidelined.

I managed to drive back across the bridge with one eye shut at closing to deposit my new friends back in their neighborhood. What now? I didn't want the night to end. Plunged into the dark underworld that always began at the Galley, I realized I only had two lonely beers in my refrigerator. Damn. Nothing left but to go home, alone. The barflies had briefly filled my desperate need for someone—anyone.

The next day I awoke with paralyzing terror. I opened my eyes and felt the gaping mouth of hell at my side. *Why had I driven drunk again?* If I got busted again, I would probably get fired from my job and do serious jail time. My post-drinking paranoia was back, a fire-breathing dragon threading every fiber of my being with fright. Alcohol brought my worst fears to life. Death, disease, or loss of my daughter; drinking would make it all real if I didn't stop. I was on a train to destruction and needed a serious intervention to alter the course.

When I watched myself on TV, I knew that I existed. When I read my name in print, I was real. Otherwise, I had absolutely no idea who Melissa was. The saddest part of all, though, was that I didn't realize I wasn't an orphan. I was a precious daughter of the King with immeasurable worth.

The month of June 2003 was hazy. I wasn't actively trying to quit drinking, but knew the end was near. One thing was true—I was going to stop, or booze was going to take my life. Chunks of sobriety strung together a few days, but nothing stuck. The theme of the past fifteen years had not changed: I'd

sometimes gather a couple of unremarkable drinking nights—
but the insidious reality always returned. The night of July 3rd
stood out like a big, black exclamation point.

I'd been alcohol-free a few days, but then an empty night
appeared and the drinking switch flipped to "game on." What to
do? Hope was tucked safely away at Seth's—I'd fetch her the following afternoon for Bayfront fireworks and was therefore cleared
for a night of drunken revelry. With the afternoon wide open, I
enjoyed running a few errands with no pressure to be anywhere.
The delight of the pending evening continued to trickle in as I
wrapped up the day browsing through a Target store.

Anticipating a steamy night complete with excitement, mystery, and the man of my dreams, I paused in the clothing department to hold a patriotic flag-themed bikini under my chin,
gauging how it might look on me. Eyeing the two-piece clearly
not intended for curves like mine, I entertained a vision of leaving
the bar and making a fast getaway to a secluded beach and wallowing in the Milky Way until dawn. My vision was oddly absent
of sex or drunkenness. Rather, it was a premonition of my soul-
mate, that man I'd been trying to find for the past fifteen years.

Why not? I tossed the bikini into my cart, thinking I'd hide
it under shorts and a tank top. I'd least I'd know it was there.

As I left the store, my imagination was in full force, and
everyone crowding the parking lot with their red carts was
certainly staring at me, magnetized by my charisma. I skipped
back to my car and headed to the liquor store, where I picked
up a case of beer. After shotgunning three cans, a peculiar feeling
of bodily separation flooded in, like I'd peeled right out of my
soul and stepped into a Twist-a-plot adventure book where the
reader could select the ending of the story. Only, in my case,

the blackout would determine the outcome. I was simply along for the ride.

Tonight, the beer would fuel me in a powerful way, and I felt on track to find the exception—the man God had predestined just for me. Glitter, jean shorts, sunglasses. Two shots of Sour Apple Pucker, a novelty drink masquerading much like those silly passion fruit wine coolers. Pucker was . . . what . . . ? 40 proof? I scoffed at the label before shoving it way back into the pantry, then slammed out the door and down the block to the Kettle Inn.

This shady little joint was filed way back in my mind for a night when all bets were off. *My last binge*. It was the same place I saw career alcoholics in withdrawal crouched near the back door, smoking and tipping bottles back early in the morning as I passed by on my way to work, often hungover. I wasn't that far removed from them, but I didn't quite know it yet.

Stepping inside fifteen minutes later, my arrival was not as anticipated as I had envisioned. In my mind's eye, I imagined all the seasoned drunks and backroom dealers staring in awe as I graced them with my presence that hot July night. Quite the contrary. Maybe this was just a regular old watering hole, and I'd invented all that other stuff in my head. No one stopped pulling tabs or plugging the jukebox—only glanced over briefly when the door creaked my grand entrance. Once I was settled, they quickly returned to raucous laughter and never-ending tap beer.

I was truly a master at gauging people's reactions—of appearing nonchalant and unaffected while inside acutely aware of anyone giving me the once-over. Although the inside of the Kettle Inn carefully quarantined the chaos of ruined lives right there on a busy street corner, no one made any judgments. I could disappear.

A curious scene juxtaposed inside the bar. Fantastic oil paintings illustrating the history of Duluth adorned the particle-board walls, but right beneath the superior artistry, a wasted couple engaged in a public display of affection. Body shots of tequila enabled the woman to expose herself, free of charge. Three beers certainly weren't enough to immerse me into the culture of the Kettle Inn. I seriously needed to pick up the pace, so my first order involved a triple shot of Pucker paired with a 32-ounce beer. Draining the glass with satisfaction ten minutes later, I figured I'd easily gain the acceptance of my fellow bar patrons because I certainly was no lightweight.

Still finely crafting my buzz, I hadn't tried socializing with anyone yet, and I was vaguely pleased that I was being left alone. The blaring jukebox bled through raised voices as I sat content for the next hour. Like a paper doll propped at the bar, I was allowed to prepare myself fully before coming to life. The more I drank, the better I seemed to myself.

I headed to the back of the bar to visit the restroom, and as I lingered at the mirror, I seemed to be taking on a new presence of a beautiful and desirable wayward traveler. Pausing to apply a heavy coat of lip gloss, I imagined myself a rare jewel among a crowd of boll weevils.

Back at the bar, I ordered another beer and then noticed someone had taken the stool next to me. He was tall and lanky with a beautiful ornate watch that instantly drew my eyes to his wrist, something like that symbolic gold cross Jack had worn long ago. Obviously, this fine gentleman didn't belong here, either. My eyes trailed from his wrist to the rest of his body. He noticed.

"Whatcha got there?" he asked, winking at my litter of shot glasses.

"It's called Pucker. Schnapps, I guess. Have you heard of it? They've got all these flavors." I gestured to the wall of bottles behind the bar. Biding my time with a potential suitor required careful disinterest and minimal engagement. I swilled my beer as he scanned the liquor offerings.

"Can I get you one? You like grape?"

"How about a triple shot? It's a lot better if you mix it."

He took my suggestion and ordered a couple of slammers. Meanwhile, the alcohol hit me, and impulsivity began reigning my impaired brain.

"Soooo, tell me about yourself," I slurred. "So, do you, like, have a drinking problem? Do you like . . . hang here? This place is kind of unruly."

With a harsh cackle, I downed the shot, hoping he'd assure me he wasn't a regular.

"Nope. I work construction in the area. Stop by from time to time. It's just a bar."

His comment seemed to convey there was no shame in being there. We were in the same boat. Nothing wrong with a no-frills establishment, right? I thought briefly of a Superior tavern with a sign that boasted, "DRINKING DONE HERE." No nonsense. I could get behind that.

Resting his elbow on the bar, my new love interest sipped his beer with an air of confidence. *He* was the exception to my usual tavern failures, I just knew it.

I think his name was James. Or Jerry? At least it started with a J, I was sure later. Had he slipped roofies in my drink or was that just me rationalizing the severe and crippling blackout I was headed into?

My money ran dry, but I had to keep the party going. I

assured J I had more cash just a few blocks away, so we headed back to the stash I kept on top of the refrigerator—rent payment for my landlord. Getting kicked out of my home was a concern more distant than the asteroid belt, especially when my immediate focus was the attention of a man. I vaguely recall grabbing the money and then returning to the bar—but not before I shamelessly produced the report from one of my DWI arrests for J's review. My final memory for the next several hours would be our laughter at my extremely high blood alcohol content.

Sometime before dawn, I woke in my bed in a panic, naked beneath my pink robe and without memory of returning to the apartment after closing time. I was lying in a puddle of my own urine.

The scene that greeted me was similar to what happens when electricity resumes after several hours of power loss. Studying my surroundings with horror, I begged them to share the untold story that was written while I was absent from my body. Two unopened cans of beer sat on the windowsill, looking as though they were waiting for someone. Every light in the apartment was blazing, the fan beside my bed blew one harsh stream of air at the ceiling. I stumbled down the stairs, clutching the scratchy robe I rarely wore around me, making a mad dash for what the growing ball of apprehension in the pit of my stomach already knew.

The deadbolt was unlocked. *Someone was here.* I crawled back upstairs and into the bathroom, peeled off the robe, and evaluated every inch of my body with a deep feeling of emptiness and spiritual bankruptcy. As I grasped for any faint recollection to ease my hysteria, I found nothing to nudge my reckless thoughts from their path to lunacy. Gently and thoroughly, I examined myself, but no resolution was found—nothing that could definitively tell me a thing. Had I been sexually assaulted? Why was I naked? I would never know for sure.

43

I tried to escape the aftermath of the night in my apartment with the unknown stranger, someone I could remember very little about and would never see again. I couldn't even identify him from a police lineup if I wanted to. The whole episode had been like a sort of psychosis, a deeply disturbing waking dream that, to my horror, had been real.

Over the next several months, I obsessed mercilessly about a possible sexually transmitted disease, but would later find out I was perfectly fine and had nothing to worry about in terms of health problems. Still, I continued to torture myself with pointless and expensive testing over the lost night. A very real sort of post-traumatic stress had consumed me, and not just from this one isolated incident. The wounding had been years in the making, the past decade and a half of my life punctuated by numerous blackouts, lost hours, and excruciating unknowns. I'd failed miserably at finding the magic formula—there was absolutely no way for me to safely drink.

On August 20, 2003, my landlord invited me to his birthday dinner at the Timber Lodge steakhouse in Canal Park. I was still trying to recover from what I thought was the worst blackout of my life along with the gnawing fear that I may have been assaulted.

"Do you and Hope want to join us for dinner?" Gerard had asked. I'd recently revealed to him that I had a drinking problem (hence the nonexistent rent) and planned to stop.

"Beck will be there. You two could hang out together," he winked.

He knew his friend and I had a little history. Maybe there was still time to turn over a new leaf with Beck. I agreed to join the party, thinking: *You need to learn to behave and be normal when other people are having a couple of beers.* Hope was my sidekick.

"Want a beer?" Beck offered as soon as I arrived at the restaurant.

My daughter scowled as I flashed a bright smile.

"No, thanks. I'm drinking coffee tonight." I gestured to my cup as if it held my very favorite beverage in the entire world. Beck and I chatted while he and the others drank socially.

"You ever been to the Minnesota State Fair?"

Poor Beck was trying to make small talk. It was late August, and the Great Minnesota Get-Together was in full swing down in St. Paul. I'd been considering a day trip alone; honestly I couldn't think of a soul who'd want to go with me. I still needed to check the concert lineup.

"Nope, but I'd like to go sometime."

The conversation dragged as Beck poured himself another beer.

"Boston's there tomorrow night, I hear. I love those guys."

"Really? Boston? I've *always* been into Boston!"

Man, I loved Brad Delp's voice. He was probably my very favorite male vocalist of all time. My mind wandered through the rest of the gathering, but I was able to distract it from the beer.

Later on, after Hope was in bed, I thought of the State Fair again and impulsively decided to give Beck a call.

"Hey! What's up? Didn't I just see you?" he laughed.

"I was just wondering . . . how we were talking about Boston and the fair earlier? Do you want to go with me?"

"I'm off work tomorrow. Yeah! Let's do it. Sounds like fun."

I've talked about the empty pawns the enemy used in his quest to destroy me—and he surely does. But remember—God takes what the enemy meant for evil and turns it for good. I am convinced He also used Beck to keep me from dying that night.

I had no plans to drink until Beck and I were heading down I-35, bound for St. Paul, and one final fiery dart plunged into my mind and lodged there. Soon headlong into the mother of all blackouts, August 21, 2003, was the night I said to myself, *Just one more time.*

44

SEPTEMBER 9, 2003

Memories of that final night of drinking would haunt me for a long time, and learning to live in reality didn't come right away. But an overwhelming conviction persisted—a *knowing* that I was done with alcohol forever. The liquor cabinet was deadbolted, the key lost at sea. What had changed? I wouldn't be able to pinpoint it for years to come, but eventually, I realized the difference was *repentance*. That big, fancy church command that sounded like condemnation and restriction to many had actually been the gateway to freedom. Overwhelmed by a deep yearning to turn from my sin after that last horrible night of drinking at the Minnesota State Fair, Jesus had met me with his grace.

A few weeks later, I still hadn't wavered in my commitment

to sobriety. I'd spent eighteen days thanking God I hadn't died that August night and pledging to live for Him for the rest of my life. Heading into work that afternoon, I had renewed energy and purpose. It was primary Election Day, and I was ready for action.

Seeking fresh material for the resume tape I still believed could free me from the drudgery of Duluth (honestly, I hadn't yet asked God about *His* ideas), I arrived at work hungry for a big story, a live shot, and an historic night out in the field. Using the Judy Garland festival as the centerpiece of my highlight reel wasn't exactly wooing news directors—but a frenetic after-party with a hot new political star might be just the ticket to getting noticed. Escaping my hometown had been my goal for the past year, and I'd successfully attracted notice from a few news executives. Despite several phone interviews, nothing monumental had resulted from dozens of VHS tapes sent all over the country.

"You read the news well, and you're attractive," one director commented about my submission, "But we're looking for *exotic*."

The lyrics to "Dirty Laundry" echoed in my head as I contemplated the field of talent—tons of stunning anchor wannabes vying for every open job. How could I compete?

Serendipity had smiled upon me nevertheless, and I'd beaten the odds that reflected the low chances of a production assistant making it to the anchor desk. Primary day was mine for the taking. I'd paid my dues.

The evening anchor was even more in control than usual though, performing double duty as producer made Annette responsible for stacking the show AND doling out the day's assignments.

The whiteboard that commanded the west wall of the

newsroom displayed each story and its level of coverage. I'd be live for the late news, but what about the six o'clock show? The post-election party I'd broadcast from at ten looked exciting, though the six o'clock assignment was a lot tamer. Annette had jotted *Viking/Packer Bet* beside my name.

Instantly annoyed, I gave her the side-eye as I scanned the board. With three local newspapers strewn out in front and the scanner blaring over her left shoulder, she hunkered below the counter of the assignment desk with just the crown of her red head peeking out. A tirade of objections threatened to erupt as I considered my history with Annette. She had mentored me for the past couple of years and provided instruction on succinct writing, spot news, and the art of approaching a grieving family for an on-camera interview. The great respect she'd earned was not enough to harness my building aggravation.

"Annette, what's the Packer-Viking thing? Won't I be live somewhere at six?"

"You're live at ten," she answered sweetly, ignoring the first question. "First, I need you to go across the street for a great photo op. The Packer fans lost a bet on the game and have to take pies in the face!"

Rolling my eyes, I turned away. Hadn't I put in enough time to be spared the lame fluff stories? What was next, a prairie dog parade at the local zoo?

I sulked at my desk until three o'clock, then begrudgingly followed Dennis, my photographer, across the street for the pastry extravaganza. I even had to haul the big clunky tripod, something I'd grown to loathe.

Out front on Superior Street, a chaotic scene awaited with a crowd of people wearing Viking jerseys and giant garbage bags.

Most of the participants were women in their late 40s, leading to a fast assumption I was heading into a gig pitifully void of excitement.

The situation quickly unfolded: the garbage bag wearers had won the bet, so the unlucky Packer people had only the flimsy protection of Viking T-shirts and jerseys designed for double shaming—both through mess, and the excruciating reality of advertising their most hated rival to the public. The bag-wearing Viking lovers were happily preparing a cart of pies for battle and appeared even more thrilled to spot Dennis and me trudging over.

"Here comes the news!" someone yelled with excitement.

A snappy sound bite was my goal—then I could get the heck out of Dodge. Scanning the crowd for an interview subject, I spotted a lone male around my age among the older ladies.

He seemed to have been plucked from the pages of *Sports Illustrated*—two minutes of side-eye was plenty for a discreet once-over. A youth-sized Viking shirt was stretched over his torso, his face painted with an obnoxious red target, a beacon of embarrassment. He seemed familiar, and we continued to make eye contact as the event coordinators fussed around dusting pies with purple glitter.

The recipients of the brimming pastries finally shuffled into place, cringing in anticipation as the red-painted guy wedged beside the others who'd lost the bet. The Hefty-bag women assembled the goodies, and Dennis readied himself at the camera.

"Help us out with a little countdown for the sorry Packer fans!" someone cajoled the crowd. "3-2-1 . . . GO!"

Pies flew and connected with the row of Viking haters, mild humiliation and cream now running down their faces. Eyes fixed on *that guy,* I had forgotten about the lackluster assignment. Seeing him drenched in whipped topping was totally worth the price of admission.

Blinded to everyone else, I dragged Dennis over to Mr. *Sports Illustrated,* watching with delight as he wiped his face with the bottom of that tiny, shameful T-shirt.

As I approached, he moved toward me with outstretched arms, threatening to spread the pie mess through a great big bear hug. Just when I was hoping to look smooth, I tripped gracelessly over the mic cord and stumbled back, laughing—a silly moment I will never forget.

"Whoa, you've got a lot of whipped cream in your eyes!" was my fumbling and awkward greeting.

"I can handle it." He grinned. "I've had experience with this before."

Uhhh, okay . . . Was that supposed to be suggestive?

"Funny. I bet you have. Can I ask you a few questions?"

Feigning a serious, businesslike aura, I recovered while diving into my notebook in search of a blank page. Dennis stood poised over the camera, trying to hide his impatience.

"What's your name?"

"Mike Huray."

The serious journalist vibe crumbled and I lowered the mic slowly, waving the white flag of surrender. Had I encountered him in a bar—or a blackout? Mild panic raced through me as I tried to determine whether we had any history I should be ashamed about. The softball questions about the Viking-Packer bet kept me numb and on autopilot as my distracted mind careened off the rails.

Mike Huray. *Mike Huray.* Then it hit me. Mike had once

dated my old roommate Anna from the Alamo. We'd crossed paths five years back—when I was charging ninety miles an hour toward full-blown addiction.

Mike was illuminated in an irresistible way now. Something had shifted, and I lagged behind to talk as Dennis packed up.

"So, what's new? Are you still dating Anna?"

Unable to resist the urge to pry into his personal life, I fumbled for my old point of connection. The last time I'd seen Mike, he'd just parted ways with my roommate—but years later, we stood in completely different places.

"Anna . . . " he chuckled awkwardly. "Nope. We were off and on for a while, but it's been over probably three years now. How about you? You married?"

"Divorced," I answered, struggling to hide my excitement. "But you already knew that. That was years ago. Did you mean am I *remarried*? No, I'm not. If that's what you meant."

Our conversation stalled, and Dennis cleared his throat as if to say, *"Do your man-hunting on your own time."* No chance of being alone with Mike, and no hope of an answer to the question now weighing heavily on my mind: *Was he dating anyone now?*

"We'd better head back to the station, but it was great seeing you again," I managed.

Mike smiled, seeming to share my secret thoughts.

45

"That pie-throwing thing will make a great kicker for the end of the newscast," Dennis remarked as we trudged back across Superior Street, after having captured the border battle spectacle.

I nodded distractedly, but my mind was fixed on Mike Huray.

Back at my desk, I logged online and scanned through the stream of emails I'd received over the past hour.

A bold subject line caught my attention: BEST SCOOP EVER. Clicking on the message with excitement, I read, "You made my day. Thanks for taking the time to cover our silly little event."

Mike Huray! Instantly overanalyzing his intentions, I considered the effort he'd made in unearthing my not-so-easy-to-locate email address with a feeling something supernatural brewing. I was still a local celebrity and had to watch out for stalkers, after all—finding my contact information was no easy task.

We soon began exchanging emails throughout the day. Mike was goofy, quirky, and quick-witted. Not to mention very handsome. Our senses of humor were similar, and we finished each other's sentences.

"How about meeting me for lunch?" he asked a week later.

We decided on the Top of the Harbor, an iconic revolving rooftop restaurant just down the block from our workplaces that offered dramatic views of Lake Superior and the Duluth Hillside.

Everything was clipping along, but a nagging thought persisted. Five years earlier, I'd been a huge party animal, and for all Mike knew, I still was. As we shared a fancy cloth napkin meal, I laid my cards down and told the story of my battle with drinking and how I'd closed the door to alcohol for good. Mike was supportive and encouraging; my past was certainly not a deal-breaker in his eyes.

"Wow, I had no idea," he finally said when I'd finished spilling my guts. "I never would have guessed . . . I mean, I used to watch you on the news and tell my buddies, 'hey I know that girl.'" He chuckled with slight embarrassment. "I don't think they believed me. Anyway, I'm proud of you! For quitting, and everything else you've done with your life. I would definitely like to offer support . . . and also get to know you better," he winked.

I melted.

Soon inseparable, we talked constantly on the phone and through email, and with excitement shared every moment we could. I was still bound to AA meetings, though. After my last night of drinking on August 22, I wasted no time calling Katy while still in the throes of alcohol withdrawal to confess my relapse. Deep inside, I knew that coming clean was the right thing and in alignment with repentance. Katy had tried to help me for a couple of years now, but I kept her at arm's length. Now, I owed her some answers and honesty. She was kind and nonjudgmental, and recommended I get my butt back to meetings. I swallowed my pride and went—and even shared a letter I had written about what I'd been through with the group— although I felt zero desire to drink and knew deliverance had come the moment I had cried out to Jesus.

I was like an alien at the tables now, and could not relate to the stories passed around about slips, cravings, self-pity, and yearnings for the old days. Alcohol seemed a million miles away, like someone I'd known years ago but couldn't even picture being with anymore. Deep down I was completely convinced I'd never drink again, and the meetings felt pointless and unnecessary. When I told people I had been radically delivered of all urges, they studied me like I'd been beamed straight to the smoky old room from the starship Enterprise, and offered dark reminders about everyone being only one drink away from a drunk. Once an alcoholic, always an alcoholic, they said.

One Saturday during the morning gathering of ex-drinkers, I mentioned I'd met a really great guy. My admission to the group was met with much muttering and discontent. Later on, an old-timer named Sadie pulled me aside.

"You really shouldn't be seeing anyone," she said sharply. "You know that, right? You just *relapsed*."

Feeling like a scolded child, I pondered her comments for a few days while Mike and I continued exchanging emails and getting to know each other. One day, he invited me for a walk in the park.

"My AA group is discouraging me about dating," I admitted, as we strolled around the Barker's Island marina. "I don't want to listen to them, but they're so serious about it. They keep saying I'm going to drink again if I don't do all these things . . . ninety meetings in ninety days, meeting with a sponsor several times a week . . . Honestly, I don't know what to think. I'm so confused. I've made a lot of mistakes, and I really want to do things right this time."

Mike was quiet, staring off at a late season sailboat circling through the bay.

"Well, that's a bummer. Looking at that boat . . . " he gestured out over the water, "I feel like the wind just got sucked out of my sails. But I understand if you want me to back off."

"I guess maybe we should just be friends for a while?" I ventured, hating the sound of the words.

Mike's look of disappointment was unmistakable. "Sure . . . I can always use another friend," he finally agreed with an empty laugh, sounding as defeated as a ruptured balloon.

For the next week, I was saddled with a terrible feeling that I was making a huge mistake. The AA meetings were accomplishing absolutely nothing, I just didn't want to let Katy down by giving up on them.

"It's a bad idea to become complacent," many had said. "While you're here in the room, your 'disease' is out in the parking lot doing push-ups."

Disease? I didn't have any symptoms of any disease. I knew I'd been delivered.

Dutifully, I continued showing up "to the rooms" a couple of times a week. One day, I sat at the table trying to determine why I felt so ill at ease. I couldn't focus on anyone's stories of past drinking exploits or offer any insight. All I could think of was Mike.

Please God, show me if I am making a mistake by putting the brakes on the relationship with Mike.

When the meeting ended, I couldn't wait to escape to my car. My green Nokia cell phone was sitting in the center console, flashing a missed call.

Hi Melissa, it's Mike. I am sorry to bother you, I know you want space, and I am willing to give you that, I. . .um, I just—well, I know you said you like Aerosmith. I just heard on the radio they're coming to the Twin Cities in November, and I wondered if you wanted to go. No pressure."

With glee, I didn't waste a second calling Mike back. I knew God had answered my prayer. This was the man He had saved for me, and I was letting the opinions of the world interfere with what I knew in my heart was the right path.

After I accepted his invitation, we were again inseparable—spending time talking on the phone, taking walks, and learning about each other on a deep level. Mike shared that he had been praying at his mother's grave and asking God if he should continue pursuing me or move on—then got into his car and heard the commercial for the Aerosmith concert and decided to propose *one* more date. It's funny to think about God working through Steven Tyler, but I believe He uses whatever means necessary and whatever we're into at the time to get our attention. Mike's soul-searching had happened at exactly the same time I was sitting in the AA meeting, feeling unsettled and asking God to reveal whether Mike was the one!

Unlike any man I'd ever dated in the past—Mike and I developed a strong bond built on a foundation of trust,

closeness, and shared values long before anything physical happened. Our extensive phone and email conversations enabled
us to connect in an extremely deep way. For once in my life, I
had met my match—and we were falling for each other at the
same pace. I wasn't approaching the relationship backwards
like I had with so many others, where I was attracted to the
person's looks or magnetism but knew nothing about them on
an intimate spiritual level. Because of our obedience in putting
God first, He saturated everything we did with his blessing, and
our courtship was a total meeting of the minds. I was just as
drawn to Mike mentally as I was physically—most powerfully
because of our shared desire to pursue a spiritual path and to
have children raised with a Christian foundation.

"I really want to get back into church," I told Mike one day.
"It's super important to me—I just haven't found the right one
yet. Where are you at with God?"

"Well, I was raised Catholic . . . but it was pretty much
just memorizing stuff . . . once I completed all the classes my
parents didn't make me go anymore. I haven't been part of
it in decades."

"Same for me," I agreed. "I was confirmed Presbyterian—but
once I got that certificate I was literally out the door headed for
a keg party. Sad, huh? I also went to church a few years back—I
did like it, but ended up drinking again and quit."

Mike and I soon settled on a Lutheran church—coincidentally the same one that had hosted my kindergarten class
in the basement.

In March of 2004, we planned a dream vacation to the
Florida Keys, something I'd wanted to do since the days of
Dad sharing stories of the beauty of the Seven Mile Bridge. We

had an incredible time, driving amazing Highway 1 in a rented convertible, taking long walks on the beach, and getting our Ernest Hemingway on.

Our last day in Florida, we spent the day at the beach and were sweaty, sandy, and sunbaked once the evening came. Ravenous, too.

"Let's find some little place on the wharf and get some crab legs or something," I suggested. "Somewhere that doesn't mind damp swimsuits and towels."

Mike didn't like this idea, instead advocating for a change of clothes and a fancy dinner. "What for?" I argued. "I'll have to change in the car somehow!"

He was so insistent that we get dressed up that I couldn't get him to budge, so I ended up wrestling out of my sandy swimsuit in the backseat and managing to put on a black shift dress and black crocheted sweater. After a wonderful dinner, Mike suggested stopping on the Seven Mile Bridge.

"It's kind of dark," I protested. "I don't know if we'll be able to see anything."

We pulled into the parking area and walked out to the bridge in the fading light. I clutched my sweater around the gusty wind as I scanned the sky.

"Bummer, I can't see anything,"

Mike hovered behind me as I looked out over the water.

"Maybe some stars are out. Do you see any?"

I had been wanting to see the Southern Cross for years, and continued looking skyward.

"Do you see anything?" Mike asked again.

I turned around, and he was down on one knee, holding out a ring box.

"The sky is cloudy, but all I can see is stars," he grinned. "Will you marry me?"

"OH MY GOSH! YES!"

Mike slipped the most beautiful half-carat diamond onto my finger, and afterwards we did our best to capture one of our most incredible moments through selfies.

We married six months later on a gorgeous September day.

Mike and Hope developed a strong bond, and he became a wonderful stepfather and friend to her. Our whirlwind courtship spiraled into years of wedded bliss, and our little blended family of three thrived—growing to a household of five over the next six years.

46

My pursuit of Jesus and willingness to make Him Lord of my life had finally unleashed His great blessings, and I tapped an incredible power through the true and genuine acts of submission, repentance, and forgiveness.

That's it? You may be wondering . . . Jesus just radically freed you, and that's *it?*

The morning of August 22, 2003, I came out of the most horrible blackout of my life, feeling crushed to the point of no return. I repented in a moment of complete desperation. To *repent* means to leave what God has prohibited, sincerely ask for forgiveness, and return to what He has commanded. In that moment of total brokenness where I was intensely aware that

HE was the only One who could save me, Jesus supernaturally removed my addictions to both alcohol and cigarettes. You'll recall from my story that I had *never* been able to put alcohol down for good through the things of the world or my own self-will. The treatment protocols, meetings, books, therapists, and other remedies were temporarily helpful, but in the end, simply Band-Aids that did not bring complete freedom. For Jesus to meet me, I had to put him FIRST, something I had never done—*and* I needed to come to a place where I had exhausted every attempt to fix my problem without supernatural help. I had to invite Him in, and to BELIEVE He would help me. I had to have childlike faith.

The most powerful example of my radical freedom and the Lord's awesome power is almost twenty years of complete freedom from addictive drives. I have been delivered of cravings, obsession, compulsion, and the paralyzing physical, emotional, and mental bondage that comes from a stronghold like addiction. The drive to drink was supernaturally lifted from me. The stresses of life still pop up, and I've even gone through a couple of brutal catastrophes, but I've never *once* thought drinking would be a cure for anything.

Recovery groups will insist, "You're never completely free of addiction." That has not been my experience at all. Once I submitted to the Great Healer, I began living from a place of total restoration, knowing without a shadow of a doubt that I am more than a conqueror in Christ and as long as I stay close to Him, I have nothing to fear. I became a victor instead of a victim. Jesus has been faithful every single day to provide me with the necessary guidance to live a sober, purposeful, and Spirit-filled life. I don't white-knuckle it through the day—ever.

I was truly delivered from the dark and demonic bondage of alcohol blackouts and the behaviors that accompanied them when I sincerely asked and believed in God's power to do for me what I could not do for myself.

Relief from the crippling preoccupation of finding my next drink was a blessing like no other. But I still needed to learn how to walk with the Lord and to live in His will, a process I will continue to pursue until my last breath, but being instantly delivered of the physical and mental aspects was an enormous blessing. These are gut-wrenching battles many people face when trying to quit without the help of God.

I would like to share some of the most important and vital aspects of "what happened after" the Lord delivered me that August morning of 2003. Perhaps the strategies I used will help you find freedom from sin, addiction, or a demonic stronghold.

I had started my TV job as a salve for my nonexistent identity, and still continued in the news media as a dayside reporter and Weekend Anchor after quitting drinking and meeting Mike, but something strange began to happen. I no longer found satisfaction or validation in the world of broadcast news, and didn't yearn for the hit of euphoria I would once get when recognized out in public. I didn't even *care* if I lost my job, which was stunning, considering that the thought of it going away was once my most crippling fear. God had removed the need to be seen, and replaced it with a desire to do His will. In fact, I began to greatly dislike the stress, rat race, and grind of the entire news world, to crave quiet solitude, and to desperately seek escape from my present duties.

My job continued for a couple of years after I met Jesus, and during that time Mike and I attended a small group study at our church. The goal of the class was to help us find our God-given purpose. In 2005 while taking the church class, the newsroom was bought out and merged with another local station in a revenue-sharing agreement, and the entire staff was laid off. Some were devastated, but I was ready. Looking back, it blows my mind to think of how strenuously I tried to leave Duluth for a big market media gig, when God kept me in town so Mike and I could meet. The church study began offering preparation for what God had planned next—unearthing a powerful desire to help others through my life experience. I did return to radio as a midday host with an oldies station for six months, and then helped a dear friend of mine start up a high-quality television station in Ashland, Wisconsin, where I was very proud to be part of a team who won an Emmy award for "Best Small Market Newscast." My heart wasn't really in the world of broadcasting anymore, though.

When my friend's station was forced to close due to unforeseen circumstances, I suddenly knew it was time for my next chapter to begin. God was strongly impressing upon me I was to become an addiction counselor. The severance package I received from KDLH-TV had helped Mike and me purchase our first home, and it also afforded a dislocated worker benefit which would cover school costs to obtain my counseling license. There were no barriers, and God opened each and every door— as He always does when we are operating in His will! I went on to receive a masters degree in exercise physiology in 2011. My substandard undergraduate performance at UWS had always been a source of embarrassment, and obtaining an MS was a personal goal. I developed a great desire to help others care for their body temple through the power of diet and exercise, and worked in intensive outpatient treatment centers for the next twelve years—leading hundreds of recovery groups as well as individual counseling sessions.

The most important ingredients to usher me into the presence of God were **surrender, repentance, and forgiveness**. At the beginning of this book, I have a quote from a well-loved pastor named Mark Olson. He once said we are only able to meet God in three ways: desperation, surrender, and eternity. Those words carried a powerful impact because at the time I heard them, I was working with a lot of people who were not ready for change, and I couldn't understand why so many— including my own father—did not *want* to get well or chose not to accept the free gift of Jesus. Instead, they were surrounded by a lot of well-intentioned people wanting it *for* them. When we enable people, we may interfere with them experiencing a necessary consequence that is essential to their growth. Throughout my journey through addiction, I'd had a lot of people tell me my drinking was problematic and that I should quit—but their words fell on deaf ears. I was not capable of change until I fully internalized the depth of my problem and had exhausted every last option of the world. Through submitting my will and my life, forgiving others even if they still held something against me, and sincerely desiring to stop my sin patterns and instead walk in God's ways, I could finally rest in the assurance that God would do the rest. HE would point me to the things necessary to sustain a lifetime of sobriety—the key was putting him FIRST in that process, instead of looking everywhere else for answers. In the book of Jeremiah, it says: "Cursed are those who put their trust in mere humans, who rely on human strength, and turn their hearts away from the Lord" (Jer. 17:5; NIV). I was stunned when the Lord showed me that verse! When we don't put God first, we are unknowingly placing ourselves under a curse! Much of the world today does exactly this, however, and is filled with people desperately searching for answers through powerless man-made creations. The world is filled with brilliant people and professionals who may be able to teach behavior modification, tips, and techniques—but every single one of them—no matter how blessed, gifted, or successful—lacks the supernatural power of the One True God.

You may also remember from my story that being alone with myself was next to impossible—I needed constant distraction and numbing to kill the intrusive thoughts that came both from my own flesh and the voice of the enemy. My paralyzing inner dialogue stemmed from a severe lack of identity and massive abandonment wound I attempted to fill with the praise of others, alcohol, and the attention of men. **I had to get alone with God**, for the first time in my life. At first it felt awkward, but soon our daily talks became something I desperately needed and could not live without. During this time, He began to heal me, and proved Himself faithful again and again as he demonstrated His desire to be involved in every single detail of my life. I am a strong believer in giving the first part of your day to the Lord, just like you would offer a tithe, or first ten percent of your earnings. I began a practice of sitting with God, worshiping, singing, praying, and journaling first thing in the morning, as well as reading the Bible. I began with Proverbs, and found a treasure trove of wisdom I wished I had known about years ago. I have since been through the entire Bible and continue to read it in its entirety a couple of times each year. It never gets old, and the Holy Spirit continues to illuminate and reveal new things.

Not only that, but the Living Word consistently speaks directly into my life situations!

As with any relationship, my bond with the Lord has grown deeper over time and is directly contingent upon my intentionality and willingness to give him priority over other things. I do everything possible to give God the first hour of my day, before outside circumstances begin to steer me off the kingdom course. This is cherished time for me and Jesus, and I do not miss it. During these intimate conversations with the Holy Trinity and getting to know the three Persons on a one-to-one basis, I found that the solution for **every single life problem** I could ever have is right in my prayer closet. There is no fear of relapse, making the wrong decision, or the things of the world when you are in lock step with God! Praying, journaling, and reading the Bible have become the most essential elements to healing my past brokenness and trauma, and have provided immeasurably more than any therapy, treatment, or evidence-based practice of the world.

Let me be clear, I am *not* against addiction treatment or therapy. I would just caution you to be very selective in choosing your provider or your program. Many Christian therapists or "Christ-centered" programs are as worldly as they come, and many providers (and sponsors) are unhealed themselves—just doing their best to get through the day while also trying to help people with severe and persistent addiction and spiritual problems. That is not to say there are not great therapists, sponsors, and treatment programs out there. I have many friends who do great work to help struggling people and further the kingdom of Jesus Christ at the same time. Just make sure you pray, seek God, and exercise discernment regarding your decision to find help. Pastoral counseling and church recovery programs and

Bible studies can also provide great assistance with breaking the bondage of addiction. Spiritual deliverance from demonic forces or generational sin may also be needed. You do not need to pay ridiculous amounts of money to enter high-end treatment facilities. Start with the lowest level of care, and work up as your need requires. I've seen many set free in church, Bible studies, or even in their own kitchen through a sincere prayer, but some may need the safety of a structured program when outside support is lacking or toxic circumstances that block the person from breaking free are present at home. And, we all need others—a support system of healthy, Christian people who will help us stay on the path. If you don't have this through friends or family right now, do not despair. You can build a new network through church and other outlets.

As a sidenote, do not abruptly stop using alcohol if you have been drinking daily or excessively, as you could suffer severe and life-threatening withdrawal. A medically supervised detoxification followed by a Christ-centered discipleship program has been the road to freedom for many people. God is limitless though—and can also deliver you of everything in a split second. I have met and interviewed many who've experienced the miraculous!

Warnings abound in AA to avoid "people, places, and things" that led to addictive behaviors, and I have to agree with that. It was different for me, though, in that I just no longer desired those things, I had no "want" to go to bars, and over time other worldly pursuits I used to enjoy started to lose their appeal and I instead wanted to pursue the things of God. You might find it funny that God used an Aerosmith concert to show me Mike was "the one," but I firmly believe he meets us where we are and uses whatever is available to get our attention. My preferences and activities have definitely changed a great deal in the past twenty years, and one gauge I use to determine how to spend time is to ask myself, "Is this God-honoring?" and, "Does this activity bring me closer to God or further away?"

Early on in sobriety, I began to cultivate a strong connection to a Bible-based church and the fellowship of other believers. I was drawn to the house of God like a moth to a flame; it was not dull, boring, or a requirement—I truly *wanted* to be there, and needed the spiritual food of solid Bible teaching and communion with others believers. "Being in church" for me used to mean going to service occasionally, sitting in the back row, and hurrying out at the end only to immediately resume my old way of thinking and behaving. That is not repentance. I had to change this old mindset, which meant "taking off my bib and putting on an apron," as another former pastor once said. We aren't just in church to get "fed" and to have our own needs met, we are there to contribute to the body of Christ through serving, tithing, fellowshipping, and worshipping together. There are no perfect churches, and we are to share in the labor so the presence of God and the people who are filled with the love of Jesus will be there when others are in need.

The final steps that helped forge a new life in recovery were implementing a regular, structured exercise regimen, having goals and attractive alternatives that were incompatible with the blackout drinking lifestyle I used to live, and finding hobbies that both filled me and glorified God. Writing this now, it sounds very technical and staged, but honestly—at the time, I didn't know that was what I was doing—I was simply getting with God first thing in the morning every day, and He was faithful to lead me where I needed to go as well as to introduce me to the right people and opportunities.

One day, in the early weeks following my last drink, I was out doing some errands and got a flat tire. I didn't have a phone with me at the time, but wasn't far from my apartment so I decided to just walk back. Well, my walk broke into a jog over fear of having my car towed before I could make arrangements for it, and before long I had jogged a half-mile and arrived at my doorstep sweaty, jubilant, and euphoric. My drinking had been accompanied by extremely unhealthy behavior that led to massive weight gain—poor sleep, binge eating, a steady diet of fast food, Mountain Dew, and candy in an attempt to power through hangovers and feel better, and a *very* sedentary lifestyle of sitting at a news desk every day and a bar stool several nights a week. That little half-mile jog birthed a love of running and relationship with the only sport that has never let me down. I've never been much of an athlete or someone sought after for a team, but the solitary activity of logging miles on the road was perfect, and I actually came to realize I was not a big, fat weakling as I once thought—I was actually a pretty good runner! Running has helped me solve many problems, produces endorphins that create a good feeling without the chemical overdose, and retrained my brain to work for a reward. I could go on all day about the physical and mental benefits—but they don't stop there! I am at one with Jesus when I am out in nature exploring the trails by my house or just pounding the good old pavement along the highway. Running and fitness were also interests Mike and I shared, and we have been competing in races of all kinds including marathons since we met. Fitness is a foundational part of my daily life, along with a healthy diet and one of my favorite activities—sleep! My weight has been stable for many, many years through consistency with just a few basic things.

Setting goals and building a streak of positive behavior also helped. I remember in the early recovery, each day I was sober I would put a sticker on the calendar, and Hope and I would both rejoice over another day clean. Before I knew it, I had amassed ninety stickers, and wasn't looking back. When you began creating a new, healthy habit—you become more invested as time goes by. Your determination grows as you build a life far greater and move from the drink or the slip into a sin pattern.

Lastly, I moved from self-service to self-sacrifice. I began to look at my life through eyes of gratitude for all the Lord had brought me through, and to take joy in everyday things. I got into serving others, listening, volunteering at church, and getting my thoughts off myself. Less preoccupation with self also enabled me to enjoy my family and the growth of my children, and I returned to my love of singing without pressure to perform, because I knew the Lord loved the sound of my voice! God loves it when you sing!

Back in 1999 when I experienced two severe drunk driving arrests in one year, I had no clue that God had anticipated everything in advance and that Romans 8:28 would later become a potent reality for me: "And we know that in all things God works for the good of those who love him, who have been called according to his purpose" (Romans 8:28; NIV).

My life is no longer teetering on the shifting sands of addiction or infatuation. It is built on a solid foundation, the rock of the Lord. After God heard my cry and plucked me from the jaws of addiction, He faithfully used every bit of my past to catapult me into a life I never thought possible. I will never be the same again. I am reborn. From a slithering pit of filth, Jesus placed me on a rock and put a new song in my mouth. Submitting my struggle to Him allowed me to accept the life-saving gift of grace.

"Therefore, if anyone is in Christ, the new creation has come: The old has gone, the new is here!" (2 Corinthians 5:17 NIV).

EPILOGUE

"For we are God's handiwork, created in Christ Jesus to do good works, which God prepared in advance for us to do."

—EPHESIANS 2:10 (NIV)

For almost twenty years, I have not looked back. That long of a track record post-deliverance from addiction is no small feat among an epidemic with skyrocketing relapse rates—but all glory goes to God. Before I submitted to Him, I was dependent upon manmade systems and my own willpower for another day of sobriety.

Getting there took a lot of painful lessons. Most of the men I dated who are mentioned in my story have been married for years, and appear to be happy—among them Beck, Mitch, Drake, Seth, Brady, Dennis, Rick, and Bryce. Others I've lost track of, and some are gone from this earth—Darren, Christy, Jed, and several bar friends not mentioned all died due to alcohol or drug-related events, and just a few months ago, a same-aged friend passed away suddenly after aspirating in her sleep from an accidental opioid overdose. Not a day goes by that I do not thank my Lord and Savior Jesus Christ for protection from the devil's plans. I think of Marge, and the enormous blessing of her presence in my formidable early years. Somehow, I escaped the fate of so many, and all I can do is accept God's grace with gratitude.

I've learned to release the past and to forgive others and myself. So many people live with regret, forever dwelling on lost years or commiserating over a situation they cannot escape. Whether they brought it upon themselves or were innocent victims of someone else's choices matters little. Either way, they harbor a victim mentality—often paralyzed by a reality they perceive to be inescapable. Their very existence is clouded with "if onlys." *If only I hadn't married that guy, taken that job, believed that lie, committed that sin, made that mistake. Things would be different. If only.*

Believing their best days are long gone, they live in bondage, allowing the "thing" or person that changed the entire trajectory of their lives so much power—not realizing that every single moment holds the potential to think differently, to submit, to repent, to forgive. You can't alter what's already happened, but you *can* change where you're headed.

What would you think if I told you that it's *impossible* to screw things up so badly that Jesus cannot redeem you? He promises in Joel 2:25: "I will repay you for the years the locusts have eaten" (NIV). I've watched this beloved verse play out repeatedly in my own life as well as the lives of others who've submitted to God. Stop labeling your detours wasted time because God can do amazing things with a submitted life!

My favorite Bible verse then becomes operational, and He will faithfully use every wrong turn to bring an incredible end. Romans 8:28 says, "And we know that in ALL things GOD WORKS for the good of those who love Him, who have been called according to His purposes" (NIV).

Notice that this promise does not apply to *all* people—*only* those who love God and are walking in His calling!

I used to wish I hadn't blown so many years fighting Jesus and stubbornly insisting on my own way, but I've come to realize not a single mistake was wasted—God used them all to propel me forward into works He had planned in advance. As I reach fifty years old, I am more convinced than ever of God's great faithfulness and guidance in all areas of my earthly walk. I once doubted I'd make it to 30—given the rebellious course I was charting—and now I am beyond blessed that Jesus has seen fit to use me on the earth for half a century.

Though my life changed supernaturally when I submitted to the authority of Jesus, trials didn't cease forever because I got sober and married my soul mate. The other day, I sat at a picnic table in the park near my house and prayed. Alone in the quiet greenspace, I talked out loud to God—like one would a trusted confidant—reminded of how I used to do just that as a small child playing in my sand pile. Back then, He surely heard me, but I didn't know how to hear Him. This intimate relationship would not have been possible without pursuing time alone with my Creator.

Even the years of holding the red hymnal doubting God existed were impactful. My parents exposed my brother and me to church and did their best to lay a foundation in their own limited way, and I learned life lessons in each house of worship I passed through. I have learned to see my parents through the lens of the baggage they carried, and to know they did their best, as I am doing as a parent.

Marge and Harold, my neighbors, were the first to show me the Holy Spirit in action—offering an incredible safety net to help diffuse the anxiety and insecurity plaguing me. God used them to bring me the Good News of Jesus Christ in a way that would birth an intense passion for him years later.

Looking back is a potently eye-opening experience—and God's handiwork is illustrated through the tapestry of my life. The protective hedge was always constant, regardless of whether I felt it, along with His love, faithfulness, and intentionality.

My life turned an amazing corner after Jesus and I began moving together on parallel tracks that morning of August 22, 2003, when I begged him to remove my desire for alcohol. Hiding an addiction is extremely hard work, and once you've overcome the intense bondage of such a stronghold, the freedom is exhilarating. Just eighteen days after that earnest prayer and vow to never touch alcohol again, God brought my future husband Mike in his divine timing. We hadn't seen each other for five long years, but one supernatural touch changed everything.

My heart's desire could not come until I was serious and submitted. Surrender is powerful, and once my will was in his hands, God brought my kingdom husband.

A few years later, God blessed us with two daughters, born in 2008 and 2010. I envisioned my amazing life continuing on a proverbial upward swing. The values Mike and I shared prompted us to root deeply in Jesus, and we became heavily invested in a local church.

My current pastor always jokes that the couples he marries are not in love yet, they're infatuated. For years, Mike and I rode high on that wave of euphoria—butterflies and constant thrills simply at the sight of each other—but then, year seven arrived, and the baggage we'd both hauled into the relationship began to cause serious problems.

Raising two young children and navigating a blended family by that time, Hope was 16 and struggling with normal teenage issues, it wasn't long before Mike and I found church inconvenient. Soon, we were harboring resentments toward it and just about everything that happened there was a reason for offense. Limited finances and lack of support from family made salvaging a night alone next to impossible. We began to drift apart.

Mike and I had the perfect generational setup to become champion conflict avoiders, and tension mounted within our marriage as we continued the deeply ingrained pattern of avoiding any topic that was uncomfortable or difficult.

Near the end of 2010, Mike's father passed away after a long illness. Since he was elderly, I imagined Mike quickly recovering from the loss. Instead, he turned depressed and distant. I'd started graduate school by that time and was deeply invested in the rigors of the program, and the stress of juggling kids and a household were taking a toll. We no longer connected in the ways that had bonded us at the beginning—long talks, funny emails, and knowing glances were exchanged for surface talk, bickering, and petty slights. Instead of confronting what was happening, we ignored the growing divide.

During my lowest moment, drinking again never crossed my mind, but my relationship with Jesus weakened, and I slowly fell prey to the pressures of the world. Over time, *Mike* had become the Lord of my life—and the fallout was incredible. I had made my husband an idol, and God was not happy.

Our marriage completely tanked from late 2011 through 2012, ushering in a very lonely and painful period. Two separations took a brutal toll, but through it all the Holy Spirit still reigned in me, along with flicker of faith for my best friend—the Lord Jesus. I knew on a deep level that He had ordained our marriage and could bring the turnaround—but not until I laid everything on the altar.

My second mother Marge also resurfaced at just the right time, and we reconnected without missing a beat. Through many deep conversations, she opened my eyes to the devil's goal of destroying my marriage and showed me how to fight back.

Recognizing Satan's warfare also revealed how my disobedience had turned me into a vessel for fear, doubt, mistrust, disbelief, confusion, control, paranoia, anxiety, and jealousy. The battle was not with my husband or with people or things in the world—it was a fight in the spiritual realm. Ephesians 6:12 says: "For our struggle is not against flesh and blood, but against the rulers, against the authorities, against the powers of this dark world and against the spiritual forces of evil in the heavenly realms" (NIV).

Suiting up with the armor of God became a daily ritual—praying against the attacks of the enemy was critical. Slowly, the situation began to shift, and I started to see my husband and others in my life through the eyes of Jesus. I needed to truly repent for making Mike an idol and trust God with the outcome.

Romans 8:28 says: "And we know that in *all* things God works for the good of those who love him, who have been called according to his purpose."

All things. Not just some things.

These words took hold as I slowly began to trust God with every aspect of my life. Early spring 2012, we moved from northern Minnesota to a southwestern suburb of Minneapolis-St. Paul. Desperate to do something to fix our relationship, we hadn't weighed the decision carefully—looking back, I understand God had anticipated it all and had an amazing plan up ahead. We just needed to step out in faith.

It was awful timing, but at every turn, God responded with an open door. We received job transfers—then traveled to the Cities to investigate housing and childcare. The cost of living was shocking, and we returned to Duluth defeated—convinced we'd have to scrap our plan.

One day at work, I was lost in thought and paralyzed with indecision. The move was still on the table, even though we'd be flat broke trying to make ends meet. Mike sent me an email that morning asking if I wanted to back out.

I closed the door to my office, knelt on the floor, and threw out a desperate prayer.

A few hours later, Mike called to let me know his boss wanted to discuss changes with upper management. He wasn't aware of my plea to God.

A couple of days later, my husband was given a promotion and a pay raise for a new position in the Twin Cities. God had confirmed the move. *He's already there . . . what do you have to fear?*

I became a clinical supervisor for a substance use disorder

program in Apple Valley. As I struggled to acclimate and our marriage continued to flounder, a new client mentioned a prayer service she'd attended called Jesus Heals.

Later on, I passively searched for the name, but was confused and continued to look for Jesus *Hills*, soon growing frustrated when my quest yielded nothing.

A few days later, a different person I counseled mentioned an intercessory prayer group called "Jesus HEALS!" Apparently, the Lord really wanted me to get the memo on this place.

This haven was calling me, and after my first visit, I realized it was an incredible and powerful healing ministry. Each week, I met with a team who lovingly guided me through various issues from the past and taught me how to trust the Lord completely.

Our family needed a house of worship, and many people pointed us to a popular local church. Initially, Mike wasn't very interested in attending; we both carried religious battle scars. The kids and I visited a few times without Mike, while I tried not to pester him.

Finally, he did agree to give it a shot. Little did I know, God was about to engage him without any assistance from me! He knows what will interest us, and He's a master at meeting us right where we are.

Mike's first Sunday at church, the worship team came out on stage, and I almost fell off my chair when I heard the opening drums and keyboards to "Livin' on a Prayer" by Bon Jovi, one of Mike's all-time favorite bands. The worship team performed an incredible cover of the song, complete with Jon Bon Jovi on the big screen—that surely got Mike's attention!

But the enemy was wreaking havoc on my mind just a week later. Romans 12:2 warns us to guard our thought life. "Do not conform to the pattern of this world, but be transformed by the renewing of your mind" (NIV).

That morning while dressing for service, I flipped on the radio. Depressing rain pelted the windows as "Don't Stop Believin'" by Journey strained through my little alarm clock. Cranking the volume a little higher, my mood slowly lifted.

An hour later, we arrived at church, and the pastor greeted everyone: "If you're feeling down, don't stop believing. If things aren't going your way, don't stop believing. If your life is in shambles and you want to give up, *DON'T STOP BELIEVING!*

The band took center stage and played that song, and God touched me deeply—impressing the words: BELIEF IS THE KEY. With tears streaming down my face, I thought, *Jesus likes Journey!*

That day, God sealed a powerful promise in my heart, confirming everything I'd so far been struggling to do; *I have ordained your marriage and I will sustain it if you submit it to Me.* Suddenly, I was more committed than ever to fighting for our precious covenant.

Soon afterward, Jesus arranged more amazing things, and Mike began joining me for intercessory prayer at Jesus Heals where we'd spend our lunch hours with the gifted prayer warriors. One week after prayer time, Mike returned to his car to find his radio tuned to KTIS, a Christian station in the area he'd never listened to before that day. He later told me that the next three songs spoke directly to him about our personal situation and that he felt God was talking to him. Gratitude flowed in as I saw the Lord answer very specific prayers after hoping for so long for a special tug at Mike's heart.

Memorial Weekend 2013, Mike and I had a breakthrough

moment. Our hearts became tender once again as the love of Jesus flooded them. No longer keeping score about who was more in the wrong, we closed the door on the past for good and moved forward together. Only the Holy Spirit could accomplish this heart transplant.

One week in early June, Mike was not able to join me at Jesus Heals. That day, the team offered prayer to receive the gifts of the Holy Spirit. After they finished, they told me what to expect next. Nothing happened right away.

June 20th, 2013, I'd just finished leading a treatment group and was alone in the office finishing up daily progress notes. As the setting sun streamed through my window, I bowed my head and suddenly the advice of the Jesus Heals prayer team popped into mind. *I need to invite the Holy Spirit.* After they'd imparted the gifts in prayer the previous week, they'd encouraged openness to the movement of Him while engaged in prayer. Remembering their directives, I began to hum in a low voice, my tongue slowly loosening from the roof of my mouth and moving on its own and making a pattern of sounds and phrases I was not creating.

Alone, sober, and alert—in my office praying—I encountered the Living God—not in church, nor the presence of people caught up in a movement, revival, or emotion. It was the most powerful supernatural experience I had ever had—I truly felt enveloped in the peaceful, loving presence of God. This extremely private moment happened between myself, Father God, Jesus, and the Holy Spirit—an amazing confirmation of my heavenly Father bringing an end to a very difficult season.

Afterward, the enemy sowed seeds of doubt about what I knew had happened, trying to instill fear, but each time he did the Lord repeated: (I told you) "IT IS FINISHED."

Everything would be fine between Mike and me. The Lord was our cornerstone once again, and I had finally repented of my idol worship of my husband and marriage. Jesus was in first place to stay. A few months later, we were baptized together in water immersion and rededicated ourselves to the Lord and service for Him. We went on to serve in a church marriage ministry and have been helping struggling couples for almost ten years.

My family of origin never talked about the gifts of the Spirit, especially not speaking in tongues! This was reserved only for "Holy Rollers." Now I was one of them! And I loved it.

Learning to trust the Lord completely with not only my marriage, but my entire life—was truly the key to freedom. The crisis with Mike forced me to press into God like never before, fasting and praying, feasting on the Bible, praying bold prayers, and waiting expectantly on Him for the turnaround. I even became okay with whatever God decided to do, I only wanted HIS plans for me, finally understanding them to be far greater than anything I could project. Total submission was the antidote to my crippling preoccupation with self.

Since then, I have not doubted for a second that the Lord is a very real presence at work in my life every single moment. THE LIVING GOD. The Bible is not just some old, dusty book of stories that happened thousands of years ago, it is the LIVING WORD, holding the power to speak into every life situation.

Mike and I spent five years attending the church that played such a huge role in our healing, and it met our needs beautifully for a season. As our spiritual walk deepened, we moved on to an Assemblies of God congregation—first for a Bible study and later becoming members.

True recovery of mind, body, spirit, and preoccupation with self wouldn't find me until I sought God's power to run my life with everything I had, and strangely—that meant giving everything up to follow Him. Nothing in this world could bring true deliverance or completely fill the void—only Jesus.

My soul mate Mike and I continue to navigate this earthly life tothether, and I am so grateful for him and my three beautiful daughters. Jesus has brought us all through so much.

Being on a parallel track with the Lord is an amazing ride. About four years ago (after spending twelve years working as a counselor in outpatient treatment programs), I was experiencing major compassion fatigue with most nights after work spent wrestling in my prayer closet. Though I didn't doubt God's call to help people with addictions, I was burnt out and weary of attending funerals for clients who'd lost their battles.

One Sunday afternoon, Mike and I wandered by the MyPillow store while shopping at the Burnsville Mall. With his infamous bedding empire and infectious commercial jingle, Mike Lindell is perhaps the most well-known Minnesotan. That day, his cutout grabbed my attention—trademark silver cross twinkling like a beacon. I was left wondering: *Why does he wear it outside of his shirt?*

For the next few weeks, I researched everything I could find about Mike Lindell—stunned to discover his past as a crack cocaine addict. For months, I spent all my free time brainstorming a path into his company. Despite my best efforts, I only met dead ends.

My last-ditch attempt was to apply for a retail job at the pillow store in the mall where I'd seen Mike's cut-out weeks before. Immediately, I was called for an interview. But as the appointed day drew near, I pondered canceling. Adding a part-time job to my already hectic schedule seemed absurd.

The Holy Spirit, however, would not let me back out. So, I showed up to the store at the scheduled time, ready to call everything off. But as the interviewer began to review my resume, everything shifted.

"I know a lot about Mike Lindell, and I really wanted to work for his company," I explained as she studied my paper-work, "but juggling two jobs isn't going to work. I apologize for wasting your time today."

"You're an addiction counselor?" she asked, almost in disbe-lief. "Mike is launching a platform to help addicts."

In this defining moment, the past several weeks finally made sense.

Much to my shock, a short time later I was contacted for an interview at the corporate office with Mike Lindell.

As I was led to his personal conference room, I couldn't get over how surreal it all was. Every single door had been flipped open by God: my only task was obedience to the promptings of the Holy Spirit.

The enemy continued his assaults—*You don't have what it takes, there are so many other more qualified people out there . . .* but when God opens a door, no man can shut it! For a reason I could not yet define, God had hand selected this opportunity for me. Yes, ME! (That showing grace and mercy on whomever he chooses thing again!)

Mike burst into the room, unaware of my extreme nervous-ness, and then spent two hours unveiling his latest brainchild: an amazing platform to help people with addictions. Pausing for breath, he concluded: "Well, I want to hire ya."

My jaw about hit the floor.

"Don't you want to ask me anything? Do an interview?"

Mike erupted into his unmistakable trademark laugh.

"I already know I wanna hire ya. This is a divine appointment! Your name has come up three times in the past week. Do you have any idea how many people apply here, and how many resumes I get? I can't possibly meet with a fraction of them. I'm not even in the office much these days. It's really a one-in-a-million chance that you're sitting here."

What were the odds?

My new position as Executive Director of the Lindell Recovery Network started in the fall of 2018. Most days, I sat there pinching myself and looking around, hoping it was all real.

When I told my mother about my new role, she bluntly declared, "I think Dad helped you get hired."

"Dad?" I laughed. "He was gone long before MyPillow came on the scene."

"No, not the pillow. The jingle. The Sweet Adelines, right? Dad would've loved that."

As you know, Dad was a Barbershopper. And I've since become a Sweet Adeline! After his death, my alcohol addiction was terrifically magnified, Jesus stepped up His pursuits, and my struggle finally ended eight months after his passing.

Dad would've loved the MyPillow jingle (he was a huge fan of the Sweet Adelines), and I am convinced he would have been just as proud of my work for Mike Lindell as he had been of my television career.

Sometimes I think, *What if I had done that bachelor's degree right out of high school? What if I never picked up a drink, said "I do" the first time, or rear-ended that lady in a blackout?* God used it all to bring me to an expected end—all in His perfect timing.

Mike Huray was the man God had chosen for me all along, I impatiently forced a marriage beforehand. God still used it—delivering the most beautiful blessing from that broken arrangement—my beautiful Hope!

My years of addiction brought much pain and heartache, but all of it would eventually be used to develop a strength and resilience I never thought possible—as well as to bring compassion to other addicts. Mightily equipped to relate to others who are walking that same path of hopelessness, my trials and struggles produced rare insight straight from the school of hard knocks.

And, if Mike and I had not experienced our marriage problems, we would never have realized our great need for Jesus Christ, grown so deeply as a couple, or experienced the incredible call God had to help others feeling hopeless in their marriages. We would've been content to continue as lukewarm Christians, never fully experiencing God's power and kingdom calling upon our lives.

Everything to this very day has brought me to the most important conclusion, I am nothing, have nothing, and can do nothing apart from Christ. If I trust in Him, He truly will use everything for the good, bringing all of this earthly life into perfect harmony through his sovereignty.

He doesn't say it will always be easy—but He is always faithful, and never changes!

"I have told you these things, so that in Me you may have peace. In this world you will have trouble. But take heart! I have overcome the world" (John 16:33; NIV).

More than anything, my friend—I want to see *you* in eternity. The earth is just a temporary home we may inhabit for eighty or ninety years if we are lucky; do not fool yourself into believing it all ends when you die. We will all spend eternity somewhere: heaven or hell. People who reject our Lord and Savior Jesus Christ will end up in eternal torment, but it doesn't have to be that way. He gave us the opportunity to follow Him! I would love more than anything to find you among the saints and to know my story played some small role in your journey. It is all for His glory that I tell it, and if my past sins and broken pieces can help someone else abandon a path of destruction, that is more than enough. From my heart, I want you to know that Jesus will never abandon or forsake you. All my life, I was looking for love in all the wrong places and trying to fill up the deep well that only Jesus could satisfy. We've come to the end of my story—but I hope it's just beginning for you. Will you pray with me?

Dear Jesus, I know I am a sinner who needs a Savior. I believe, as it says in Romans, that if I confess with my mouth that you, Jesus, are Lord and believe in my heart that God raised you from the dead, I will be saved (Romans 10:9; NIV). Jesus, I do believe this, and I need your help with any unbelief I am struggling with and also to grow my faith. Please wash away my sins and help me to walk in your ways. I invite you in to be my Lord and Savior. In Jesus's name, amen!

Congratulations! Now get yourself into a good Bible-based church, start reading the Bible, and submit to the Lord every day. Thank you for reading my story! I pray that it blessed you!

—MELISSA HURAY